STARSHINE

STARSHINE

BY

WINTER ZAKWOLF

www.whitefalconpublishing.com

Starshine
Winter Zakwolf

www.whitefalconpublishing.com

First Edition, 2020

The contents of this book have been timestamped on the Ethereum blockchain as a permanent proof of existence. Scan the QR code or visit the URL given on the back cover to verify the blockchain certification for this book.

Requests for permission should be addressed to
zakariak.engg@gmail.com

ISBN - 978-93-89932-18-8

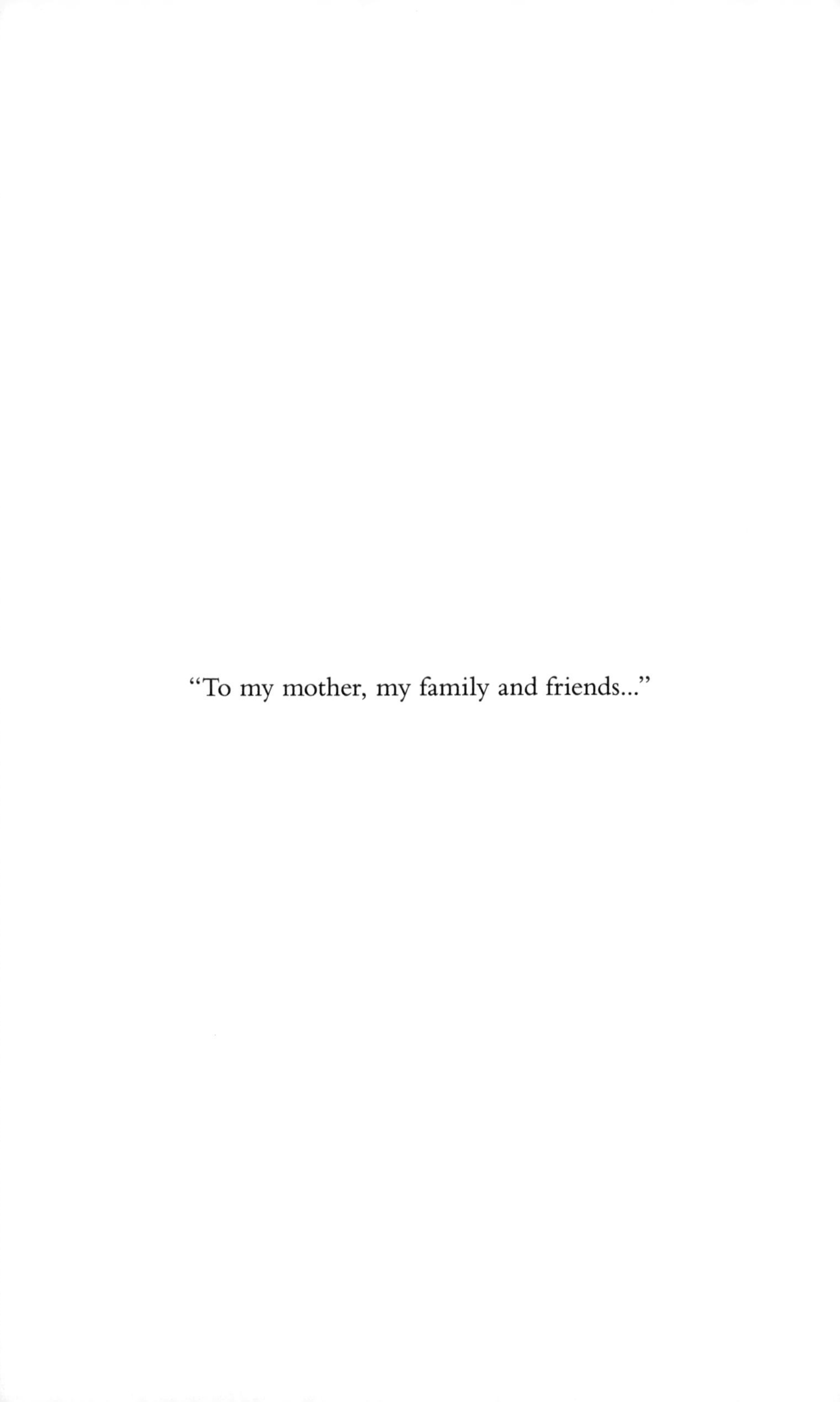

"To my mother, my family and friends..."

CONTENTS

1

A Walk through the Path to the Lost Kingdom

It took me by great surprise when I was selected to work with the research group of Professor Ralph Tennyson on my Master's Thesis during my final semester. Although a semester usually runs for one half of a year, I was in direct contact with Prof Tennyson for a shorter span of a little more than two weeks. Nevertheless, the time had some great influences in my life, forming interference through the years - both positive and negative. Prof Ralph Tennyson is among the most noted academicians in the fields of medieval history and culture of respective Europe. I, Alan Smith, was in the University of Glasgow, struggling with my semesters and most of all, the domain of my thesis. I must admit I was a bit confused when Prof Tennyson and his team started working on the parochial history of a long lost kingdom of England, a kingdom lost in time and translation from the fifteenth-century. Despite that, I was feeling something auspicious about my future with it and therefore, I mailed Prof Tennyson anyway and asked for the 'exaggerated' opportunity. About one year after my thesis was accepted, because of the interminable requests by the reviewers of my thesis as well as from my colleagues and friends, I finally have decided to write it down for the sake of general public - the story of Michael Chapman, the swordsman of the fifteenth century. I am aware of the fact that if I were to write another thesis or a paper on it, my readers would stop reading it from the very second page. That is why I have tried to ornate it, excluding the research and including the stories, to make it reach the general public for their perusal.

It was about a year and a half ago when my supervisor of my university deliberately caught me in the coffee session. I also had been intentionally avoiding him for the past few days as we had to submit an abstract of our thesis by some previous weeks and I had still been in the uncharted ocean.

The sun was setting at the flaming horizon of the dying afternoon. The length of the shadows of the chairs and tables in the canteen, engendered from the last sunlight of the day coming through the open windows, was increasing and fading away as well under the growing darkness. The official smell of the coffee and the beans were enhancing the mood. A few scholars were sitting here and there in this large room and enjoying their afternoon with the delicious Cappuccino, Latte and Expresso. One could hear the incognisable and deep sound of discussion from the scholars talking amongst themselves about their works of the day. I was sitting on a lonely couch at a corner while hiding my face behind my laptop. And I saw my supervisor approaching towards me.

"Mr. Smith, you do know that your delaying is only exacerbating the situation," he alerted me. I already was mentally exhausted with the topic and so his warning and the cold glare did nothing to ameliorate anything.

"Sir, I am trying to find a topic I can work on and I am sure you can help me out," I tried to cover myself up.

"Like this by the time you find a topic, I will have found myself buried," he bowed a sarcastic comment.

"No Sir, I already have checked all the previous and the on-going projects of the university, and also of Cardiff. I was hoping for something original," I tried to show that I had done background work.

"Did not you find a single project from all the projects listed?" My supervisor was utterly surprised.

"I did, Sir. But, with all due respect, all of them were extensions of other works. Such things are going on all over the world in all academic fields. One can never write an original research paper from them, but just a review article. I want something original." I was a rebel.

My supervisor kept looking at me for a minute. I knew that he was a little resented. But, I did not back off.

"I have heard that Dr Ralph Tennyson is with his team in Canterbury. They are working on a project. And they have a post open. They actually are looking for someone to decipher the language," being someone who knew my specialty in the medieval English and sub-languages, he said that.

"That would be great Sir!" Only Prof Tennyson's name was enough to cheer me up and I started to look for good hope again.

"I will mail you about the project by tonight. Please have a good study before you write to him," my supervisor warned me from doing any mistake.

That night I got the email from my supervisor stating the gist of the project which Prof Tennyson was working on, with some web links and two PDFs attached therewith. Professor Tennyson, if you are reading this right now then I sincerely apologise to you and I assure you that it is just an honest revelation of my past self. I spent the whole night reading, studying and performing my research on the topic of the project - that included the histories of the Kingdom, the Kings and contemporary interesting courses of events.

The kingdom, as I studied, was situated near the English Channel, somewhat south from Canterbury and on a hilly terrain. The only two kings whom one could study are King Phillip V and King George IV, whose times were some half a century apart from each other's; both of them ruled in the 15th century. Unlike most other kingdoms of UK, it did not have any long run war (or, did it?), any unique or noted development in terms of science and technology or literature and it did not even have any revolution too to study. Although while going through the documents and googling the links I did find mentions of some French invasions over and over again and fierce fights with them in the 'Forbidden Forest' or the 'Forest of Death', but I did not really get into it. With the whole opaque idea about the project, I was having a dilemma writing to Professor Tennyson, however, I did not have any other choice. Like any other application, I had to go through the exhausting processes of sending the statement of purpose and letter of recommendation. But finally and fortunately, I got the job. I would like to take some space to thank the authority for granting me this amazing opportunity that was going to change my life.

After some painful journey via London from Glasgow during that time of the year, I finally reached Canterbury. From Canterbury, it was about two hours of the road via train towards the Channel. The journey through the cathedral cities in southeast England with all the ancient walls, originally built by the Romans in the middle ages, encircling its medieval centre with cobbled streets and timber-framed houses made itself worthy of spending. Moreover, the time of the year with cold winds and the ephemeral dark clouds with sporadic rain were changing the place into ethereal beauty. I was having the definite goosebumps and the feeling of a possible great prospective research and of as if the train was not traveling distances but was traveling in time. The feeling was making the portrait within my unconscious mind go back by a century for every mile traversed.

I am skipping the parts of my arrival and all the initial greetings with my new colleagues including Prof Tennyson for my readers as these are relatively less interesting. Upon starting our discussion on a possible project topic, Prof Tennyson stated something which appeared to be very disheartening and disappointing to me. Michael Chapman, the swordsman and horseman of King George IV, and also my topic of research, seemed to be too narrow to have the scope of making a promising Master's Thesis. And quite naturally, I was hoping for something more intense, like the wars that had been fought. However, I could not have been more wrong if I had rejected the project. Not only it secured me a challenging Master's Thesis but also offered me much more in my life.

It is very strange of us humans that our preference is based on the descending order of fame. Otherwise, this place would certainly have become a focal point to native and international tourists. The sublime place had the touch of cathedral constructions as well as the remnants of a fifteenth-century city, lost in time and translation. There was an old church nearby and I could hear the high bell in its tower ringing every respective hour. It had been ringing in the Christ and ringing out the grief, sins and the faithless coldness of the times to the pleasant and wild skies for seasons that one had lost count of. A hilly terrain was there at the centre of the place, encircling which all the other natural and manmade developments had come out like the petals from the stigma of a rose or the arms from the core of a galaxy. Of the remaining artificial beauties from some hundreds of years ago, the graveyard offering the places to the Kings of the medieval times for resting at the north of the hill, and the City Hall at the west were some examples of precocious developments of the medieval societies. Among the offerings from nature herself, I could note the gatherings of Alder, Ash, Maple, Beech and Oaks, the empty fields at the south which once had consisted of commanding barracks and formidable stables, and the remainder of the forest at the most south, more than some miles wide - the memory of the Forbidden Forest, the Forest of Death of the fifteenth century.

And almost at the top of the hill, somewhat in the southern slope, there stood the Castle, founded in the era of King Phillip V and prospered during the reign of King George IV.

The venerable castle did not actually age with respect to time. The impregnable walls made of stones and rocks of the fortress still were standing their ground of defence. The four watchtowers at the four main directions of North-East-South-West and each at each corner of the stronghold were still scanning for intruders over miles.

Of all of them, the tower at the south was the tallest, dominating the skyline of the place. It was almost a clear indication that the south had been the most disturbing and most probable direction of unfamiliar movements and attacks. This assumption quite obviously pointed our attention towards the Forest of Death and the ocean beyond as the sources of intrusions.

I want my readers to particularly note the tower at the South because a majority of this story will involve and revolve around it throughout the following chapters.

The towers, or should I call them the Keeps, were standalone structures made of stone and were the last line of defence against a siege. There were arrow loops almost at the top of them, which were of a window-like shape. Skilled archers used to attend these places with sharpened arrows waiting to stun any intruder's heart. Tall walls were there covering everything in the stronghold. There were

Embrasures and Merlons, openings and parts respectively at the top of the walls where archers could hide and siege. These were actually the first line of defence if the castle was under direct attack. Efficient archers and watchmen used to patrol on the top of these walls twenty-four hours a day. Parts of the keeps were attached to the walls forming parts of the walls' interior as well as exterior portions. Except for the towers within the walls' perimeter, the main engineering of the fortress had been architectured, surrounded by towers and designed by the genius minds of the fifteenth century- the Greathall which actually was the main building, showing panache in both benefits and beauty. In addition to this, there were Baileys - open courtyard fields within the walls and were used for many purposes. There were actually two of them, the North and the South Baileys. Where the North had constituents of battle and nature with armed force as well as one beautiful garden, the South entirely was with the army. The Greathall was in the middle, separating the North and South Baileys. The gatehouse, a huge iron gate protected by Barbican, which was a stone structure established to buttress the gate, was at the southern walls in the southern gradient of the hill. The Barbican itself was a part of the walls and the gatehouse was under it. Their construction in the southern part was a strategic intelligence as it had allowed the soldiers to join the fights mainly coming from the Forest of Death and the ocean beyond with ease. The North Bailey had a marble statue of an Angel, an idol of a beautiful lady with wings spread, hands praying and head down towards earth; she was the Guardian Angel of the castle protecting it from all evils. The South Bailey was all about commanding barracks, stables and other warehouses. However, because of their construction with wood rather than stones, there were very little remnants left of these warehouses when I was in there. The more southern gradient of the hill had contained even greater number of such warehouses which had included siege factories and large-scale armoires. The Greathall, the widest and one of the tallest of all the constructions, had been the place of the King and his family and always had been attended meticulously by the most skilled archers and horsemen called the King's Men. And about thirty kilometres away from the castle, with war-ridden villages to separate them, was where had stood the Forest of Death, The Forbidden One, and the main stage of our story.

To begin with, I was called into the library in the Greathall, almost at the apex floor, which had been built away from the noises of patrolling soldiers and cracking of the swords of the trainees. The library contained books of such a myriad kind that an enthusiastic student could spend days studying. There were books on literature, biographies of the Kings, astronomy, alchemy, medicine, etc.

It was a big and old library. There were almost five columns and ten rows of shelves for books. The books contained the proofs of the unprecedented achievements made by the civilization from some hundreds of years ago. Most of the books, still waiting to be gone through for the very first time in the modern age, were five hundred years old. About half of those books were unfortunate - time had already played its penultimate game on them. And they had lost their ability to tell their stories that they had been saving for so long. The dust and dirt from dates of the centuries had differentiated their pages and called on their deaths. But the mummified chapters of the stories were still enlightening the library like how the dead Castle was glorifying the village. Recently, precautions were taken to save the rest of the books from the evil eyes of dust and pests.

Being a member of Prof Tennyson's team, I was given the opportunity to roam around the library and peruse any book I wanted.

Prof Tennyson delivered me over a tome. It was an extremely worn book with fragile bindings but with costly covers made of cow skin. The once decent quality white pages were yellowish today, with even darker spots in some of them including multiple black spots in some, and broken and rusted edges. This was evident that the book had been of a lot of importance to the King but with time the significance and attention had been overlooked and nobody in the later periods had cared about copying it over to somewhere else or to ameliorate its appalling condition.

"I want you to go through this book and translate the whole to Modern English. Now before you start, remember that it is not written by any scholar but by a common soldier. That's why the language has a robust inclination towards that of a village man. Thus, the job is going to be hard," Prof Tennyson said to me.

"Professor, what is so important about this soldier?" I had to ask.

"Well, I was hoping you would ask that. As a student of History, you do know how biased the writings, biographies and books by the historians and philosophers of different times are, right? They always have tried to show how great their Kings and Queens were. Their works always were in support of the economies, social and religious conditions of their respective nations. Any downfall in the conditions was blamed on natural disasters, even sometimes when it was all the King's worthlessness. There were writers who called Julius Caesar 'Great'. Even Adolf Hitler was once nominated for the Nobel Peace Prize. These are all political. But, this unpublished work is totally unbiased, and I have an intuition that this one is a masterpiece and is wealthy of information stored for us."

That night I started my project on the translation in the library itself. The solitude and the ambience were taking me back to the time of the reign of King George IV. I had some other books from the library to assist me over the job. I could see the scholars arguing over Plato and his theories, I could see the soldiers patrolling, I could see the King being escorted and accompanied by his Men, I could see the Queen, the lovely Princess, I could see King's Man Michael Chapman sitting on the stairs.

By the slope of the snowy highlands,
The four grey walls and grey towers stand,
The breezing river and the barley bands,
The birds fly high to sky in clans,
Away from the fire and fury;
The soldiers marching here and there,
The roaring wind loud and clear,
Waiting for a horsestep familiar
The Lady of Canterbury.

The tome had been written by swordsman, horseman and King's Man Michael Chapman and had been addressed to an anonymous called James. The very first page, without any previous introduction or prefix, started with, "Dear James,"...

2

Michael, James and the Forest of Death

When the two horsemen entered the roadside inn on their way, it had been raining for more than some hours at a stretch. The weather, the storm and the night herself were worsening their already rigorous and stringent work of following their path. Thus, upon seeing the roadside inn, they decided to pause their journey through the resistances and riddles, and go into the inn.

The raindrops were plummeting ruthlessly, mercilessly fast and conforming their path from the Heaven to the Earth on the wet soil. The pristine water on the soil was creating a petrichor. It was erasing the odour of wet leaves. The sky was dominated by black clouds and lightning. The cold in the air was deadly, accompanied by the plutonic silence in the streets. The regular warm clothes of the time of the year were not sufficient to be a threshold against the irregular cold. There was a laziness in the environment; one would like to spend it on his chair next to the fireplace with cigar in his mouth.

The travellers' cloaks, without any crest at the back which was denoting that they were not from the King's Men, were completely wet and so were their horses. It was going to take the long night to dry the other little accessories that they were carrying.

After entering the inn, they discovered themselves on the ground floor which was a bar-cum-restaurant of the three-storyed building. Local farmers, soldiers, natives of other professions and even some people who looked like pirates were helping themselves with rum. Some of them were also having their moments with prostitutes and slaves and were making the place a perfect one for the occurrences of so many crimes including rapes and murders. The shouting by the drunks, their fighting including duels over meaningless issues, the open sex or should I call rapes, and joining the party by other aroused drunks were creating an uncontrollable and interminable hostility and anarchy.

It was not a big room, neither was the inn itself. The width and length of the edges of the place were surprisingly smaller than the height of the inn, which too was not big. A part of this room was for the innkeeper, one adjacent smaller part was the dirty, smelly and smoky kitchen, and the third, the biggest part of the room was for people to dine. There were wooden roundtables and chairs for the guests. And at one corner of the room, there was a very narrow staircase.

The drunks were in groups around roundtables. And they had no ability to realise how violently they were behaving and acting. There were boys who were serving large jars of rum to these 'gentlemen'.

Suddenly, two of the drunks started fighting and fell down on the floor.

"How dare you drink from my glass?" One shouted while fighting.

"Who said it was your glass? It was mine. I paid for it!" The other tried to defend the argument and himself.

-"You did not, you sick bastard! I paid for it. I already had warned you not to drink from it. You lying whore!"

-"I am warning you. Do not talk to me like that. I will kill you!"

-"I will fuck your mother and your sister. I will destroy you if you drink from my glass." This was followed by many foul words addressing the second drunk's family.

The rest of the crowd started cheering. "Kill him" "Yes, go you fools", etc. were chanted with the advices on where to punch. The weak and almost unable punches could barely put on damage to a normal person, but the fighting and under-conscious drunks were getting seriously injured. They were punching, hitting, kicking and breaking glasses. The wrestling floor was getting dangerously covered with the broken pieces of glass and slippery rum. At last, one of them became too tired to continue. The victorious one began almost roaring - a wild expression. And the audience started laughing at and coercing their drinks over the fallen one - the shame of defeat.

The two youthful horsemen went forward towards the innkeeper. The hostile ambience seemed inconspicuous to them as they were least affected by the situation. However, underneath, they were blaming the worthless innkeeper for the situation that was being caused in the bar. The innkeeper himself was completely wasted, and they needed to punch the innkeeper's table hard to snatch his attention. The innkeeper had been taking a nap and the sound generated from hitting the table annoyed him. He looked at the two young men in front of him. He was irritated but also amazed as he was not hoping for young people in that bar during that time of night and weather.

"I beg your pardon?" the drunk innkeeper showed his annoyance, followed by a slang.

"We want a room for two and a shelter for our horses for tonight," one of the two horsemen said to the innkeeper. He almost had to shout while saying the words to assure that the sleepy innkeeper could listen to him despite the hostile environment generated by the drunks.

"We do have a room for you, and a place for the horses. Tell me your names, where you are coming from and where you are heading to," the innkeeper said while opening a book to register the guests.

-"James Wheeler and Michael Chapman. We are from the north and we are to the King's."

The King's name diverted the attention of the drunks from rum, prostitutes and slaves to the young newcomers. They noticed the swords of the swordsmen and decided not to create any scene that might disturb the newcomers for their own good.

After registering their names to the innkeeper, the two horsemen and swordsmen ordered for bread, soup and rum for dinner. They chose a table at one corner, away from the ones of the drunks and the animosity. Getting extremely dissatisfied with the cold food that was served to them, they decided not to make any complaints but to go to their room after leading the horses to the stable.

Their room was as dark, dusty and dirty as the bar downstairs. There also was a foul smell, which might be coming from a dead rat. The men had to clean their beds which otherwise were unworthy to sleep on because of insects. The rainwater coming in through the two open windows of the small room already had created a mess. There was something in that room which was like an omen. It felt like the last day alive on the dying earth. The men could not hear anything else other than the thrumming and impinging rain on the roof, and the cracking thunder. A chair was there with a broken leg which seemed to signify how helplessly disabled and paranoid the men were within the room of damnation. They tried to gaze from the windows but could only see a vengeance of blood red clouds at the horizon of the dark night.

"How long will it take to the castle?" Michael asked while lighting a half-dead candle.

"It will take a few more hours. We will start at dawn. But first we need this goodnight sleep. The horses need a rest too," James replied.

James threw his exhausted body on his bed in a carefree manner. Conscious Michael locked the door and had a second check at it and the small windows. James brought out a tiny bottle of rum, had a slip, passed it to Michael and took it back as Michael had one slip. Then, he started to drink more until Michael rebuked and stopped him.

"I wish I had cigars now," disappointed James said while looking at his wet cigars.

Michael Chapman, 22, was from long of the north. He never knew who his father was and never had the opportunity to ask his mother about this question. What he had heard from others, he was born in a voluntary centre where his mother had come for the delivery at the last stage of her pregnancy. Similar to the storm, snow and cold of that night, Michael himself had always been unwanted to his mother. She, as Michael heard later in his life, had wanted to abort him just after giving the birth. Like the breast milk of his mother, Michael had lacked the care and love. Fortunately, the maids and boys of the centre were there to supervise his mother and take care of little Michael. When he was only five, his mother had left him in the centre and never came back. He had been seeing the darkest of sorrow, pain and loneliness of life since then. Although he did not know the words 'bastard' and 'leftover' back then but even a child like him became aware of the amplitude of these stigmas. As days were passing, he started to become exhausted of the lambasting and chastising of the people of the society as well as that of the centre for being one cumbersome nuisance. It was just before his tenth uncelebrated birthday that he left the centre to find a job in a firm and mill where the workers did not have any knowledge and information of his previous life.

There he had to wake up with the sun, join others in the fields and work till the dusk every day. His every day started with the desire for the end of the day so that he could have the soup and return to his bed. The unprecedented hard work was rapidly erasing the grain of ambition to live that was left within him where he already had lost faith in love and merry. The ring of churches never succeeded to engender the trust that he had lost when he had got tired of looking at the streets and waiting for his mother to come back to the voluntary centre. However, at the end of every day's drudgery and labour, he used to join the others in the party of cigars and rum and listened to the amazing stories of the King of the South, the kingdom, the bravery and efficacy of the King's Men, etc.

"Years ago, there was a time. Our country was not like this then. There were very few people living in our village. The Dark Age of plague had killed so many people. The disease had started with a man in the village. He had got fever. After that, blood had come out of his mouth. From him to his family, from the family to the village - the epidemic had spread. And it was dangerous. But, the time I am talking about, the disease had gone away. People started to come back to the fields. But, our forefathers did not have their own lands like us. There were owners with vast lands. Our forefathers worked for them. And they did not have shoes to wear on the fields. The South was dark then. There were wars between good and evil in there. One day, the King in there heard that the enemy was coming. The troop was endless. Their flags flying in the sky were covering all the white clouds till the end where the sky and land met. The enemy was destroying everything they found. And they were coming to take the throne from the King. They took lives of many people and soldiers. Everyone was helpless. Then, ten King's Men came forward. They went to fight the endless enemies. They hoisted their cloaks of King's Men. And they ran their horses towards the enemies," the oldest of the mill used to tell stories. Michael used to imagine himself as a King's Man running his horse to the war. With determination to visit the South, he started to save from the little that he was earning.

Despite having the relief that here nobody ever had bothered to ask about the source of the name 'Chapman' and about his mother, and furthermore he himself never actually had given up to the donkey work, five years later Michael left the firm to London. In London, Michael met young blacksmith James Wheeler in a workshop where James used to manufacture swords.

Michael was working at a cloth dyeing factory. And he was living in a slum. Like all the other rooms, his room there was tiny and without a security. The broken windows at the falling walls of rusted wood nevertheless never attracted a thief as there almost was nothing to steal. He only had some old clothes and a crooked bowl. During heavy rain, the place would go under flood and water would come into the rooms of the slum of that low land. All the people would have to abandon their rooms and take a shelter at a high land. Keeping themselves dry would become their topmost priority where parents would also strive to find a nut for their crying starving child. The unhygienic place was covered with contaminating mosquitoes and other insects. Diseases and deaths were part of their daily lives.

The hard works of the day in the hot and moist chamber of the factory were nothing better than the job at the firm. Michael was afraid to leave the job. There were nights when he went to sleep without a piece of bread. The wheel of his fortune was not turning at all. But, was not it?

It was a lazy afternoon of a late summer. The sun was setting at the warm west. Michael was at a market to buy his bread and eggs. The small market was a place only for the slumdogs. The rich crowd of London had no intention to visit this poverty-stricken market to buy rotting foods. Suddenly, Michael heard a noise.

"Thief, thief," a shopkeeper was shouting at a small boy running away with some apples. Some other shopkeepers started to chase the kid. He tried to run away, but the tiny legs gave up to the boisterous muscles. The men started to beat the kid.

Michael took up a big and narrow piece of wood, and jumped at the men. He used the piece like a sword to attack them and save the kid. After a few moments, the men ran away.

"We will see you soon," they were warning him.

The next day, Michael was there again to buy that night's grocery. And he was confronted by the men. Today, the men had weapons for themselves. Unarmed Michael tried to defend himself. But, the men were beating him up badly.

"Who will come to save you now?", "I know he is also with the kid", "Break the arm. He will never lift anything again", they were saying while hitting Michael with their iron rods and pieces of wood. Every hit was effective and he was bleeding. No one came to his rescue even when there were people at the market. They merely were observing the incident. But, all of a sudden, someone came up with an actual sword. Fallen Michael could see him beating the men with the sword. His defence and footwork also were noteworthy.

The men were still trying to hit him for the first time. At last, they gave it up and ran away.

The swordsman helped Michael to stand up. And he was very angry at the observing crowd. He used a slang at them and shouted at them to go away. Now, Michael could see him properly. He was wearing a brown cloak and a black hat. And the sword was shining. This was the first time he was seeing an actual sword. It was a sword like the ones of the King's Men.

"Are you alright? My God, there is blood all over you. You need to see a doctor," he said.

"I am okay. And I do not need a doctor," Michael replied, although he was very tensed and was shaking seeing the blood.

-"Let me help you get back to your house. What do you do for a living?"

-"I work at a factory."

-"I saw you yesterday. Those men were beating the boy and you helped him. I was having a cigar and I heard the noise. I was just thinking of going to save the boy when I saw you with the wood. You fought well. You are very talented. Why don't you come with me? I am a blacksmith. I make swords. You can also work with me. Besides, I sincerely doubt this place is ever going to be safe for you again."

Michael thought for a moment about the sudden invitation. He was reluctant to follow a stranger. However, the entire London was a stranger and unfriendly to him. And, swords fighting was the goal for which he had come to London.

"I am Wheeler. Call me James. And you?" The skilled swordsman with the brown cloak and black hat had taken Michael's silence as a yes.

James was an orphan living in London and had been working in the workshop for a long time. Michael managed to get a job in the workshop and became James' acquaintance. James, who was a year older than Michael, soon became his guide in this new and carefree society and the wanting best friend that Michael always had needed.

The fifteenth century London was becoming the capital of Europe very fast. Soon, it was going to become the capital of the nation where the sun never set. It was going to capture and colonise countries, continents and subcontinents from different parts of the globe. And it was going to rule the world in terms of arts, literature, drama, science and technology, medicine, and even alchemy and astrology. Now, the torch was being lit with the growth of the population and wealth that were fuelled by a vast expansion in trade. London was having trade in woollen clothes and dyes, processed food and furniture - both wooden and metallic. The period was seeing London rising as the most important among Europe's commercial centres. Trade expanded beyond Western Europe to the Americas, and beyond Eastern Europe of Germany's Bremen, Hamburg to Russia. Mercantilism and monopoly trading companies such as the Muscovy Company and the precursors of British East India Company were getting established by Royal Charter. The latter was going to arrive in the Indian territory to trade and later, to rule. Immigrants were coming from Wales, Northern Ireland and also from Portugal and France. During the Reformation, the city was the principal early centre of Protestantism in England. Nearly half of the properties belonged to different monasteries.

All of these were happening in exchange of child labourers, slaves and the inhuman torture on a deprived majority of the city. One could watch children making a crowd in front of slaughterhouses for a piece of meat, men working all day in factories and firms without food and rest, pregnant women begging on streets. On one side of the wide roads, there were commendable City Halls and on the other side, there were poignant slums forcefully separated from the rest of the societies. Where one side of the roads was lightened by torches and street lights, the other one was dark, non-airy and densely populated. Murders, assassinations and rapes were as common as daylight.

There were early fortifications of the London Bridge and the Tower of London on the Thames River. The river was an important medium of transportation and trade. The growth of the population greatly increased the amount of waste entering the river - human waste, waste from slaughterhouses and that from the processing factories. Corpses also seldom floated up on the water surface. Throughout its history, the tower had been used as a settlement of Kings as well as to imprison a wide range of prisoners, from deposed monarchs to more common criminals. The two sons of late King Edward IV, imprisoned in here, had never come out alive yet.

Although the work in the workshop was as hard as in the firm and the factory, Michael here got the chances towards his dream - every day after the shutdown of the workshop, James and he got into friendly duels to sharpen their skills. Moreover, he had gotten accustomed to the labour of the works a long time ago and so it did not affect him. The innate and natural talent of James and his prospect as a possible swordsman were praised a lot by natives whereas Michael had to go through tough calls with it. Sometimes, locals gathered around to enjoy the duels of Michael and James and cheered for both of them. At the beginning of every duel, Michael was able to match James both in techniques and power, however, as time forwarded with the duel, Michael started to get overwhelmed. He had got a terrible birthmark - a difficulty to adjust with blood which resisted him to continue duels for long as duels had obvious injuries followed by blood. James was aware of this condition of his friend and supported him in every possible way. Michael himself, on the other hand, always refused to call it the reason behind his failure and looked at it as an excuse behind his poor talents. Every loss to James inspired like flame within him to train for an hour more than James. He became fixated on the fact that the only way he could catch up with James was by spending more time and sweat. He knew it was the only way he could achieve his dream of becoming a King's Man. His best friend James always took some workload off him to practically support his extra training.

Both of their experiences in sword-fighting helped them in manufacturing quality swords and vice versa. Some of their best outputs were imported by the King for his army, and for the King's Men. This gave them their auspicious opportunity of a lifetime when Michael was 21 and James was 22 and were still working in the workshop. One fine afternoon, two men in cloaks entered the workshop. Their cloaks had crests on their back - a sword on a circle, the crest of the King, the crest to wear by the King's Men. They had ridden here from the southern kingdom on horses and decided to stop at a familiar environment of battles, duels and swords. They were Commander Black, the commander of the King's Men, and Sir Arnold Light, one of the most skilled, experienced and powerful, second in command after Commander Black and one of the topmost in the hierarchy. They were quite impressed with the workers of the workshop, especially with Michael and James, for the aspects and features of the swords made by them. They also shared some suggestions on the key characteristics of swords that they preferred and expected. Every soldier had his own preference on the weight, length and width ratios of different parts of a sword - the Hilt which included the Pommel or bottom end of the grip, the grip itself and the Guard which separated the grip from the metal, the metal part which included the edges, the Fuller which was the axis of the metal and the upper point. However, some of the preferences are scientifically more accurate and those of these two King's Men were some of them.

The owner of the workshop asked Michael and James to spend more time with the King's Men in order to increase his chances of having a contract with the King. The King's Men were sitting and observing the works of the workshop when the owner approached towards them.

"My respected Sirs, these are Michael Chapman and James Wheeler," he said while introducing Michael and James. And he continued, "They are two of my finest workers. And they are swords-fighters themselves. They know how to make the bests of all swords."

"Is that so?" Commander Black seemed to be impressed, "you boys are into swords fighting? Where did you learn?"

"We taught ourselves, Sir," James answered.

"Well, well! There are some basic rules in swords fighting. One needs to start after learning those. They are like the primary education that a fighter has to pass. But, when someone is into duels without learning those orthodox rules, something original is born within him. I would like to see you two duel!" Sir Light was equally impressed.

Michael and James could not have let this chance go away and they appealed to the Men for a friendly duel. To their great surprise, the Men accepted it. It was the Commander against James and Sir Light against Michael.

"Look, I am not going to tell Sir Light about your condition. But you need to promise me that when things get worse, you quit," James asked Michael.

"Thank you for the gesture. But you know, now I really should stop running away from it. Sorry, I cannot promise this to you," Michael replied with a sigh.

The duels started. The pains of practices and works of every single day for the last six years were finally paying off for Michael and James. The extra time and effort by Michael were proving out to be excellent decisions of the past. Both of them were compelling two of the best veterans of the Great Island to bring out their bests. However, it became unfortunate to Michael when he started getting nervous and overwhelmed after getting a cut on his left and non-combat arm. This resulted in his defeat. On the other side, James fought for longer and his skills were perfectly cancelling out that of the commander. The stamina that he had built for the long time was also benefiting him. Furthermore, he was fighting audaciously, with bold techniques and movements. But, a small mistake in a move called on his defeat too.

Both of the King's Men were moved by their oppositions.

"I cannot remember the last time I fought this hard against someone who is not a soldier. You two totally forced us to give our best. The kingdom at the South direly needs soldiers as strong as you. Michael and James, how would you like to join the army of South in the future?" the Commander asked.

"It has been our dream for a long time, Sir," the boys said in unison.

The proud audience of the workshop were looking at the two youngest workers when the Commander took white parchments out of his bag. And he gave written recommendations with the seal of King's Crest - the sword on the circle, to the boys. That night Michael and James decided to work more in the workshop in order to save money because of the need of buying horses to ride to the South. The recommendation was the hope beyond disappointment to Michael for losing the battle due to the same old reason. And he promised himself to work even harder to get over. And this was the past of Michael and James.

It was almost midnight when Michael and James, the two newcomer swordsmen in the roadside inn, woke up on hearing a noise from downstairs. It was coming from the bar. The noise was loud enough to distinguish itself from any of those created by the drunks. The young men even heard swords cracking, women screaming, and someone shouting out in agony. For a moment, both of the two young men thought in minds that it was another anarchy by the intoxicated people enjoying the night. However, they decided to go downstairs to check the situation out.

Keeping in mind the possible gravity of the on-going situation, Michael and James were coming downstairs while watching for their feet, without making a noise and hiding as much as they could. Before they almost came down, James waved his hand to make a gesture to stop. He wanted to know the situation well before actually getting into it. They started looking at it while hiding behind the wall of the stairs.

The sound indeed was an aberration from that of the drunks. Michael and James could see three men in black cloaks, wet which was proving that they recently had come in from rain. They had swords pointed towards the frightened audience - the drunks, the prostitutes, the slave girls and the innkeeper in a night gown and a lantern in one hand. And someone in blood was lying on the floor- a headless corpse with a sword in a hand. The two young swordsmen could guess that this man was the one who had gotten into the duel and they had heard their swords cracking. One of the three intruding murderers was holding the head of the unfortunate loser of the duel as the medal of his triumph. The frightened and shocked audience were all standing at one corner of the room, staring at the murderers and trying to be as far away from them as they could. Some of them were holding swords themselves, but they were too wasted and panicked to inaugurate a fight against the skilled murderers who had just committed a serious crime. The broken chairs and tables and the broken glasses of the bottles of rum on the floor were highlighting the amplitude of the recent duel.

One of the three murderers, who was holding the head of the dead, threw it at the audience aiming for the innkeeper and said, "We told you we would go in there and come back. And we did it. The stupid bastard should never have played the bet. He lost it and then refused to pay. So, he deserves it. His head will pay me."

The second of the murderers walked towards the frightened audience, pointing the sword towards them, and said, "Give us everything that you have." Looking at the innkeeper he continued, "Why don't you start, Mr. Bummer? Give us all that you have earned."

The third one of them walked towards the audience, grabbed the hand of a slave girl firmly and pulled her forcefully, saying, "Why don't you please me tonight?" Despite all her efforts, shouting and crying, the poor girl could not free herself from the grip of him.

Judging that the situation was crossing the lines, Michael and James finally decided to show up.

"Listen fellas, you already have made a lot of mess. We will give you half of the water clock time to clean all this up and leave," James gave the ultimatum.

The three murderers looked at the two young men in cloaks and swords in hands.

"The King's Men!" someone of the frightened drunks said out loud. This was enough to snatch the broad attention of the murderers from the mess, money and the poor slave girl to the two young men with swords and cloaks challenging them. Although they were aware of the fact that if in fact their challengers were from the King's Men of the Castle then they would have no chance in a combat, they were unwilling to give up after being insulted.

"And who are challenging us if I may know?" the first of the three murderers asked.

"Sir Michael Chapman and Sir James Wheeler from the King's Men, from the seventh regiment of the South Tower," Michael took the vantage position of being called the King's Men.

Preparing himself mentally for the upcoming robust battle, the first of the three murderers alerted, "No one messes with us. If it is needed, we will have two more heads today."

It was a moment of high tension. The audience was preparing itself for the round two of the battle of the night, a more intense one than the previous one, between the two King's Men and the three murderers. The crowd was going to witness more damages to the place and more deaths.

At that moment something happened which was beyond any expectations of both the audience and the duellers. The third of the three murderers collapsed down on his knees grabbing his chest, panting heavily and trying to breathe desperately. Michael and James understood that he was having difficulty breathing. Suddenly, the man started to hit and stab his chest with his fist as if he was urgently trying to ease the unbearable ache he was having. However, it only exacerbated the condition, rather than ameliorating, and he started vomiting blood. Shocked, his two companions of the nexus grabbed his arms, tried to lift him up, saying, "Steven, are you alright? What is happening?"

James was the earliest to adapt to the circumstances and was the fastest to react to it. He quickly grabbed a glass, poured rum into it from a barrel and gave it to Steven to drink. Because of the healing quality of rum and the hangover which could ease the pain, it was one ingenious gesture. However, unfortunately, Steven could not finish the glass. His lifeless body was lying partly on his companions' arms and mostly on the floor. The two companions of Steven continued to shout calling his name in the last attempt to wake him up.

When everyone was still looking at Steven and failing in endeavours to understand what just had happened, someone from the crowd shouted out, "You are cursed! You went into the forest. You will disappear. You will be spirited away."

It was a drunk from the crowd, almost at the corner, behind almost everyone else. He had a cross made of stone in hand; he was shocked to death and was praying without a break.

"It happened again, like last fifty years. You should not have come back. But as you are here, you will die, soon. Your final destination is recorded," he continued to stammer.

For a moment, everyone else's attention was fixed at the stammering drunk. And, they finally were finding the link missing between the mysterious death and the bold move that the three murderers had taken some time ago. Although Michael and James were still in uncharted territory, they were guessing that the three murderers had done something impudent which became the reason of Steven's death. Both of them were surprised and shocked; they looked at each other with an attempt to ask the other to comprehend what the stammering drunk was talking about.

This was the moment when the second of the murderers stood up. He was looking pallid, his legs were shaking badly and he was putting all his force to stand. The sword from his hand fell down on the floor because of the loose grip of his weak hand. It was just past midnight, with heavy and cold rain without any break and strong wind accompanying it. He went out of the inn, ran to the unfriendly environment and shouted, "I don't want to die. Forgive me, God." Repeating this over and over again, he climbed up on his horse and started running away. Very soon he got out of everyone's sight because of the recondite rain and storm.

It took the first of the murderers some time to get over everything. Nonetheless, he knew that it was the last time he was seeing his companion of nexus, the second murderer. Being betrayed, outnumbered and after losing his companions, he lost control over himself. Calling the innocent stammering drunk culpable for his losses, he cried out, "You! Old fool! You are the reason for this. None but you should die. You should be spirited away." He rushed towards him carrying the sharpened sword with the thirst for the second kill of the night, however, was blocked by James on his way. Their swords tackled against each other. This time the first of the murderers could see the back of James's cloak and recognised it.

"You don't have the crest. You don't have the King's Crest. You are not King's Men," he laughed. "I will kill you!"

And thus the much awaited and inevitable duel of the night finally inaugurated. The first of the murderers was mentally stressed and physically fatigued where James was defying the laws of nature. From the very first of the blows, the outcome seemed predictable. And as expected, the duel did not last long as James's sword penetrated through the man's chest. As Michael already knew about James's power, perfection and panache, he was not surprised. On the other side, it was also the most probable result to the crowd because they already had been waiting for the destined death of the last of the murderers, the trespasser to the Forest.

Michael was the one to break the silence followed by the last death of the night. James was cleaning blood from his sword with the dead man's cloak. The crowd finally started to feel ease and relief as the magnitude of the intensity of the night started to decline. Some of the drunks including the innkeeper came out of the amassed crowd from the corner of the room as their nightmare was over. "As we meet the King, we will not say that anything happened here. In fact, we will not say that we spent the night here. But you need to take care of the dead," Michael said.

James was finally done with cleaning his sword. He went to the cash register box, took some money and said, "And as we have never been here, I think we should be paid back for the stay and for the awful dinner." No one including the innkeeper protested this open theft by James but was looking at them with respect and gratefulness.

"Can I make you men some nice hot drinks?" the innkeeper tried to impress the two young men or bribe them for something; it might be a payback for the unimpressive dinner of the night that had been served or for saving his inn from the murderers or as a bribe for not revealing the poor condition of the inn both in hygiene and morality to the King.

"No, we are good", James said while climbing the stairs.

"But yes, you should keep it down, your party, we will be sleeping," Michael smiled and gave a friendly warning while following James.

The next morning with the sunrise, Michael and James left the inn to ride to the castle. It took them some hours on horses, as James had predicted, and they reached the hilly terrain at noon.

As they were heading closer towards the stronghold, the terrain under the horses' heals was getting more and more ups and downs. From their way to where their eyesight met the horizon, it was all green highlands. There were seldom giant rocks amassed on the ground, created by some unknown ancient natural phenomena. There also were scattered grasslands with wild horses roaming. Whenever the two horsemen were up on a hill of the highlands' many peaks, they could survey a larger part of the vast terrain. They could also hear the high bell of a church ringing from somewhere close.

At last, they could see the apex of the four towers of the castle, the flags with the King's Crest flying high kissing the sky and some of the many regiments outside the castle from the other side of the hill. As they moved forward, they were stopped by soldiers of the fifth regiment of the North Tower for interrogation. The nomenclature or numbering of the regiments close to a respective tower or Keep was in ascending order as one moved away from the castle along the respective of the four directions. The North Tower had five regiments in front of it and thus the fifth one was the northernmost one and the first regiment of the North Tower was the closest one to it. Similar was the scene for the West and East Towers. The South Tower had two more regiments, making the seventh regiment of the South as the southernmost regiment and the one closest to the Forest of Death. Each regiment was a half kilometre away from the nearest regiment and thus the seventh regiment of the South was three-and-a-half-kilometres away from the castle. Each regiment consisted of barracks, stables, workshops, arsenals, watchtowers and torches. Moreover, each regiment had its own soldiers - swordsmen, horsemen, archers, and a commander to lead.

As Michael and James came close enough so that the soldiers of the fifth regiment of the North could observe them from their watchtowers, some soldiers came riding on horses and blocked the way to the castle. There were five of them - one was in the front and others were behind him in a guarding position. Two of them were bearing the hoisted flags of the King with the crest.

"Who are you, passing? Tell us your names and why you are here," the leader of them said out.

"We are James Wheeler and Michael Chapman. We are from London. We are here to join the seventh regiment of the South," James vehemently replied.

Giving it a little discontinuity, the leader looked back at his comrades. Then he said, "Do you know you do not get to pick the regiment? After your thorough examination, the army gets to pick it."

-"We have written recommendations from Commander Black of the King's Men. We hope that by his name the army can make two exceptions."

The soldiers looked at each other after hearing James' reply. It was obvious that they were impressed at the two young aspirants' achievements. Without making any delay, the leader ordered two of his soldiers and one flag bearer to escort Michael and James to the seventh regiment of the South.

It was more than six kilometres perpendicular from the fifth regiment of the North to the seventh regiment of the South. However, the fifth regiment of the North was in the northern slope of the hill whereas the seventh regiment of the South was on the other side of the hill,that is the southern slope. Moreover, the castle itself was on the southern slope and they needed to bypass its territory. All of these made their road even longer.

On their way, Michael and James saw the ten other regiments that were on their path. They witnessed the barracks, stables, workshops and arsenals. They saw the hoisted flags, there were many of them. They saw the training grounds, the horsemen on the horses duelling, archers aiming for their targets, devoted workers in the workshops. They encountered the commanders of the regiments ordering the fallen and tired trainees to get up again, pick their swords up and go back to the hardships one more time. They glimpsed defeated soldiers to get back on their horses, spend more sweats, highlight disaffected attention and show impregnable determination to claim their feats again. The soldiers of the large army of those regiments also looked back at the two unknown men on the horses. Nonetheless, finding their own comrades and the flag bearer with them, the soldiers realised that the two unfamiliar faces were of no concern and must have been here for some genuine reason. Therefore, they went back to the training.

In the middle of their road, Michael and James reached the castle just after they had crossed the pinnacle of the hill to go from the northern gradient to the southern one. The gigantic engineered architecture was obstructing their way and they had to bypass it. The monstrous walls of it were separating them from the interior of the stronghold. And the width of the fortress, as well as the height of the walls, only allowed them to enjoy a little glimpse of the vertex of the Greathall. They looked up to see patrolling archers on the walls and the Keeps, examining their every move with alert eyes and targeted arrows. And as they passed the castle, they found the tallest of all the structures - the Tower of the South.

As they finally reached the seventh regiment of the South, they found a similar scene as in the other regiments they had crossed - soldiers spending time in the training grounds and workers doing the same in the workshops. Michael, James and their companion soldiers stopped their horses and came down. Watching this, the soldiers of the regiment paused their training to look after the situation. There were three of the soldiers who came towards them.

"Wait here," said one of the companion soldiers of Michael and James, and went towards the three soldiers of this regiment and said something in a low tone.

Hearing whatever he said, the three veterans looked back at Michael and James. One of them came, moved his hand ahead as a gesture to shake hands and said, "Nice to meet you two. I am Benjamin. Call me Ben." Michael and James shook hands and introduced themselves.

"We want to join this regiment. I think we should meet the Commander," Michael told about their interest.

"Someone call Molly. She is in her tent," the second of the three soldiers ordered. "Hello, I am Daniel. I am the second in Command after Commander Molly here. I am happy to welcome you," he said while introducing himself.

"Hi, I am Raphael," the third of them said. They shook hands.

A soldier from the ones who had been training went into a tent nearby. And after a moment, he came out with Commander Molly - a young attractive lady in armour suit but with a glass of wine in one hand. It definitely was ironic and contradictory as it was unusual to see a soldier in armour to drink. Michael and James were a little surprised to find their possible leader a woman. But at the same time they admitted their loyalty to her silently. They were impressed and had fun looking at her and because of the wine.

"Yo, yo! Who is welcoming whom into the regiment? Is it you Daniel, you fool?" she asked. She was walking in a funny way. Definitely, she was drunk.

"I am James Wheeler and this is my friend Michael Chapman. We are from London. We are here to join the seventh regiment of the South," James said vividly.

-"Wait a minute. Do you really believe you can just join us? Do you think you have what it takes to be in this regiment? Don't you know this is the hardest of all the regiments?" Molly asked. She tied her dark brown hair behind her head and tried to look serious at last.

-"We know ma'am. That's the reason why we chose this regiment of all."

Molly stopped for a moment, looked at the two bold men in front of her for an instant, gave the glass of wine to the soldier standing next to her and said, "But you just cannot be recruited. Well, if it were a regiment of North then it would have been possible. Of course, they also would judge your determination, loyalty, etc. But here you need to prove that you are capable of being here."

James walked towards her, brought out the recommendations from Commander Black, Commander of the King's Men, and gave them to Molly. "Here, we are referred by the highest of the entire army, Commander Black," he said with self-satisfaction.

Molly took the papers and went through. The papers were Commander Black's letter, with costly ink and King's Crest sealed at the bottom. The letters stated, "To whom it may concern. This is to certify that the bearer of this letter is an excellent sword fighter. I, hereby, confirm that he can be an excellent swordsman of the army."

After reading the letters, Molly gave them back to James and said, "Look, I understand that these are strong recommendations. However, to me, still you have to prove yourselves," she insisted.

Michael was a little annoyed and confused with Molly. He said, "You are not joking, right? These are from the Commander of the King's Men!"

-"Listen to me. Do you know what the most threatened place of the entire stronghold is? This regiment. Care to guess why? Well, you should know it. Know it later, ask someone about it. And there are these King's Men, always within the castle, within the rocky walls. They barely come out to fight the actual fights. This is the reason why I cannot trust the value of these recommendations. And if in fact they are worthy of being believed, then why don't you prove it one more time?"

"It's fine. We are ready to go for it. Tell us what you want us to do," James said with confidence.

Molly smiled hearing this and her eyes sparkled. "I think you have hitherto met Daniel and Benjamin. They are my best soldiers. I want you two to fight them. Show me your skills. Prove your worth," she said.

"We will be delighted to," said Michael and James, picked up their swords and entered the open field. They were feeling the urge within themselves, the flame to prove every drop of the sweats they had lost over the last many years. It was the first step towards achieving their goal and they were prepared to give all they had to make it come true. Both Daniel and Ben also joined them after receiving the order from their Commander.

Michael was taking the challenge of Daniel and James was against Ben. Molly indeed was correct and was not exaggerating. The seventh regiment of the South undoubtedly had the best soldiers of the entire army and Daniel and Ben unquestionably were two of them.

To pass Molly's tests, Michael and James needed to fight duels on foot as well as while riding their horses. All the other soldiers of the regiment were observing the duels while Molly herself was closely examining them.

Footwork was one key aspect that distinguished a great swordsman from the ordinary ones. Along with the movements of arms and shoulders, the reaction of the legs against the opposition's was one feature that affected the outcome of the battle. Like the playing of a piece of a challenging game of chess, the movement of legs ensured a constant pressure on the opposition after perfectly securing the defensive position for the dueller himself. The metaphor of chess held true again as the efficient movement of legs required prediction of opposition's upcoming movements and with the tendency to thwart them from the very beginning. On the other hand, a battle between horsemen was mostly about the pace of both the man and the horse. Their perfect skills relied on the speed and how to respond to the speed. An ethereal but slow skill could not be much of a requisite in here. However, skills of a high category definitely were needed too, especially when the duellers matched in speed. It was like a game of clocked chess - the duel inaugurated with some basic moves which the duellers mostly remembered like the grammar of the duel. However, as the duel proceeded, it needed efficacy in skills and pace.

As they battled the duel on foot, Michael and Daniel found their strengths to equally match and thus after giving it a lot of tries, they had to call it a tie. However, the battle while riding their horses had an inclined outcome as Daniel came out as victorious. Although it had been a popular phrase for long that 'not the horse but the horseman matters', but here it turned out to be a fallacy. Daniel's horse was way too powerful and quick, giving him an extra advantage. In contrast, Michael's horse was not meant for intense battles like this. For James, the outcomes were almost similar. His inborn talent and precocity made him gain victory in the duel on foot. However, he also lost his duel on his horse.

Both Michael and James fell down from their horses, resulting in their defeat, and their opponents came down from their horses to offer them helping hands to stand up.

So far, all the other soldiers including Raphael were cheering for their favourites, they even had gambled the following night's dinner and finally, everybody enjoyed the duels. Molly was, however, distant from being a mere audience and had taken the role of a judge. At the end of the duels she clapped slowly. She was satisfied with the two enthusiasts and her big smile was proving that.

"Bravo, my boys. You too, James and Michael. I am proud of you all," she said. "However," she continued, "I need some changes before you two are recruited into my team. First, I want you to have actual armours, not those fashionable cloaks you are wearing. Secondly, I want you to have actual war horses, not those old ones."

"We could only buy them with whatever we had. Besides, they have been with us for many fights," James was reluctant to let his horse go.

-"Now now, don't be a cry baby," Molly laughed. "You can keep those in our stables. But I want you to have two other horses from there. In fact, I'll recommend which horses to pick."

"So I think we are in the team?" Michael asked with ambition.

Molly took some time to look at both of them, took the glass of wine and drank one ounce, did her hair for a moment and then said smiling, "Yes, you too are in."

"I, Commander of the seventh regiment of the South Tower, hereby, welcome Michael Chapman and James Wheeler to our regiment. Take pride in yourself to be a part of the Seventh Regiment of the South. You are the descendants of real heroes who have fought and sacrificed their lives for our country. Be proud that you will walk through the same grounds, share same tents that once those legendary soldiers of this regiment and this country did, before they bravely died fighting against humongous enemies," she announced, and then turned back to Daniel and said in a lower tone, "See, this is how you welcome someone in the team!"

Daniel could not help laughing. "I learn from you, Molly!" he said.

"By the way, James, before going to your tents, how would you like to dance with me?" Molly offered while picking up her sword.

Although James was a bit tired because of the entire journey and the duels, he could not deny the offer from his Commander. "I surely will follow your lead, my Lady," he intentionally flirted back while picking up his own sword.

It was the night. Michael and James were sharing the same tent with Daniel, Ben and Raphael. They all were celebrating the night for the recent recruitment of Michael and James into the regiment. Only a few moments ago, they had roasted chicken and parts of beef outside the tent, and now they were enjoying them with bread, fruits and rum. Michael and James were loving the barbarian style dinner. It must be mentioned that soldiers traditionally did not get to have parties like that but today, Molly had permitted them with a special exception. Michael and James were feeling lucky to have found friends in this new place so sooner than what they had expected.

The piles of wood to cook outside the tents had burned away a while ago; they were still producing smoke which was going up to the sky. Some of the pieces of coal were still emitting a red hot heat wave. Most of the soldiers had gone into their tents to have a good night sleep. The horses had been brought to their stables. Even the blacksmiths of the workshops and armoires had locked their workplaces and gone to their homes nearby or respective tents. Only a few archers were outside, on the watchtowers, alert and awake. They were wearing warm clothes. The torches of this regiment were tearing off the ocean of darkness in this vast hostile land.

"I think you could beat Molly if you were not tired. It was completely your battle," Raphael said to James about his fight against Molly that afternoon where he had to call it a day after fighting for long.

"Yes. Of course, she is the strongest of us all. But you were even better. You clearly had the chances. I have no idea what Molly is thinking after finally finding her match," Daniel agreed.

"No, no. I don't think so," James denied himself. "She also was drunk. She fought like that in spite of being wasted. I don't know how good she normally is. I might have no chance against her if she hadn't had wine. This was a defeat today, fair and square," he conceded.

"Yes, I must say she is strong. I mean, at first, I should admit, I was confused how strong a woman like her could be," Michael shared his thought.

"She is the strongest of our regiment. In fact, she is one of the strongest of all the regiments. Although she is only a little older than us, she is one of the most experienced. She has fought actual war - a civil war some years back. She also has been outside of this kingdom. She has visited from the north of this Great Island to the south. And by south, I mean she has been very close to the forest," Ben informed.

-"But don't you think she is too rude to all of you?"

-"That's Molly. Actually, she never knew what love or care is. We have heard of her story. She doesn't even know how it feels to be cared for or to care for someone else. However, I personally think that she does care for us, her regiment and this kingdom in her own lifeless way."

"Why did you say she doesn't know what love or care is?" James showed interest.

"Because she is a bastard daughter of a former King's Man. Her father had her with a prostitute of the North when he had explored that place for a mission. And he came back with Molly, but without the mother. As we heard, she had refused to come. From the very beginning, Molly was alone. Her father was always hardworking and engaged with his work and used to live either in the castle or outside in missions. Molly was left behind and she started training on her own. She faced brutal truth of life and had to survive on her own. Before long, her father was killed in action. See, she never got loved. And I think she hated her father," Raphael said.

James looked at Michael for a moment to review how he was doing. James already knew the story of Michael's childhood. A similarity with that of Molly inevitably reminded Michael of his own distorted childhood. He, quite surprisingly, did not exhibit any emotions to reveal himself.

"Is that the reason why she has such hatred towards the King's Men? Because of her father?" Michael asked.

-"Yes partly. But again, she believes that King's Men do not deserve the acclaims and accolades they get. After all, we face the hardest of the missions."

-"Because we have the forest?"

"Correct!"

"So what is the deal with the forest anyway? Why is it called the Forbidden One, the Forest of Death?" James asked with curiosity.

The three soldiers rotated their eyes at each other. It appeared that all of them wanted to split out everything, but again hesitated to say anything at the same time. At last, Daniel, the second in command, took the lead and the responsibility. He finished his glass of wine, took a piece of beef at hand, held it instead of eating, breathed heavily in and exhaled out. Coincidentally, a perturbation in the weather occurred at the moment calling in the wind and mild rainfall. The fire radiating the heat and light so far in the tent extinguished due to the impact of a sudden wind, leaving the natives of it in total darkness. Michael and James felt an unusual downfall in temperature due to the light going off or the nature or something completely supernatural. Ben stood up and shut the entrance of the tent to prevent the cold from coming in. Raphael took some buffalo wax and lighted it up to generate a feeble flame. And Daniel started.

"There is a reason why it is called the Forbidden Forest, the Forest of Death. First, I am going to tell you about something that happened fifty years ago. Back then, this place was not like what we are seeing now. The castle had lower walls, the Keeps were not this tall and strong, the army was not this big. There were no such separate regiments every half a kilometre away, although it did have the constructions. The kingdom, in fact, was not this troubled by war. Back then, it was King Phillip V. He was the one who founded this castle and this kingdom. Now, from our regiment to the forest, there exist some villages. Back then they existed too but were in far better shape. One day, I must say fifty years ago, something unexpected happened. Nobody from here was ready for it. Soldiers and pirates from the other side of the forest started to invade into the villages. They came overcoming the Great Sea on the other side of the forest. They were countless. The villagers got outnumbered. The soldiers and the pirates looted, killed and raped. Many innocuous villagers were taken back into the forest. After hearing the news, the King sent his best soldiers. Initially, it worked. But soon, everything just elapsed. More enemies started to come than the ones who were killed. The King had to dispatch his entire army. He even took the risk of leaving his own castle almost defenceless. Soon, the army itself started to be hackneyed. To commensurate the loss, the King was compelled to send non-military citizens to fight. And obviously, as they did not have any prior training, the endeavour was going in vain. A big part of the war occurred in the forest. Even the highly skilled soldiers faced difficulties to fight in there where sunlight cannot penetrate, where the depth is so intense that one suffocates, where it is like a maze and one easily gets lost. The enemy pirates who were inured to fight in such scenarios were getting the dominance. And it was impossible for the non-military citizens to habituate themselves with this condition. Anyway, the war went on for a year. And at last, the enemy fell back. Everything took a while to get back to normal from aberration. The enormous casualties could not be suppressed from affecting the nation. There were economic recessions, a hike in the costs, and after all, a great loss of humans from all sectors - from military to agrarian.

However, something did not go back to normal. It was the forest itself. The natives found that it had changed. They started to hear unnatural sounds from the forest coming at nights. There were howling, cracking of swords, patrolling of soldiers, and sounds of running horses. It seemed like the dead were coming back to life at night. It was like they were resurrected to conclude their war that they had left unfinished. The curse started covering the villages. People started going crazy. There was an increase in anarchy. The villages totally got separated from the rest of the nation. Many people went into the forest. Some went after becoming crazy, some went to see the truth, and some played bets. But no one of them made it back from the forest. Till today, it is called the Forbidden Forest, the Forest of Death. Till today, the dead soldiers wake up at night to continue their fights. Till today, its curse is there on the villages, even on us. We, the soldiers of this regiment, are also involved. Every time something happens in the villages or in the forest, it is us who are called. We try to avoid the forest. But as soon as you are recruited here, you are part of the curse. We need to be ready, always, to fight not only the next possible attack from the other side of the forest but also the supernatural within it. We know why you have chosen this regiment over all. Yes, it is the quickest way to get promoted to King's Men as it has the maximum number of chances. However, be informed that it, in addition, contains the maximum possible death threats."

The incident of the previous night, the behaviour of the drunks towards the murderers, the constant mourning of the stammering drunk and everything else were clarifying themselves to Michael and James at last. They finally were establishing the link amongst the occurrences of last night that had been missing so far. From the moment the murderers had gone into the forest they had become cursed and destined to die - to disappear and be spirited away. It was not James who killed the first of them, it had been already profited.

After taking time to recall the incident from last night, at last James said, "Do you really believe in this? Sounds like a story to me."

-"Well, I admit, it does sound like that. But you will know it too, very soon. I will, as your friend, ask you not to enter the forest."

Raphael tried to reduce the intensity of the atmosphere. "Hey, what do you think about Molly?" He tried changing the context.

"Huh! I think she is very arrogant, and a fool too. She should not hate all the King's Men only because of her father. And she is treating her soldiers the way her father used to treat her - with apathy. So how is she different from her father?" Michael said promptly. The first interaction between Molly and him was unfriendly to him.

"I think you don't like her," James said laughing.

-"Oh! I think you like her too much!" Michael did not like how James was becoming fond of her.

-"Hey! It is not like that! I respect her as our leader," James tried to cover himself.

"Well, I think someone is having a feeling for her," Ben added humour.

The others were going to add something too, but everyone had to stop as they heard Molly from outside.

"Hey, Daniel. Is Michael in there?" she shouted.

"Yes, Commander Molly, I am here," Michael replied.

-"Just call me Molly, come out and join me in my tent for some wine. I need to talk to you."

Michael was surprised because of the unexpected invitation. He looked at the others while leaving the tent. The others including James, however, were unconcerned about the topic of the possible talk or the reason of the inauspicious invitation.

"Hey, she didn't hear us, right?" James asked in a low tone while laughing.

Michael followed Molly to her tent. Her tent was like any other soldier's, without any unnecessary amenity, messy, and with military equipment and wine. This tent did have some extra amenities, not because Molly was the commander but as she was a woman - like a toilet. There was a table and a chair, with a map of the kingdom on the table.

Molly poured wine into two glasses and asked Michael to have a seat. Offering him a glass, she gave Michael a span to drink some. After that, she asked, "So, now tell me about your problem. Why are you afraid of blood?"

Hearing the question, Michael got amazed which amused Molly. Michael was sure that neither James had told anyone nor he himself had panicked enough to call unnecessary attention during the duels.

Judging his face Molly said, "What did you think? I am the Commander only as I am the strongest? You should know that I can see through your forte and fears."

She took a knife from the table, deliberately made a cut in her right thumb, came closer to him and held it in front of his eyes. "Don't look away, I dare you. Don't close your eyes," she challenged him.

Michael was trying his best not to get overwhelmed by the blood. But it was out of his control. He felt as if it was not only a fear but also a torture that he could not tolerate. He felt like he was being cut into pieces in a dungeon by a crazy serial killer. And he was getting upset that still, even after so many years of hard work, the fear was manipulating him. At last, he could not withstand it anymore and closed his eyes.

Watching Michael failing like this, Molly sighed and said, "Sad." She took her hand away, rapped a piece of cloth around the cut to prevent it from festering and asked Michael to open his eyes.

Michael was embarrassed and humiliated. He was furious at himself. He could not help himself from hitting the table hard in anger.

"Now now, don't get too excited," Molly said. "You are a magnificent soldier. Unluckily, with this condition, you are no good in actual war. If you cannot stand a paper cut how can you fight when there are corpses and blood everywhere beside you?" She shared her concerns.

"With this condition, you are only a pawn and cannot take the position of the Queen in a fight," she used a metaphor from the game of chess. "However, you can overcome it with my help, although you will need to go through inhuman exercises. Can you do it?"

"I will do anything to overcome it. I will undertake anything to be the best," Michael was determined to give all he had.

3

A Day of a Soldier of the 7th Regiment of South

In this chapter, I am going to write about something which does not go directly with the flow of our story, but certainly is pertinent. I thought excluding this chapter would not be a justice to both my readers and the soldiers I am writing about, although a big part of me was equally opposing this decision as this chapter has no direct effect on the outcome of the story. However, this chapter is like the missing piece of your puzzle, a free word given to your crossword, a critical number of your Sudoku. That is, though this small chapter may have a small significance, without it the big picture is incomplete. This chapter is like one mundane day of a year with three hundred and sixty four days more; this day has no historic event which can make it worth remembering. But, this day is the mirror image of the norm; this day depicts the lives of the soldiers most successfully.

This chapter is surely about a day, a normal day of a common soldier of the seventh regiment of the South.

When I was with Prof Tennyson and his group, there was only one thing I was interested to study for the first few days. The thing was the battles fought during the reign of

King George IV. I was coming to know about the Forest of Death and the excitement was thrilling. "Was there a curse in reality?" I used to ask myself a lot. I came to know about the effects of the forest on the daily lives of the soldiers of the southern regiments. And it forced me to learn about the lives of those soldiers.

Now, before I explain more about the chapter, I would like to argue why, after having a big clash with myself, I finally have decided to include it in our story. This chapter depicts not only a normal day in the seventh regiment of the South as mentioned before, it also highlights the hard work that a normal soldier went through on a daily basis. One essential aspect that I would like my readers to notice is that the chapter is written from a normal soldier's viewpoint, who may not be our protagonist and even more, he may not have any significance to the outcome of the story.

The seventh regiment of the South was the southernmost of all the regiments; among all the towers, the South Tower was the closest to this regiment. However, only the apex of the tower could be seen from here and that was only because the tower was on higher lands with respect to the regiment. This regiment was not that close to the fortress. And this regiment was not too far away from the Forest of Death, the Forbidden One. There were so many sayings about the forest and its curses. And these sayings were among the common people for about half a century. "Those who go into the forest will never come back", "Any living being to go into the forest will die before the following sunrise", "Trespassers will be spirited away" - these adages were very common in the sentences of a common man for some generations. There were some villages in between the seventh regiment of the South and the forest that always lived a poignant and squalor quality of life.

And it was the curse from the forest that was called responsible for this condition by the natives.

There were, in general, a total of about fifty soldiers in this regiment. Of them, around thirty five were swordsmen-horsemen, and the rest were archers-horsemen. The number of swordsmen-horsemen was higher than that of archers-horsemen as the first type of soldiers were more efficient in combats, absolutely in the close range ones. The ratio was inclined towards the swordsmen-horsemen, definitely, but the number of the second type of soldiers was also significantly high. It was principally to ensure the availability of watchmen on the watchtower twenty-four hours a day. And the watchmen always were archers as here they needed the skills of long range combats. The arrows from their bows were always prepared to aim for the hearts of intruders. In addition, the watchmen themselves were always aware of any possible siege.

The regiment consisted of barracks and training grounds for the soldiers, stables for their horses, armouries and workshops with specialist blacksmiths and arsenals. The regiment also had a watchtower and torches. There also were fifteen tents for the soldiers. A subgroup of about three tents and one from each of the armouries, workshops, stables and arsenals made a larger group. Each of these groups was separated from the adjacent groups in order to claim a larger area of space for the regiment. This benefited the soldiers with larger training grounds and an airy atmosphere. The formation of the groups with these warehouses mentioned was made such that any soldier could get ready for action in no time in case of an emergency. The torches were constructed in spaces such that they were few in numbers but could efficiently brighten the entire regiment even in the darkest nights.

On an average day, a normal soldier woke up with the sun. The first thing which he considered as his duty was to pour water in buckets for the horses, give them the water and feed them. Some specific soldiers were assigned to supervise a specific stable. However, it was every soldier's duty to take the responsibility and act on his own despite if he was assigned to the stable or not. Next, the soldier would have some meal himself. This morning meal usually contained slices of bread, fruits and eggs - pure and fresh. They were enough to provide sufficient energy for the soldier to withstand the upcoming training.

At a specific time of every day, the training would begin. The swordsmen would go to their place of training and the archers would go to theirs. But, at first, the training would begin with basic exercises that included running, walking by carrying cumbersomely heavy objects on the back, wrestling, etc. These exercises and workouts were performed to warm up one's body. Without these exercises, the latter trainings would not be much effective. The soldier would have muscle stiffness, quick exhaustion and even easy fatal injuries like torn muscles, broken bones, dislocated joints, etc. because of the unaccustomed body. And with the exercises, the warm blood flowing through the veins would bring the best of the soldier, both from his physical and mental abilities. Surely, these exercises were most effective during winters.

The final and actual training would start as soon as the soldier was capable to go. It was not the commander of the regiment to order to commence the actual training but the soldier himself. This certainly was because only the soldier himself could accurately understand if he was ready for that day's actual training. This was the time when the soldier could withdraw if he felt any unnatural fatigue or pain. The actual training would be so arduous that it might deteriorate the soldier's health and so any kind of unusual sensation would be notified to the commander at once before the soldier would join the actual training. Everyone understood that it was very logical for a soldier to feel sick and it definitely was not a reason of being ashamed.

As the soldier would join the onerous actual training, he would go towards either the archery fields or the close combat training fields. In the archery fields, the archers would aim from different distances towards their targets which periodically were something similar to what is used in modern day shooting sports. Again, the targets intermittently were idols, in the form of enemy soldiers, made of mud, wood, dead plant parts, etc. In the close combat training grounds, the swordsmen would train by fighting amongst themselves. This part of the training would always become a hard test for all the soldiers. This was because they had to train at a stretch for a long time without any break. A little water and no food were served. And the soldiers were not given any rest. Once one training was over, the soldiers would be sent to the next part of the training right away. Suppose, there was a pair of battling swordsmen and their battle came to an end at last as one became victorious and the other defeated. In the next moment, they would join their next battle with the same or any other available opposition. The goal of this hard training was to artificially develop an environment of a realistic warfare where the soldiers were supposed to spend a lot of time fighting in the fronts without rest and food.

The commander or the leader and coach of the regiment would supervise the training and would observe for anything noteworthy. This might be any special forte of a soldier that he himself was unaware about or a part of his fighting techniques that needed improvements. It was the commander's duty to ensure that his soldiers could bring out the very best from themselves. It also was his responsibility to make sure that no soldier of his team was getting unnecessarily injured. However, being completely unfazed and unscathed from such a training was impossible and was a daydream. So, the commander had the power to stop a battle any time he wanted to skip injuries or to notify some information to the soldiers about their techniques. The commander himself could join a fight and in that case any other soldier who was experienced, skilled and was high in the hierarchy in the regiment would supervise that battle.

This training would end before the lunch hours. During the medieval times, this part of meal was not called 'lunch' like what we do now. And this meal also was not as heavy as we have now. The only heavy meal that people of that period would have was 'dinner'. And unlike today's 'dinner', that dinner could be eaten at any time of the day. That is, the heaviest meal of a day, no matter when it was taken, was called a 'dinner'. If someone would have a heavy 'lunch', he would say that he had a 'dinner'. But usually people preferred to eat a 'dinner' in the evening period as they came back home from work.

For the soldiers, 'lunch' was a light meal with a lot of water. During this time, a soldier was given some free time of some hours that he could utilise by visiting someplace else from the regiment, take a rest, have some gossips with his fellow soldiers and many more. The intention of this break was to rejuvenate the soldiers before the second part of the hard training. This refresh time was for soldier's body as well as for his mind. The rest was essential for his physical as well as mental health. This was a high requisite for him to get over from a possible stagnation and suffocation of battles. I must mention that they also had to feed the horses during this allotted break.

For the second stage of the actual training, now, the soldiers would bring their respective horses out of their settlements. This part of the training required horses and the soldiers would start with basic horse riding followed by run. Sometimes they would also go for a friendly contest against each other. After that, similar to the previous training before the break, soldiers would go for battles by swords or aiming for their targets, while riding horses in both cases. And this training would be as exhausting as the previous one. With sun setting in the West, the training would conclude as the Commander would call it a day.

Sometimes, a soldier would have a duty or a mission assigned to him from his Commander or even higher authorities. The missions typically included from investigating a murder, robbery, theft, etc. to joining the less skilled forces of the towns or villages within the kingdom on various issues like a mob and ransack. In such a condition, the soldiers would be given some special break before the mission for preparation. During this specified break, a soldier would go through the maps of the area of his duty, would talk to his colleagues of that mission, talk to people or other soldiers/natives of that place or who had previously visited that place - all of these were to familiarize himself in order to have an edge to make the mission a success. And, judging the gravity of the mission, a soldier might get a break even after the mission so that he could overcome the aftermath.

The usual activities of the soldiers would vary seasonally. Summers were the best times to all of them; it was a time without any hustle and bustle from nature. The winters, however, had some different pictures. During winter, the temperature would go down to freezing followed by snow and even blizzard. Seasonal rainfall and heavy showers would occur sporadically. These natural calamities would make anyone's life a challenge. They inevitably would hamper the training of the soldiers, the forging of swords, arrows and armours by the blacksmiths as well as the supervision of the horses. Getting fresh water and food would become difficult during this time of the year and the soldiers had to constantly worry about storing fresh water, food as well as animal fat and oil to burn during the cold nights in their tents. They also would have to make special arrangements for their tents. They would keep the tents about a foot above the ground to circumvent the wet soil and any uncalled flood. Another troublesome result of the winter along with the shower and blizzard was epidemics. Special treatments for all the citizens including the soldiers were offered from the King to cure diseases and also to have precautions. But finally, it was a soldier's duty to keep himself as well as his horse fit during this time of the year.

Finally, the soldiers had to deal with another situation. Not only the soldiers of the seventh regiment of the South but also the soldiers of all the other six regiments of the South and the innocuous villagers of the villages in front of the Forest of Death had to deal with it. This was not a natural calamity or hardship of a day, but it was a daily basis question from the people of the north, west and east. It was completely illogical but many people of those three directions believed that there were people amongst the mentioned soldiers and villagers who were worshipers of the evil inside the Black Forest. They thought that people from these regiments and those villages were spies for the demon inside the Forest; they thought that these people were slaves of Death who periodically and timely informed Death of everything that went on in the Kingdom. They thought that these people informed the evil inside the Forest of any invader beforehand. And they even thought that these people were the only ones to go inside the Forest of Death, do their duty and pay their debts to the evil and come back alive without others' notice. These were the reasons why a certain part of the King's strongest soldiers and many innocent people were treated as traitors by many others.

However, there also was a big part of rational citizens who looked at the soldiers of the regiments of South, especially the ones from the seventh, as heroes. Children considered them their idols more than even the King's Men. They used to make crowds on the roads to see their idols riding their horses to the important missions. People used to get moved by devotion of these soldiers beyond the fear of death and curse. Old natives used to tell stories of the bravery and patriotism of these soldiers and the legends who had fought the war half a century ago. Regardless, many of the stories were forgotten in time and translation; the bravery and sacrifices of the soldiers of these regiments since long were facts once, and then became legends and finally faded away to become myths.

4

From the Diary of Michael Chapman

For a couple of days and nights, besides my other works, I had to squander my entire time in the library. My job was to obtain a lost information that was missing from Michael Chapman's tome. The tome, despite its fragile binding and medieval age, was not in such a bad condition to lose some pages. Michael Chapman had not written about this information in the first place. However, without that information, the tome was not making much meaning and sense from the beginning to the addendum. The wanting of the information was creating a vacuous inauguration, and my perusing through the next pages was not filling the vacancy at all. Every chapter and even almost every page of the tome had strong mentions of some of the main sequence characters of our story, yet important parts of them were missing. This was developing the history quite distorting and also affecting my research. In this manner, my only hope was to find the information from any one of the thousands of other books in the library. The arduous work was the only way to know what had happened to James Wheeler and Warcress.

There was shortage of another information, and my prior knowledge on it was vague, creating an opaque image in my mind. This lack of information was on the warfare between King George IV and the invading allies of French and pirates. Exactly after fifty years from the first invasion of this kind during the reign of King Phillip V, there occurred the second invasion - warfare and the massacre of macabre of the Forest of Death, the Forbidden One. I was certain that the war was somehow related to James and Warcress's status of being M.I.A. (Missing in Action). But my prior knowledge on it alone was insufficient to draw any conclusion and proceed further, and I direly needed help from wherever I could get.

One crucial help that I got was from venerable Dr Parker Abraham. He was the senior-most of our team, a well-known philosopher and a wise historian. He had been serving the domains of History for an astounding and successful forty-plus years. Although in his long functional life he had studied many topics of History, his favourite and most visited area of interest was warfare and how it affected reigns, eras and societies in courses of time. He already had spent a significant amount of time in research on this kingdom when I got here and I never thought of anyone else to ask this question.

To my readers, I feel the responsibility to inform that when one works on a research in a team, it becomes very hard to catch the time of a senior member of the team and it requires certain sacrifices to get connected. For me, the sacrifice was a good night dinner and supper of a day as I had to wait all my evening in front of Dr Parker's room. I got the chance when it already was nine in the clock and he called me in.

"Good evening Sir, I am Alan Smith. I am here for my Master's research and I am working on deciphering the diary of Michael Chapman," I gave a brief introduction of the self.

"Oh yes! I have been hearing a lot about you. That day Prof Tennyson was talking about you at lunch," Dr Parker tried to remember something. "Yes, tell me what I can do for you," he said.

-"So, as I am working on the writing of Michael Chapman, I need some information about the war that took place in the time of King George IV. I thought you might help me."

To my great surprise, Dr Parker asked, "Which war are you talking about? More than one war took place during his time."

"Well, Sir, I don't even know that there was more than one war," I admitted my lack of information.

-"There were three actually. First two were when the French attacked the English. In the third, the English stroke back."

I got the light from here – "The first one, Sir, which happened exactly fifty years after the one during King Phillip V's time."

-"Oh!" Dr Parker took some time to remember and structure everything that he was going to say the next.

It was a long information and took an hour. Later, he also suggested some books from the library which, along with his own information, finally clarified and elucidated everything to me.

But before going into that context, firstly I would like to write about something else that I believe my readers are asking for themselves. I am presuming that introducing my readers to Warcress would be my first priority.

It was the end of the first week of Michael and James' time at the seventh regiment of the South. In this meantime, they had invested a significant amount of time duelling against more or less every other soldier of the regiment. They also had checked out every unit of the regiment - the barracks, the armoires and workshops, the arsenals, the watch tower and the torches. The barracks along with the training grounds were where the soldiers got to sharpen their skills, the armoury and the workshops were where military equipment were manufactured or repaired, the arsenals were where they kept or stored spare military equipment for possible future use. Some prolific watchmen and archers were always on the top of the watchtower. This watchtower had a considerably lower height than the Tower of South. During any attack or invasion by enemies or any similar circumstance, the torches, tall constructions with highly flammable dead crops wet with oil kept at their tops, were lightened. When the torches of one regiment were lightened, the watchmen on the watchtower of the adjacent regiments could see it, notify and order to lighten the torches of their regiment. Thus, this procedure would follow up to the castle and then to the regiments of the other three directions. This would allow sending the message of the circumstance without much delay, and this would not require a soldier on a horse to travel to every regiment to spread the news. Also hereby, the soldiers of the different regiments could follow the trail of the torches to reach the source of the disturbance in no time.

Every day after their training was over, James saw Michael to follow Molly to the South, both riding on their horses. Michael had already told James in a gist about the special training that he was going through under Molly's supervision to mollify his fear of blood. Therefore, even after finding his friend dead tired when he returned at late night, James did not ask any question.

After their first week here, Michael and James saw Molly taking a break for a couple of days. She informed her fellow soldiers of the regiment that she had some official business to take care of and left leaving Daniel in charge. After returning, she called Michael and James into a stable of the regiment. This was the stable where Michael and James had kept their horses.

They had been frequently visiting the place as well as the other stables to look after the horses as taking care of every horse of a regiment was the prime duty of every soldier of the regiment, and thus they had become familiar with all the horses.

But today, they found two new horses in the stable - one was pitch black and the other was dark brown. With their experienced eyes, they instantly realised how powerful these horses were. Both of the horses had sharp eyes, strong foreheads, long crests, sturdy shoulders, tall backs, wide croups, extensive elbows and arms, well-built knees, cannons and heels.

"As I wanted," Molly started, "for you two to have new horses for combat. Well, I had these two in my eyes for quite a long time. They typically belong to the King's Men. But I could convince them that these two are going to be in good hands. These are two of the strongest and quickest of all the horses of this nation," she introduced. Pointing at the pitch black one, she said, "This one is, as I believe, the strongest of all. James, I want you to meet Warcress." Looking at the dark brown one she continued, "This one is for you, Michael. I do believe it goes with you as it is very young and definitely is very unyielding. Michael, I want you to meet Axilior."

Both Michael and James were suitably impressed with Molly's gesture, and the first obvious thing that they wanted to do was to give the new horses the first try. They had a race and duels, and the horses exceeded everyone's expectations; Molly herself was astounded. Like how a child would react after getting a new toy, Michael and James spent the entire day with the horses in the training grounds. Michael promised to himself and to Axilior that they both would work hard to get better. At the end of the day, Michael and James left Warcress and Axilior in the stable and spent a lot of time with their old horses. Molly already had assigned them a new duty to extensively take care of every horse of that particular stable.

"I guess it is their time to call it a day, and have the rest they deserve," James said while petting his old horse.

"You are right. They have been with us since long. We saved money after meeting Commander Black and bought them. Yes, they were old when we bought them, but they have been with us since then. In every of our journey, in every of our battle," Michael recalled the past while petting his old horse.

"We will always come to visit you. You take your rest. You have done well," emotional James kissed the forehead of his old horse.

"Always," Michael replied with teary eyes while touching his head against his old horse's.

For the next few days, I extensively studied the books that Dr Parker had referred to. His suggestions, along with some other information and the least that were mentioned in Michael Chapman's tome, turned out to be really fruitful to me. Now, I need to aggregate all that I got from these by then to draw the entire picture of the warfare. It happened about a year from the time Michael and James had joined the army. And it went as follows.

It was a gusty night with strong, cold wind and blizzard. Most of the soldiers of the seventh regiment of the South had already gone to their beds in their tents after a hot dinner. The on-duty archers and watchmen were still at the top of the watchtower and were trying hard to concentrate on their sights by penetrating the weather. James and Molly were on their bed in their tent. Molly already had gone asleep in James' arms. And like every other night, James was judging his own training session of the day. But tonight, he was also thinking about how his life had revolved through the years, especially through the previous one. He was memorising his time so far in the regiment - every training, every new skill that he had achieved, his fellow soldiers, Michael and Molly. He himself was surprised that only a year ago his sole goal of life had been to be the greatest King's Man. He had shown apathy and disinterest in any mortal feeling towards someone else. Michael always had been like a brother to him that he had never had in the long past. But his life during the span of the last year had gone along a totally unexpected way because of Molly. Molly was extremely inflexible and uncompromising to James like she was to any other soldier when it was about the security of the regiment and the nation. But, he had found a soul of a beautiful woman who was caring and friendly within her. It was surprisingly pleasant to him that, now, all he wanted was to be with Molly forever and protect her at all cost; he had given up his dream to be a King's Man. Although Molly herself was not aware of the fact that James had forfeited his dream, otherwise she would not allow it, not only for the betterment of James' future but also for that of the nation. Molly still had her equivocal opinions about King's Men, however, she was certain that James was the best candidate to be the next one of them.

It had all started on last Christmas Day, the only day of the year when a soldier could get permission to do almost everything he desired. The celebration started on the Eve. Some went back to their houses, some visited their relatives, some just travelled to new places, and some even got married as it was a sign of good luck in marital life to get married during this time of the year. They believed that it was completely safe to take a break from their duty as they knew that no kind of siege would occur on the God's day.

The soldiers of the seventh regiment of the South Tower had decided to visit a village and enjoy the whole day. They had costly meals and wines that they usually did not afford to buy on the other days, and they had danced, and some even had gone to bethels. At evening, all the soldiers had already gone tired but continued to drink and dance. They had no intention of stopping as they knew they would have to wait for another year to get a holiday like that. Moreover, they had local beautiful young ladies as their dancing partners. And only a fool would throw away this opportunity of dancing with them. James saw Michael was enjoying a lot. He was drunk, was dancing with the ladies, and even was singing:

"Hey! Oh! Hey! Oh! Pick up your sword, spear and bow
Hey! Oh! Hey! Oh! Pour the wine - a drink you swallow
Get a barrel, fill the glass, the world doesn't have this beer, Alas!
Get a bread, have a meat, the world lacks the seat so neat
And drink the beer, shout and cheer, to foes and dear;
drink the wine like the end is near.
Hey! Oh! Hey! Oh! We are calling you on the dance floor
Hey! Oh! Hey! Oh! The music calls you on the dance floor
So join the Carole, take off the shoes, come in here in your barefoot
Take out the string, that you will sing, sing and sing with the zing
And sing the Flute, smoke the pipe, play the Shawm;
from this night till the dawn.
Hey! Oh! Hey! Oh!..."

They also had been dancing a traditional dance of the place where the couples danced in rhythm with the instruments played by the players. Sometimes, a couple would hold each other's hands; there were hopping, clapping, spinning on one leg.

All in a sudden, their attentions had drawn to one corner. A fellow soldier of theirs had been on his knees in front of his girlfriend. He had asked her to marry him and the girl of the moment had been in tears - the tears of joy. She had said yes. They had been hugging and kissing. The others in the party had been clapping and congratulating the newly engaged couple. James had been sitting when Molly had come and asked, “Hey, you are not dancing?”- “I was, a moment earlier,” James had lied. –“Come on, take my lead,” Molly had offered a dance. As they had been dancing, Molly had asked, “So James, whom of these pretty ladies did you like?” –“Yes, there is one. I really liked her,” James smartly had replied promptly. Molly had got interested. And she had asked about the girl, but James had refused to reveal her identity. Then Molly had asked if James had wanted to dance with that girl. “I want to dance my all dances with her,” James had replied looking directly in Molly’s eyes. Molly had become enthusiastic and had inspired James to ask that girl for that eternal and perennial dance. James had asked, “Are you sure I should ask?” –“I do,” Molly had replied. –“Alright,” James had said, “Molly, will you dance the eternal dance with me?” Molly certainly had gone surprised and James, for a moment, had started to think that it had been a mistake. However, he also had been thinking that it already had been a while and now he had to tell before it was too late. Molly had not talked for a moment, neither had James, but both had continued their dance. And then, Molly had held James, stretched her neck up to reach James’ lips and kissed him. –“I will,” she had replied.

Tonight, James was remembering all of these moments that had such significance in his life. Suddenly, a loud noise was created from the watchtower. James heard a running horse approaching and stopping. He also heard some loud conversations. Molly got awake too and she was trying to figure out what was going on. At the very moment, a soldier from outside the tent started shouting by calling Molly.

“Don’t come in!” Molly yelled at him.

James was afraid that something wrong had happened and so he asked out, “Tell us, what is it?”

“It’s an attack! They are in the villages! From the forest!” the soldier informed panting.

Both James and Molly got up from the bed. They started getting the armours on for the inevitable warfare that everyone had been waiting for fifty years.

"Call everyone else, firstly Michael and Daniel. And assemble everyone on the field," James ordered.

It was an invasion by the French and the pirates. They already had surpassed the forest and were in the villages. A native from there had ridden on a horse to spread the words to the army.

The soldier went and blew the horn. The horn was used to generate a loud sound to attract everyone's attention. It was a call for an emergency.

As soon as Michael, Daniel, Ben and Raphael heard about it, they got up, wore on their armours, collected their swords from the armoury and went to the stable to get their horses. Michael took Axilior out of there and climbed on it. Warcress had already been taken out by James.

All the soldiers assembled in the field wearing armours and with their swords or bows, and on their horses, waiting for Molly's order. Michael found Molly and James come at him.

"Michael, I have a task for you. I need you to run to the sixth regiment and then the fifth and so on and give them the news. You have Axilior - you are fast. I need you to do it," Molly ordered him.

Considering the weather with wind and blizzard, it was the best option left for them as the torches were useless.

"What?" Michael was surprised. "No! I want to join the fight. Do you think I will get petrified in the front by looking at the blood? After all this time?" He denied Molly.

-"No! That is not what I was thinking. I have faith in you. I have faith in every one of my soldiers. But this is the only option left. The other soldiers need to know. And we don't know how large our enemy is. We may need reinforcements."

"Exactly, the enemy can be large. You need me in the front from the very first. Give this order to someone else," Michael tried once more.

"Molly, let me talk to him," James said. "Michael, of all people I know how strong you are. And I know how much you have developed since last year. But, it is our only option left. I want you to inform at least the regiments of the South and then join us. If the enemy is large then we can't suppress them for long. I want you to join us with reinforcements the soonest you can. Till then, let me handle it," he said to Michael.

"Alright. But promise me that if needed, you will fall back. You are too hasty. Don't get carried away with it," Michael alerted him.

-"I promise you."

Michael got on Axilior and started towards the North - the opposite direction from the one that the rest of the soldiers were about head to.

"Don't you people die on me!" He shouted at James and Molly as he was going away.

Now, he concentrated on the very task that Molly had assigned to him. His keen eyes were at the sixth regiment of the South as he heard Molly, "It is no time for a motivational speech. You have learned enough. I trust every one of you. Make me proud. Show everyone why the seventh regiment of the South is the strongest." Her loud voice gradually faded away.

Michael rode Axilior to its highest possible speed towards the sixth regiment of the South. However, this half a kilometre road was appearing to be much more to him. Moreover, because of the weather, he was not having any torch, a wooden stick with animal fat and wax and oil at its top, to light. It was an onerous and taxing job to ride like that through the darkness and he was imagining how hard it was going to be in the front.

As he reached at the sixth regiment, he shouted out for help. As expected, the watchmen and archers on duty from the tower were the first to come down and respond.

He did not get down from Axilior and said to the soldiers, "I am Michael Chapman from the seventh regiment of the South. It is an emergency. There has been an attack. The other soldiers of my regiment already have gone towards the villages."

"What? An attack?" The soldiers were shocked. "Where? Who are they?" they asked.

-"It is in the villages before the forest. It is the French and the pirates I think, like what happened fifty years ago."

-"Blow the horn. Call everyone," one of the soldiers ordered another one of them.

-"I am going to alert the fifth regiment. I will come back after that. Get ready in the meantime. I will join you."

Michael started towards the North again, this time his destination was the fifth regiment of the South. As he was going, he heard the horn being blown. His intention was to alert the soldiers of the fifth regiment, ask someone of them to go to the fourth and carry on his job that Molly had asked for. Whereas, he would come back and join the soldiers of the sixth regiment to the battle. And he followed this and came back to the sixth regiment soon to join the force.

It had been a while since James and the others had confronted the enemies. During the first hour of their counterattack, they had been finding a few of the French and pirates here and there in the villages; most of them were torturing the villagers, looting or igniting the houses. Outnumbering and defeating them was easy. But as they were moving closer to the forest, they were facing more and more obstacles from the enemies' side. Molly was feeling that they were getting overwhelmed and they direly needed reinforcements, however, it was too early to hope for that. She was hoping that the other regiments of the South should join the battle the soonest and the regiments of the North, East and West as well as the King's Men to join as soon as possible.

While pushing the enemies further towards the South, they finally reached close to the forest. James was finally in front of the cursed Forest of Death, the Forbidden One. The darkness of the night and the cold were creating an unnatural silence in the forest. This silence was supernatural beside the roaring of the wind and blizzard, and the noises of swords clashing, horses neighing, soldiers and horses shouting in agony. The forest had achieved its dense ephemeral depth from the very beginning of itself. Every tree was tall, wide and ancient and had seen many casualties due to the curse, including the war that had happened fifty years ago. The trees were blocking the least of the moonlight that was trying to come down after penetrating the thick clouds, and thus making the forest even darker. Snow covered all over the leaves and branches of the tall trees and the darkness along with the snow of the Black Forest made it even colder. The trees blocked the voracious wind and it resulted in a completely steady state within the forest.

However, the supernatural silence of the Forest of Death, the Forbidden One was torn down suddenly as James and the others heard a fierce howling from deep of the black forest. It had a terrifying effect on everyone and it caught everyone's attention from the battle; the horses started shouting in fear too. James saw that even a strong horse like Warcress was also acting abnormal. The sound was disturbing to everyone in the battleground. The blizzard and storm got stronger. The soldiers felt as if their blood under the bodies was solidifying because of the plutonic cold. They felt like they could no longer move a muscle. And as if thick clouds were covering the air in front of their eyes. Every emotion including happiness, sorrow and anger had gone extinct; the only fear there was – was of a painful death.

"Are the dead reincarnating? They are coming back to fight!" A soldier cried out.

"We are doomed. Get out of here," another one said.

"No one is going anywhere. We are not in the forest. Continue your fights, you cowards," Molly, who already had experiences of being to the forest's close vicinity, ordered.

The howling from the forest had created an impulsive deviation for all the soldiers of both the parties. The English were the ones who took the paid advantage of it. Before the invaders got their minds back, the English had put themselves as heavyweights on the opposition. Soon after this, all the enemies were killed.

It was about two hours from the commencement of the operation and everyone was relieved to see it ending before any serious casualties. The soldiers were happy and they started celebrating. Everyone was thinking of going back to their regiment and have a grand party. They were feeling proud that only the seventh regiment of the South had taken care of the serious siege all by itself and they could not wait to spread the news of victory to the other regiments, the King's Men and to the King himself. High rewards from the King were what they were hoping for.

However, another blasting sound from the forest gave them a quick reality check. They stopped shouting "Hurrah!" and looked at the forest. The sound was continuous and it was increasing. Something definitely was approaching them from the forest.

The source of the sound was clarified instantly. It was a pack of thousands of soldiers, coming in hundreds from the forest. They were different from the French; they were more boisterous and belligerent than them. They were riding on wild horses and instead of swords they had spears, lances and hatchets. Their stocky bodies were painted with blood - texts and ancient signs, letters and dialect. And they were shouting raucously, starving ravenously for blood; they were shouting a war cry. They were either from an unknown tribe, pirates or were certainly the dead coming back to life.

James was the one from the English side closest to the forest. He tried to defend himself from the incoming. But it did not take time for him to realise that he was nothing compared to the inhuman strength of the hundreds of the enemies who were gradually surrounding him.

He only had one option left to survive it - he dodged the enemies to circumvent being surrounded and rode Warcress fast towards the forest. The enemies did not bother letting one of the targets go when they had so many before them.

"James!" shouted Molly. She tried to follow him but was blocked by Daniel.

"Where are you going?" he yelled. He took the hackamore of Molly's horse, which was the rope tied at its nose, turned it around to the opposite way and shouted to order, "Fall back!"

The other soldiers did not dare to disobey this command from the second in command. Unfortunately, some of them including Raphael were too marked to the enemies' hands and they did not have any chance left to abandon the fight. As Molly, Daniel and others were going away, they saw the few soldiers, who were left back, getting killed by the spears, lances and hatchets of enemies. Molly turned her head back for a while to look at the forest where James had gone to, but she found no one to come back.

It had been some hours since Michael had joined the operation of defence and counter offense. He was with the soldiers of the sixth regiment of the South and they all were heading towards the forest through the villages while commencing the operation. It was also getting to be a search mission as they needed to find the enemies. And they were finding French and pirates randomly here and there in the villages. In the meantime, they assembled with the reinforcements - the soldiers of the other regiments of the South. Now, it was an army of about three hundred skilled soldiers hunting for enemies. This was very surprising and suspicious to all of them as they were finding neither Molly's team nor a large army of enemies which they had been hoping for.

Finally they reached the final village before the Forest of Death, the Forbidden One. It was the village most torn with natural disasters and wars. The villagers always lived a perilous, penniless and poignant quality of life. The forest interminably played its curse on its closest neighbour village. The villagers mostly dealt in animals breeding as the soil itself was too rough to cultivate. There were bars and inns serving whiskey and beer of the worst quality that one could ask for.

But, Michael and the other soldiers found a lot of differences in the village from a normal village living under poverty. There were corpses of dead villagers lying on the heap of snow on the ground; the snow gathered on the corpses was indicating that it was a while since they had been butchered. Blood was there everywhere on the roads and the roadsides. Some houses were completely decimated, some were gutted with fire. The remaining surviving villagers were frightened, in their houses locked from inside.

The blood and so many dead bodies could be a problem to Michael. He never had seen so much blood in the past. He would definitely get terrified and stupefied by them some other day. But tonight, he had a strong jaw. He was desperate to find the guilty and punish him for the unforgivable crime. Although it was a mystery to him that where the large army of enemy soldiers had gone. The small number of soldiers that they had faced so far was not enough to had led to such a slaughter.

They started looking for clues or any survivors among the corpses.

"Here is one alive," a soldier found a survivor.

Michael and Commanders of the six regiments went at him. He was an old man lying on the ground and panting heavily. He had a wound in his chest which was festering quickly.

The Commander of the sixth regiment asked, "Who were they?"

Hearing the words, the man tried to look up. "It was the undead, thousands of them, on horses," he tried hard to say it.

"Where did they go?" asked the Commander of the fourth regiment.

The old man pointed towards the North. However, it was strange as the English soldiers had just come from that way without finding any large army. The soldiers looked at each other; they were surprised. It was clear that they believed in the old man's words that it was the undead, which seemed to be the only logic behind what was going on.

"We might have missed them. They might have outsmarted us and headed to the castle," Michael brought up the concern.

"Alright, we need to split up in twos. One team go back towards the castle and look for the enemy. If you find them then notify to the castle and the other regiments at once. The second team follows me towards the forest. We need to find the soldiers of the seventh regiment of the South," the Commander of the sixth regiment of the South was quick to take the decision.

"Regiments one, two, three and four, let's go to the castle. Remember, we have a large army in front of us. Regiments five and six proceed to the forest in search for the soldiers," the Commander of the second regiment of the South ordered.

The entire army got divided as per the order. Michael joined the soldiers of the fifth and sixth regiments of the South in the search mission. The larger part of the entire army headed towards North. And a few decided to stay in search for more survivors and aid them.

It was about six hours since the beginning of the operation and now the darkness of the night was getting ameliorated by the rising sun. The blizzard also had turned into a common snowfall. When Michael with the other soldiers reached close to the forest, he found the fallen bodies of some of his familiar faces, the bodies of some of his fellow soldiers from the seventh regiment of the South. Their bodies had frozen in snow and because of the time that had lapsed. This made it very difficult to identify the bodies. Michael came down from Axilior anyway to try to identify the bodies. At that moment he, along with the other soldiers, heard running horses. They looked back to find the soldiers of the seventh regiment of the South; the only difference was that the team looked smaller.

Michael saw Molly, Daniel and Ben, however, he could not find James and Raphael.

"Where are the others?" he asked desperately. The silence of the team to his question compelled him to ask it again, this time shouting.

"Raphael and the others have been compromised," Daniel replied. "But we have no news of James," he added.

-"What? What happened?"

"Only when we thought we had won, a big army came from the forest. We had to fall back. But some of us could not," Ben said.

This time, Michael saw the body of unfortunate Raphael lying. A lance had gone through his heart and his face was badly broken. Poor Raphael had to endure unbearable pain before his death.

"Where is James?" Michael asked. The improper silence from the team again forced him to yell.

"Last we saw him, he went into the forest, running away from the big army. We had to fall back and we were in hiding since then. And now we are coming here. So, we don't know what happened to him," Daniel said.

All the stories about the forest that he had heard so far and the scenes of the night in the inn of the day before the one when he had joined the regiment flashbacked in Michael's eyes. He knew and believed in the curses of the forest and thus he was having a hard feeling about James. He could not suppress his anger and pointed fingers to call Molly culpable for it.

"And you let him go? After all these times? You do know about the forest - once one goes in, he does not come back. But you did not stop James. And you call yourself the Commander of the strongest regiment of all! And it was James! How selfish of you? If I were here, I would have tried to stop him. Even if it priced me my life!" he shouted at Molly.

Molly had been silent so far, but Michael's words triggered her.

"Stop it! Know who you are talking to! I am still your Commander, you like it or not. And if you don't like it, you are free to leave. I'll remain the Commander as long as I live and the King lets," Molly shouted.

It was becoming an embarrassing situation for the soldiers of the seventh regiment of the South to see their teammates fighting and of course, it was not the time for it. So they tried to calm Michael and Molly down.

After some time, Molly said, "It was James. I know. But there were so many of them. We had no chance. Where were the reinforcements? James also knew about the forest. I thought someone as smart as James would figure something out in order to get out of the forest. I understand Michael, that he was like your brother, but he also was all I had!" Saying this and without wasting any more word, Molly got on her horse and rode it towards the North.

As Molly on her horse got out of everyone's sight, the Commander of the sixth regiment of the South asked Daniel, "So you faced the large army, right?"

"Yes," Daniel replied.

-"How were they?"

-"There were so many of them, coming interminably from the forest. They were coming and coming, and it had no end. I don't think they were living humans."

-"And, you fell back and went into hiding. And the army went North, right?"

-"I think so."

-"However, as we came from the North, we did not face any large army. We also thought of the possibility that they somehow took some other road and headed towards the castle. Rest of our army rode back to there. But, we have not heard any alerting news so far."

-"What? That is impossible! The army of that size! How could you miss that?" Daniel was astonished.

-"But we did. I don't have a clue on what is going on. Now we need to operate a search mission. Every one of the regiments five and six spread out. Also, we need the other regiments from North, West and East to join. We need to search the entire kingdom. And the soldiers of the seventh regiment, go back to your regiment and take rest. Otherwise, you will die of exhaustion," the Commander of the sixth regiment of the South ordered.

Michael was going to oppose this decision, but he was stopped by Ben. He came at Michael and hugged him. In his ears Ben said in low, "Michael, I understand what you are going through. But we need to go back. Raphael and the others need a proper farewell. And if James is alive, then the other soldiers will be looking for him. We will come again tomorrow."

The first few pages of Michael Chapman's diary were very difficult to make out. These were the first one or two letters from him to James and they did not have a link with each other and also with the few following ones. I tried going through them over and over again in order to understand them. But, the work was going in vain. Such a blow at the very beginning of my research frustrated me in a terrible way. I cut myself off from any sort of human contacts for a couple of days. I even got the news of the first wave of Brexit long after it had got a hit in the news. At first, I assumed that the diary was a result of an amateur author trying to write on a complex issue. However, after two days of immense stupidity, I decided to read the following few letters as well. And things started to make sense for the first time. The incognizable nature of the first few pages of the tome was not due to Michael Chapman's lack of experience in writing, but was an outcome of his emotional breakdown. Moreover, the letters were meant in such a way that they were addressing something the reader had already known. Michael Chapman had written them in such a pattern that they only were reminding James Wheeler of some emotional parts of a fact already known to Wheeler. And, being someone who did not even know the most mundane pieces of the story, I was struggling to focus on the Hands of God and Adam. Going through the next few letters and some other evidence provided and suggested by my supervisors was the only way by which I could grasp how Michael Chapman had painted the overall Sistine Chapel ceiling. For my readers, here I am assembling them.

The next morning, Michael got up too early. It was still dark and the other soldiers were still sleeping. Their tent looked empty as Raphael's bed was unoccupied. Michael tried to go back to sleep but he was being too restive. He felt that his heart was pounding quickly and he was being desperate and restless for a reason. He wanted to get up, take Axilior and look for James and Warcress. The last night itself had been painful. He could barely sleep. And he had a dream that James and he were in the workshop in London, making swords. The dream was beautiful. The peace in that dream also was making the dream a nightmare because of the cruel reality - the dream was not real, it was a flashback of a memory only to Michael's unconscious mind and Michael could not go back to those beautiful days in reality. He intentionally was thinking about the memories although they were hurting him.

He got out of the tent. It was a long time since he had been this lonely. He remembered about his times with James, the times in London, the trainings in there and in here, spending the adventurous night in the inn. He walked with a pace all around the regiment, not thinking clearly, and hoping for the morning to end and the following night to end as well. He was frightened underneath. He was fast losing his zeal to become the best swordsman, horseman and the King's Man.

"What lies ahead?" he asked himself.

The burial ground was just in front of him where Raphael and the others were sleeping for eternity. Michael went in there to pay respect. Raphael not only was a good swordsman but was also a great friend and teammate. Michael had fought many battles against him during the training and he had to admit that Raphael had praiseworthy talents. Michael was afraid that the tent would never be the same again without Raphael.

Raphael's major work of stopping Asmodeus was done. Now, it was time for the archangel to return home - heaven. And now, it was Michael's turn to stop Lucifer of the army of the dead.

While walking around aimlessly, Michael came in front of Molly's tent. He had not seen her since she had left the previous day. And after recalling her last words, Michael was feeling sorry. Molly had suffered a lot since her childhood. She had lost everyone, and now, probably James too. Michael really had liked seeing Molly and James together, even when he disliked Molly underneath. Although he was always annoyed with Molly's arrogance, but there was no way he would deny that Molly was the best Commander. She was one of the most powerful and was also great at leadership. His training to overcome his fear under Molly's supervision for the last year had been extremely fruitful. And so, Michael was feeling sorry for questioning Molly's worth as a Commander in front of the other Commanders.

He entered into the tent. The bed was clean which made Michael realise that Molly had not come back last night. Although Molly did not care about the cleanliness of the place but James did.

Michael was getting a little worried about Molly while looking at the place. At that moment, he heard the familiar voice he had been wanting to hear for long. "What are you doing in my tent?"

It was Molly herself, standing at the entrance.

There was a long awkward silence as both of them looked at each other for that long time span and tried to find words to say. At last, Michael started with the obvious, "Where have you been?"

"Near the forest, the whole day. Waiting for James," Molly replied something which was beyond Michael's expectations. He was feeling ashamed of himself. Not only had he questioned Molly's love for James but he himself had not gone to find James yet. On the other hand, Molly had been there the whole time.

Looking at Michael's face and predicting what he was going to say, Molly said again, "Save it. Listen, the King has called the Commanders of the regiments of the South. At noon today. It is about the war. I will go. And I will leave the regiment to Daniel for the time. I want you to accompany me. It will be a long and important discussion."

At noon, the seven Commanders of the seven regiments of the South with seven horsemen, each of whom was accompanying his respective Commander, went to the castle to meet the King. The huge gatehouse was opened for them. Michael was in the fortress for the first time. He saw the South Bailey where there were barracks, stables, armoires and arsenals. There were training grounds where the King's Men were fighting. And the King's Men were wearing cloaks with the crest on the back - a sword on a circle, the King's Crest.

As the team was entering the stronghold, some King's Men stopped by to greet. Michael saw the trainings of the King's Men at a glimpse. It was even more intense than his. The practicing Men were acting as if they were in an actual war. Their techniques, footwork, skills and mentality stunned Michael. And, he was coming to the realisation that he still was miles away from becoming worthy of wearing the cloak with the crest.

They were in front of the Greathall when they got down from the horses. And they entered. From here, they were accompanied by some King's Men to the room where the King was waiting for them - the Grand Hall.

The Grand Hall was on the third floor and they needed to take the huge staircases. There were idols of marbles depicting humans, soldiers, animals, Angels and Madonna, artefacts made of animal skin and bones, precious stones, metals and shiny wood in the castle to ornate it. The small artefacts were placed on stone or marble tops which themselves were beautified by artificial carvings. There were also soldier armours, swords, lances, bows and arrows to give the place a different kind of thrill. Colossal portraits of former Kings, Queens, King's Men, other eminent personalities and of natural beauties on medium of oil on poplar panel hung from the monolithic walls.

Michael Chapman had written about the arts in the castle as he had seen them - fresh and enchanting. When I was examining them, most of them had lost their originality in colour and meticulous crafting because of chemical reactions like oxidation with the air for centuries. However, one could not miss the seminal and magisterial delicacy in them. No doubt why this era was called the Renaissance in European Arts. Michael Chapman, as a novice, had said how he used to look at and enjoy these arts - a sight for his sore eyes. And I was finding immense pleasure in relating my outlook with his. I saw how Christianity had been depicted in the paintings. There were arts on the resurrection of Christ, previous Archbishops like St Thomas Becket, St Theobald and others - these were the works of Nottingham Alabaster carvers. There was this very big oil painting - an Archangel stabbing the chest of the Fallen Angel with a sword. Michael Chapman had written about the mysterious drawings on glass. I found the masterpieces of John Thornton and others. There were paintings of coronations of Kings, God, Bishops and one beautiful garden with a little girl flying with angel wings painted by them. There also was a large portrait of Geoffrey Chaucer - the father of poetry of medieval England. And there were some works that Michael Chapman had illustrated as horrifyingly aesthetic. I found the works depicting the Black Death that had occurred only a century before Michael Chapman and decimated one-third of the population of Western Europe. Michael Chapman had seen one of the liveliest strongholds in UK; I saw a sleeping beauty. But when I used to climb the stairs and close my eyes, I could feel the castle waking up after centuries. I could imagine that the time was taking me back; all the cultures, clothes and people were getting replaced by respective counterparts of that ancestral period. I could perceive the fading colours of the arts and paintings getting rejuvenated. And I could comprehend the footsteps of King's Men, the Ministry Order discussing an issue, the King ordering his servants, the laughter of the Queen and the Princess. I could see Michael Chapman sitting on a stair and looking at the glass paintings and the windows with his astonished eyes.

As the group reached the Grand Hall, everyone was already waiting for them. The Great King was on his throne, beside him, there was Commander Black - the Commander of the King's Men. There was another throne, empty today, as the King had decided not to take the Queen in today's meeting. In the room, there were other famous people sitting on the left side of the room - there were poets, writers, scientists, philosophers and artists. And on the right side, there were ten men sitting - the Order of the King. This was the bench of the ministry to assist the King with their suggestions, experiences and conspiracies. The leader of the bench, the Head of the Order, was Walther Livingston, the genius and the dwarf of the kingdom. And there were armed King's Men all over the Hall guarding it. Sir Light was among them too.

The group of the fourteen people bowed before the King and took their seats in the middle of the Hall.

Walther left his seat to come to the centre of the Hall. He inaugurated the meeting, "I hope we all know why we are here. It has been in the news that there was an attack in the Southern part of the kingdom. Which is concerning because last time when this happened, it almost took over the kingdom. The castle came under direct threat and there were thousands of casualties. However, first, we need to justify the source of this recent attack." Introducing the team of fourteen to the rest of the people in the Hall, he said, "Here we have the Commanders and soldiers of the regiments of the South. They claim that they have faced and stopped the siege. Now, tell us about the attack."

Molly started, "At the night before yesterday's, we got the news from a villager that there were French and pirate invaders. We took the initiative to spread the word to the other regiments as well to join the fight. And we faced the soldiers as expected. We went pushing them to near the forest. But something happened."

"What?" Walther curiously asked.

-"Only when we thought we won, another attack came right on us. It was thousands of soldiers. We did not have a chance and we had to fall back."

"There was an invasion of thousands of soldiers?" Commander Black asked being concerned.

"Yes, but the more troubling fact is different," the Commander of the sixth regiment of the South said, "later, we and the other regiments counter stroke and killed the rest of the French and pirates. But, we could not find the large army. We reached the forest. We found the last village to be completely destroyed. We then had thorough search operations, but still we could not find the army."

"How is that possible? They never came at the castle, otherwise someone would notice. The archers and watchmen are here all days and nights. Even if they circumvented the castle and went far North, they would face the East and West regiments on the way. Moreover, circumventing the castle is not expected," Walther said.

"So, what do you think has happened?" the King asked himself.

-"It is puzzling, Your Majesty."

"Tell us about the casualties," Brendon Ray, another member of the Order, and the oldest of them, asked.

"Besides the deaths of the villagers, twelve from of us were K.I.A (Killed In Action) and one was M.I.A. (Missing In Action)," Molly replied. "All of them were from the seventh regiment of the South," she added after a short break.

"What do you think, where did the army go?" Walther asked the team of the fourteen.

"We operated a meticulous search. They cannot be present in the southern part of the Kingdom," informed the Commander of the first regiment of the South.

"Can you describe the soldiers?" Commander Black asked.

"They were savage and sturdy. They were using wild weapons and horses. They were no ordinary soldiers and were not wearing any armour. It was like they did not care about anything but mass destruction," Molly, who was the only one in the Hall to have encountered and confronted the mysterious and large army, said.

"Mr. Ray!" Walther turned towards his team - the Order, "Do you know of any tribe living near or inside the forest who can be responsible?"

"Well, there are some tribes living near the forest, but they are not big enough to produce thousands of armies. And as I studied, there are some tribes living inside the forest too. But there is not much information about them," Ray replied.

"Wait, do you think it was a tribal army?" the Commander of the fourth regiment of the South interrupted.

"I am presuming so," Walther replied.

It sounded very shameful to Molly. "Do you really think we would get defeated by a tribal army?" She got excited.

"I am afraid so," Walther replied instantly.

"How dare? What do you know about our strength? What do you know about fighting?" Molly shouted at the imp imperviously. Michael made the quick action after seeing his Commander losing her cool in front of the King. He grabbed her hand and twisted a little to soothe her down.

"Silence! I want outcome," the King himself, who was known as the kind King, got impatient without seeing any possible results.

Walther took some time, came closer towards the team of fourteen and said, "I believe the army is from a tribe living in the forest. The forest is so unfriendly and hostile for living that they have adopted savage rules to survive. They do not fear living or death. Hence, they are far more dangerous than ordinary enemies."

"The villagers saw them and they said that they were the undead," the Commander of the fifth regiment of the South added.

-"Do you really believe that?"

-"You cannot ignore the curse of the Forest of Death."

Walther sighed. It seemed that he did not believe in the curse. "What do our scientists say about it?" he asked.

The scientists were sitting on the left side of the Hall. With this question being asked, they had a brief discussion amongst themselves. Then one of them said, "We cannot conclude here. You cannot explain everything with science. Like, you can say that the source of the snow and rain is clouds from Heaven, but what is the source of the Sun?"

Walther looked at them with disappointment. Then he walked to his team and asked Ray, "What do you think?"

"Well, I certainly liked the conclusion of tribes. But as for the Forest of Death, there are hundreds of cases where people went in there and never came back. Or, they went, came back but died in their sleep. I should say, the Statistics is not with Science today," Ray replied.

Hearing from Ray, Walther walked around in the centre of the Hall for a span of time. Sometimes he was looking at the spectators and again went back to thinking. At last, he said, "Alright. Let us consider both the possibilities. They could be tribal army or the undead. Now the important question is where did they go? I personally think that they returned back into the forest."

Walther's conclusion created a disorderly discussion amongst the people present. They both agreed and disagreed with Walther which resulted in strident and blatant accusations at each other. And yet again the King had to step up to silence them.

"Why do you think they fell back? It was a perfect opportunity to attack the castle. We were not ready and they were leading. It was a clear advantage," asked Commander Black.

"Is not it obvious? They were tribes or undead. They do not go by normal routines of battles. Mass destruction is their only goal," Walther explained.

Now was the high time of the discussion. Everyone was aware of the situation that there would be more upcoming attacks in near future. To prevent this, they direly needed a strong defence mechanism. Moreover, the raided villages needed aids. Walther, Ray, Commander Black, the Commanders of the regiments of the South and the King himself directly participated in this discussion with the agenda being a better defence mechanism.

The points that were selected as initiatives to be appointed associated with the mechanism were:

1. More soldiers recruitment to the seventh regiment of the South to compensate for the recent loss.
2. Patrolling soldiers including King's Men in the villages in front of the forest.
3. Exchange of soldiers in between the castle and the regiments of the South.

4. More advanced weapons and armours for the soldiers.
5. Initialisation of category of Cavalry - Light and Heavy Cavalry. The distinction was made on the basis of the weight of the armours that the horseman was wearing.

Besides, more resources were incorporated in defence and as the aids for the war-ridden villages. And it was decided to address the tribal army or the undead as 'Unprecedented Army' before their true identity was revealed.

And the meeting ended with a feast.

After the feast, Michael found Commander Black talking to the Queen, who had joined them later in the feast. He walked towards them and waited for their attention. He was unsure if Commander Black would remember and recognise him, but Black did recollect and greeted.

"My Queen, this is a brilliant soldier from the South regiments," Black introduced Michael to the Queen. Michael bowed before the Queen to show his respect and loyalty.

"Hello there. What is your name?" the Queen asked.

"I am Michael Chapman from the seventh regiment of the South, my Queen," Michael replied.

"Well, Michael, enjoy your feast. I'll see you around. But I need to go now. Commander, if you excuse me," the Queen was not interested in further talking. But it gave Michael the opportunity to talk to Black.

"How are you, Commander Black?" he asked.

"Fine, thank you. How are you?" Black asked.

-"I am alright. Getting ready for more warfare."

-"I am glad that you two have joined. Do your best to serve the kingdom. And where is your friend? The one I fought with?"

It was expected that Black would not know of James' poor destination. Michael gave him the news. "He is the one M.I.A. from our side, Sir."

Black was shocked at the news. "I am really sorry to hear that," he consoled.

As the meeting and the feast ended, Michael got the news that he had been appointed to patrol on the South Tower, the largest construction in the nation. He would have the duty as watchman every Monday night.

Later, Michael found the King and Walther Livingston together, the two people he was eagerly waiting to talk to. He bowed in front of the King.

"Rise, soldier," the King said.

"I am Michael Chapman from the seventh regiment of the South, Your Majesty," Michael introduced himself.

"Oh! Michael, so how long have you been in the army?" the King asked politely.

-"A little more than a year, Your Majesty."

-"That is good. Have you fought the recent battle?""

-"Yes, Your Majesty, I am the one who spread the news to the other regiments. And after that, I joined the battle with those regiments."

"So, you did not fight against the unprecedented soldiers? Like the other regiments?" asked Walther.

"No Sir, they are mystery to me too," Michael replied.

"So how do you think you will fight if you incur this army?" Walther asked a tricky question.

"Well, Sir. I'll fight with my sword. Dead or alive, undead or tribe, I believe I can kill them with my sword," Michael was confident.

The King was impressed with Michael's answer. He laughed and appreciated.

"Sir, I have a question that I was hoping to ask," Michael asked Walther in a requesting tone.

"Yes, go on," Walther permitted.

-"Sir, do you believe in the curse of the Forest of Death, the Forbidden One? I mean, it is well known that whoever went in there died a horrible death."

-"Unfortunately you are correct. Every person to go in died. And in most cases, every person who went in didn't make it out. It is like finding the taste of a poison. But the poison is so toxic that anyone who tastes it dies instantly. Thus, we do not have any way to find out the taste. I admit there is something within the forest. But unfortunately, we don't have any way to find it out, at least not yet. But if you ask me whether I believe in the curse, then I must say I am in ambiguity."

After returning to their regiment at that night, Molly's first job was to prepare her team for the upcoming works. She had to inform the soldiers whom she had selected for the exchange of soldiers' participation between the castle and the regiment. This participation was very important as it would engender and foster enthusiasm amongst the soldiers in the new work environment, reduce boredom and increase the efficiency. Michael was selected as a watchman in the South Tower every Monday. Ben was selected to guard the Western Wall every Friday. Some of the soldiers from the castle were associated to work in the seventh regiment of the South on particular days too. Furthermore, soldiers from the seventh regiment of the South were assigned duties of patrolling the villages in front of the forest with soldiers from the other regiments and that of the castle on particular days. All of Michael, Ben and Daniel got this job every Wednesday.

Molly also had to recruit at least fifteen more soldiers in the team as soon as possible. And she asked the unified team to assist her. However, Michael asked for a break for a couple of days. He wanted to explore many places of the kingdom alone. Although, it would be better for even Michael himself to stay with his friends during that time and try to overcome the grief, Molly gave her favourable response. But, she also demanded Michael to return and join the force soon as the special training of Light and Heavy Cavalry was about to begin within the following few days.

That night, when everyone was asleep, Michael visited the stable. It was the stable where Warcress used to stay. It had been M.I.A. with James for a couple of days. It was the stable which Michael and James had been assigned to take care of. It was the stable where their old horses were still there. Michael went to look after their old horses. It was an amazing yet unexplainable fact how animals could feel the concern of upcoming danger or the sorrow of loss. He found James' old horse, sick and pale. And he found teardrops at the end of its eyes.

"I wish I could say everything will be alright," he was talking to James' old horse.

On the following day, Michael went out on Axilior to travel the entire kingdom. He went to the church at the far West, and the city it belonged to. He went to the grasslands and villages of the far East. He went to the villages of the South and near the Forest of Death, the Forbidden One. He visited the regiments of the East, West and North. He also bypassed the castle and the regiments of the North to go to even far to the North. He, at last, visited the inn where he and James once had stayed. During his voyage, he met many people, observed them in their daily lives, heard them talking. Every person had a different story of his life to narrate and Michael enjoyed watching them. He met the small camps and troops of soldiers appointed to guard those places. He saw rich businessmen dealing in tobacco, diamonds and clothes on their horse carts. He also saw poor farmers in their endeavour to sell their crop. He stopped for a drink in the inn and met Mr. Bummer, the innkeeper. As expected, the innkeeper could not remember one of the two fake King's Men who once had stood up against three murderers and had saved both his life and the inn. Michael found the place to be still as noisy and raucous as it had been before. But he refused his own urge to visit London. "Some things should remain as memories. And besides, those days are long gone. I cannot get those days back even if I want and try to," he said to himself. "I already have said goodbye to those beautiful days," he was determined not to break down.

The following Monday was a big day for Michael. It was his first day as a watchman in the South Tower. He had the duty on the top of the Tower the whole night. Michael reached the fortress duly on Axilior. The Gatehouse was opened for him. He then left Axilior in one of the stables in the South Bailey. And he used the large stairs to reach the top of the tallest Tower.

The top of the Tower was conical. There were window-like shapes in the cylindrical walls. These shapes were used to look from by the watchmen and archers in search for any unfamiliar movement. The floor of the top was round and the diameter of the Tower, which constantly and slightly reduced from the bottom to the top, was enough for some watchmen and archers to stand. The place was incredibly elevated from normal sea level - it was the top of the tallest construction in the place and the construction itself was on hilly terrain.

Now, he looked outside from the windows. It was nothing like how he usually watched the ambience at night from the regiment. Today, he could see the whole earth around him. It was a night of full moon. The moon and the stars shining were reducing the blackness of the night sky and turning it with violet rays. The entire night sky was divided into two at the edge of heaven by a gathering of millions of stars starting from one side of the sky to go to the other; it was like a narrow pavement for stars on which the stars boarded and journeyed for light years - it was a Galaxy. White, red and blue were them, the stars on this pavement, and were creating a palette of so many colours in the sky. This pavement was called the Milky Way. There were parts of clouds in the sky, sometimes covering the moon and the stars from Michael, and the clouds looking like reddish waves in the dark violet ocean of sky. The whole place was under a cover of darkness. The fortress itself was illuminating like flames in some parts, but otherwise, mostly it was dark. However, due to the moon and the stars, the whole place along with the castle was not entirely under darkness, rather it was radiating a bluish field. The fire lightened in the regiments and the villages seemed like yellow dots on the dark sea of blue. In the moon's reflection, Michael could identify the things closer to him, like the trees and roads. The Black Forest of Death, so far away from him, was looking like the divisive horizon in between the sky and the land. There was a narrow river flowing in the East, from the North to the South. It looked greenish. The scenario was like a witch had played her ultimatum on the river. There was a sweet and cold breeze blowing. And the temperature was high above the freezing blizzard of the night of the war. A white owl was flying high in the sky from the Towers of the castle to the Forest foraging for food. Its seldom howling was breaking the silence of the night. And there were air dusts floating in the sky and the air; they were glowing brightly in the rays of moon and stars; they were the Stardusts in the Starshine.

Michael believed in the fact or fallacy that at night the people dying or lost in the Forest of Death reincarnated; he strongly believed in it as he wanted James to come back to life during the nights. He took out the only two non-military things that he had brought - a feather and a paper. He trusted that James would come here to read what Michael would write and leave. And so he started, "Dear James..."

Later in the future, Michael would be coming here every Monday, writing a letter addressing James and leaving it in a particular position at the top of the tower. Years from now, these letters would be discovered by the King. He would find the importance in them. They would be bound to make a book. Decades from then, archaeologists and historians would find the tome. It would gain a special place in the heart of the medieval history of England. This would become Michael Chapman's tome, Michael Chapman's diary.

But tonight, along with a simple but first letter to James, Michael also described the night himself. And as he wrote:

When the darkness spreads and the silence sprouts
And the whole world sleeping, hiding the face in shy,
Only the moon shining in sky and so shine the stars
With the waves of the Starshine that come from beyond the sky.

The moon that shines in pride, and the airdusts in the Starshine
Dancing in the wave while the music plays
The one who dances along - The Owl, on the top of the boughs
Dancing until tomorrow, on the sky's silvery bays.

The crickets flying over the greenish river
Flowing nearby; assisting it the cool breeze is blowing
The white howling owl, flying before the brightest moon
And the spiders in their webs, the night they are enjoying.

Yonder, by the end, there stands the Forest of Secrets
Where roam the legends that, for long, are not heard or told,
The melodies of the leaves, grasses and the feathers of the sleeping birds
And the girl in white gown will tell you the legends to hold.

The Forest went so violet, but the boughs silvered by -
Who dances in their voyage to the beyonds all night,
And so went silver - the spiders, the stable, the silvery owl in sky
And the unknowns, in the Forest, by the Stardusts of the Starshine.

5

INTO THE FOREST OF DEATH, THE FORBIDDEN ONE

It was a while since I was in Canterbury working on my research project. And there were many riddles of this long lost mysterious kingdom that my team and I were trying to decrypt. However, there certainly was something about this isolated island in the vast ocean of ruthless time which I was mostly interested in. So far, I had studied how the presence of that particular thing had affected the lives of Michael Chapman and others. I read how it had devoured and snatched the last breaths of many people. But, I was yet to figure that haunted thing out in depth, mostly what had been inside it, where 'it' being the Forest of Death, the Forbidden One.

So far, I have completed about thirty percent of Michael Chapman's tome without any trace of the devil within. And it was frustrating me, I was becoming reckless and restless. I must condemn myself for some major errors that I was doing because of my restless mind. Fortunately, I got myself back sound and steady very soon. And I started to spend time studying the other books in the library for the information I was looking for. But it was surprising that I found almost nothing in the library rich with so many enlightening books, parchments, letters and drawings. Even the most logical pundits of the time had been afraid to write anything about the forest; they had been afraid of being cursed and spirited away.

Thus, I decided to take a break from my work one snowy day and visit the remnant of the forest. It was about half an hour by a taxi to the place from the castle. My goal was to see what was inside the forest. "Don't you dare have any high expectation," I was alerting myself.

The car was running while passing small towns and villages. These towns and villages were different than those of the rest of the country. The buildings were small, undecorated and isolated. The roads were wider and lonely, and the fewer street lights were trying their best to lighten the roads during that snowy morning. The number of people on the roads was horrendously small even for a cold day like that, and the oaks and pine trees were belligerently watching the movements of my car. There also were expansive farm lands with many cattle grazing. I was having the feeling that the centuries-old curse was still depriving the development of this part of the country.

At last, I reached the remnant of the forest. The deep maze of the Forbidden One as described by Michael Chapman now was only some kilometres wide. It was getting lost to the ever-growing human civilization. And with that, the curses of the forest seemed long erased. The devil inside had to rest in the Hell again. And the Hell's hounds were chained again behind the Hell's Gate.

I had the courage and enthusiasm to go inside the forest. It merely was a wood. However, the remaining depth was successfully blocking the sunlight, making it woods of night. The snow was on the leaves of the trees and also on the very narrow road that had gone through the woods. And with the breezing sounds of the wind, I happened to hear something unusual coming from the denser part of it. It felt like there were tombs and temples. And there was an ancient society inside that was praying a ritual before jumping at flames altogether. The sound faded away within seconds. And I could not decipher if it was just my mind playing with my vulnerability or some surreal reality. But, the light of the day was decreasing rapidly and I had to return to my room. And Michael Chapman's tome became my only resource to know more about the forest. Upon returning, I started working on the tome once again. Little did I know that the tome had a surprise for me.

Three months had passed since the attack of the French, pirates and the unprecedented army. Everything was becoming normal again. The affected villages in front of the Forest of Death, the Forbidden One, were also recovering quickly. The soldiers of the regiments and the King's Men had shown proficiency and temperament in their jobs which turned out to be extremely necessary and constructive.

The Christmas Eve and the Christmas passed. The enjoyments of these days for the soldiers of the seventh regiment of the South were almost nothing. The recent tragedy had shocked all of them and so, this year the usual chicken, beef, pork, wine, singing, dancing and after all, getting extremely wasted were absent. The dancing women in the decorated bars could not attract them and nor could the traditional breads with three pork sausages.

The time of the year reminded Michael of last year's Eve, and the party, the dancing, the joy. James and Raphael had been with them back then. And Michael was feeling how hard the season was for Molly. So, he decided to pay her a visit in her tent.

Molly was sitting on a chair alone in her tent. Her eyes were closed. The cold spreading from the dead candle was inconspicuous to her. The glass of wine on the table in front of her was unusually full. She did not open her eyes as Michael came in.

Michael took a chair beside her and sat. And he held her hand tight. Molly still did not open her eyes, but she held his hands back. They did not say anything. However, the silence spoke thousands of words for them.

The snowfall was more intense than last year's. The snowflakes were amalgamating with each other to create ice crystals and were falling down from heaven. The Angels had taken a shelter to give rest to their exhausted wings. The clouds in the sky were hiding the sorrow of the earth from their eyes. The entire Kingdom was painted with a lifeless colour by the winter. The birds and insects had gone into hiding long ago to their nests, waiting for the first leaf of spring to come. The Castle, the regiments, the churches, the towns and the villages were under thick grief of snow. Every morning, men would come out of their houses and clear the snow to keep a track of the lost roads.

There had been some noticeable changes in the seventh regiment of the South. Fifteen more soldiers had been recruited. And all the soldiers had to undergo a tougher training than ever - training on Light and Heavy Cavalry. Personally, Michael preferred Light Cavalry; although the Heavy one was more protected, the Light one was more swift and quick. Michael, Daniel and Ben had a new tentmate - Tim, who had recently joined the regiment. Tim was the youngest of them all and was only in his teenage. Tim was from the city in the far West. Unlike most of the soldiers of the regiments, he was not from a low-income family, broke, leftover, bastard or orphan. However, he also displayed the zeal to become a member of the King's Men. And this was the reason why he had abandoned a safe and secure life to join the army. Molly had given Michael the task to supervise Tim.

Michael continued his job as watchman every Monday night at the top of the South Tower. And he left a letter to

James every night of his watch on top of the one left on the previous week in a specific place at the top of the Tower. Sometimes, he would write the letter before going to the castle, and sometimes he would write it on spot during his watch. He would write about his week, about his training, about their horses, the regiments - especially the seventh of the South, Molly and others, the new changes and challenges, etc. He also wrote about the King, the Queen, Commander Black, Walther, Ray and the others. Sometimes, during a period of light intensity, he would write and explain about the bars he had visited recently, the beers he had tasted and even the funny entertainments that he had enjoyed too. More importantly, he regularly wrote about Tim and asked suggestions for how to supervise the kid. Unfortunately and obviously, he never got the suggestions back.

One thing I must mention that I have guessed from his diary. Michael did not like Tim; probably he was turning out to be someone the army was trying to replace James with.

Michael often met Black and Walther. Walther was an eclectic as well as eccentric man. His self-confidence reminded Michael of James. Being a dwarf, Walther was pointed at numerous insults and ignorance, despite being the Head of the Order, but he always displayed disinterest in them. His responsibility towards the Kingdom also inspired Michael. One Monday night, he actually spent a quarter of the entire time with Michael on top of the South Tower. He would do such sudden visits to regiments too in search for the dedication of the soldiers and any hidden ulterior motive. With Michael, his aim had been to justify how effective it was to watch from the Towers.

Looking at the earth from the window, he had asked, "It is a grand scenery, is not it?"

"Indeed it is, Sir," Michael had replied.

Now, watching the view for a moment and closely observing it, he had said, "It really is a good place to watch. You can see a lot from here. Even the forest can be seen. Any unnatural movement of light or something like that can be notified easily, even during the no moon."

-"You are right, Sir! In the Starshine, I can also see a lot. And a large pack of soldiers is even easier to find out."

-"That is true. And a small group of soldiers cannot be much harm anyway, even if you miss them. But how do you think you will watch on a rainy or snowy day? Like the one when the last invasion happened?"

Michael had no reply to this question. This really was a loophole in the almost perfect plan and process.

On the next Wednesday, Michael, Daniel and Ben went on their scheduled patrolling in the villages in front of the forest. Tim also joined them. Although he had not been assigned to this work, he chose to accompany his friends rather than spending time alone in the tent. He could have gone through a training session during the time but he preferred real life experience over it. They were observing how slowly and steadily the villages were coming back to normal. Even the last one was prospering at last because of the attention from the authority.

The broken houses were being rebuilt, the dead farm and cattle animals were being replaced. The few farms and mills existing on the rough soil that had been annihilated during the invasion were also ameliorated. And most of all, the natives whose will to live had been obliterated started to dream again.

There was a bar in the last village that Michael and the others always preferred because of the low cost and old rum which were served. It caused a fine hangover. Today also they decided to hit it. The bar always was full of lively and energetic people from the villages. Like Michael and his friends, other soldiers often visited it too. Nothing unusual usually went on in the bar. But today was different. When Michael, Daniel, Ben and Tim were enjoying their rum, they overheard something that snatched their attention completely.

"So, more young men went in the forest. And never returned," someone from the next table said out.

"It is a shame, and it was about to happen. No one can stop it," another one from the table said.

Michael and the others gave a cessation to their drinking and turned at the table. There were four people at the table, all having drinks like them.

"Yes! I don't know why they put their lives in danger for the fucking idiot," the third one said something which was not very clear to the four soldiers.

"It is because of the father," the fourth one responded with some explanation which itself could not clarify anything.

At last, Michael and the others decided to step in and interrogate. They walked to the table, introduced themselves and asked for what the four men were talking about.

Mr. David Young, a wealthy businessman, lived in the city in the far West. He used to deal in diamonds. He was one of the most powerful and richest persons in the nation and his worth was almost the highest amongst the non-royal people. He owned a big mansion over a large area, some shops, firms and mills, his own personal soldiers, a big stable, a bench of secretaries and much more. But he was not satisfied with his life because of his only son Mr. Joe Young, a loafer and a disgust to the great family. He was extravagant, spending recklessly and excessively the superfluous money of his father. Spending time in brothels, bars, with his friends in the anti-social activities were his only schedules of a day. On any day, he saw more whores than he saw the members of his own family. He already had been arrested and had spent nights in jails several times.

This time, a few days ago, he had got intoxicated after drinking a lot, started doing inappropriate behaviour with local women, was busted by soldiers, got into a fierce fight with the friends against the soldiers, got involved into a murder and flew into the forest along with the friends and never came back. Death penalty was the inevitable fate - even Joe Young knew it.

After getting the news from some of his son's other friends, old Mr. Young announced a big pile of reward for anyone who could go into the forest and rescue his son. Some young men, searching for a future with an urge to become famous and rich overnight, took the challenge. They went into the forest in teams, and the last of them went in there at only the dawn of the on-going day. And it was not any surprise that none of them had made it back so far.

Michael and the others were getting up to ride to the King and to give him the message. However, they were stopped by another incident. A young man suddenly entered the bar and shouted out while panting. It seemed that he had run a lot from near the forest to the bar. And his news definitely was something that would drive Michael and the others to ride to near the forest in the next moment. He said that someone from the last team to go into the forest in search for Joe Young had just made it back.

Michael, Daniel, Ben and Tim rushed to the spot; many enthusiastic people from the bar and the village also joined them. At the spot, they found a huge crowd of curious natives as well as some soldiers around the survivor.

It was not any human survivor; it was a horse of one of them. The horse was pale, almost bloodless. Its eyes were coming out of their cups, the mane was cut down in some parts. The saddle seat was empty and was hanging down at the belly as the leather and breast belts, holding the seat on top of the back, were badly torn. There was blood all over its body with scratches of unusually long claws. The horse was shouting in a demonic tone - like it was being possessed. And every now and then, it was standing on the last two legs. It was shaking badly, the legs were trembling; it looked like the Devil was on its trail.

By the time, the hangover period of the drunks was gone. They refused their initial urge to go near the survivor. In fact, some of them cried out in fear and ran away leaving the cursed place.

The horse was hitting the ground haphazardly and shaking its head badly. Underneath, these actions were dislocating its bones and separating its muscles. And it was shouting tremendously in fear and agony. However, it continued to hit and nod, worsening the conditions.

All the people, who were close to the horse, got away from it. Even skilled horsemen like Michael, Daniel and Ben also were hesitating to go near it. A kick from a horse, especially from a crazy one like this, would be sufficient to kill someone. So, they waited for it to calm down because of exhaustion. Some moments later, it collapsed down. It could no longer stand because of the badly injured legs. By shouting excessively, it had severely damaged its vocal cords. And now it could no longer neigh. Still, it was trying to shout, which resulted in a silent appeal and a slight high pitch voice from it.

The soldiers took a quick action. The horse was taken on an open hood carriage run by horses. And the injured horse was taken to the stables of seventh regiment of the South for shelter and treatment. Michael went to the castle to give the King the news. And Daniel went to the city to summon Mr. Young, the senior by the name of His Majesty.

As old Mr. Young arrived in the Great Hall, the meeting started. There were the King, the Order, Michael, Daniel and some other people in the Hall besides him. It was, beyond all doubts, evident that his nonsense reward had caused the missing men and deaths.

Walther came to the point really quickly, "Mr. Young, do you understand the consequences of your reward?"

Mr. Young nodded to say no.

-"There are at least fifteen youths who went into the forest in search for your son and never returned."

"But, Your Majesty, I did not compel or ask anyone to go. This was their own choice," Mr. Young tried to defend himself.

-"You are wrong. Your reward was an action like an unintentional murder. You are guilty for it."

"But he is my only son!" Mr. Young gave a last try to save himself.

"A son who is guilty for murder and is a runaway. Our soldiers are already looking for him in the villages. And if he went to the forest then I don't think we have an option of finding him. But, I'll ask some of our best horsemen to search for him in the forest. However, they will have the right to withdraw the mission as soon as they sense any danger," Walther said to Mr. Young.

Mr. Young was not happy with the decision and he wanted to oppose. But he was stopped by Walther yelling at him. "Mr. Young, I do not want to denounce you in the public but your reward is illegal!" Walther said. "Mr. Ray, can you please explain why?" he asked.

"Well, one can easily perceive that Mr. Young is trying to protect someone who is in the black list of our army," Ray answered.

Hearing Ray's explanation, Walther turned back at old Mr. Young and gave the warning, "I want you to withdraw your reward. This is the first thing you will do as soon as you reach your place."

After the end of the meeting, Walther, Ray and two others from the Order decided to visit the stable of the seventh regiment of the South to see the injured surviving horse from the Forest of Death, the Forbidden One. They were convinced that the horse was a lead towards unravelling the mysteries behind what was behind the forest. Michael already had described the condition of the horse to the Order and they found it no different upon arriving at the destination. The dying horse was lying on the floor of the stable and the horsemen were doing their best to provide any kind of panacea. The deep scratches of long claws on its body were matters of in-depth inspection to the Order, however, they were completely in dark with them. Anyone could conclude that hounds from the hell had been chasing the poor animal in the Forest of Death.

The following night was very critical to the soldiers. Best horsemen were assigned with the job to look after the horse; one soldier from each of the first six regiments of the South and Michael from the seventh were in charge. Even Walther himself stayed the whole night in the stable.

As time went on, the condition of the horse only aggravated. Natural antibiotics were applied on the wounds and rum was provided with water. But all the endeavours were going in vain. Alas! At the dawn of next morning the horse passed away.

It was yet another example on the verity of the curse of the Forest of Death, the Forbidden One; and it was another example for the proponents against the oppositions or heretics. The phrase associated with the forest still was holding true - "Any soul to go in there will be spirited away before the next sunrise." And now, it was a rigid support on the phrase as even the meticulous hard work of some of the best horsemen of the kingdom could not save the horse, neither could they delay the death till the next morning. The phrase had been true since its origin, fifty one years ago from this time. Even the French and pirate invaders had been killed in spite of having a larger army. And still there was no scientific or logical evidence on the 'unprecedented army'.

For the last few hours, some of the best horsemen of the Kingdom had faced the macabre of the curse indigenous to the Forest of Death. The terrifying experience that they had gone through while nursing the horse crucified with the curse of the Forbidden One was inundating to all of them and it unnerved them to the most extreme just before their crucial mission. These were the soldiers selected for the rescue mission of Young Junior. And they had to ride into the forest which had been vindicated for all the massacres since a time about fifty one years before.

To the common eyes, the soldiers of the regiments who always went through the toughest exercises possible had engendered disaffection from any humanly emotions including fear. The first oath that the soldiers had to take after they joined a regiment was that the authority would not be responsible for their deaths from any military cause which could happen at any time of any day. And the vows that the soldiers put to themselves as they woke up and before they went back to sleep differentiated them, in fact, from a common man. A common man would call it - "someone with mind, eyes and heart of that of a wolf. Sharp and calm, keen and stable, merciless and fearless".

However, the reality was certainly a little detached from the fantasy. Every person has fear of death, and if it does not arise from the horror of the uncertainty of the afterlife then it must be caused from the terror of the unbearable agony that causes death itself. Long future does not usually come to the context of human considerations as it is uncertain, and people are afraid of uncertainty. That is why we make biased outcomes of the possible results of an unknown event, no matter how implausible the outcome itself is - it is a common human trait since the primordial times. However, death is not only an event of uncertainty, it is an event towards uncertainty for an unsettled amount of period. And the pain that a dying man undergoes that results in his death is something more troubling. Even the most misanthropic soldiers of the mission, therefore, were traumatized as they were afraid for their souls and bodies and nobody loves anything more than his own soul and body. To worsen the situation, the Forest of Death, the Forbidden One itself was a place of ambiguity and unpredictability with only a wishful thinking of not facing the unprecedented soldiers and the undead.

Sir Light, the King's Man, had to individually talk to each soldier of the mission in order to encourage them before the mission. Sir Light, who was going to lead the mission, had come to the stable that morning along with two other King's Men.

He talked to Michael too, "How are you feeling?"

"Excited like boiling water, Sir," Michael tried to sound confident.

-"Wow! And, are you afraid? Of death, to go in there and never return, to be detached from your friends?"

-"A little bit, Sir."

Sir Light put a comforting hand on Michael's shoulder and said, "Michael, I know you for a long time. I have fought against you. And I know what an amazing soldier you are. I know, you can make a huge difference in any mission or war. Your comrades can totally rely on you. And I trust you, so does Commander Black, and also the King himself. Tonight, a child in a village, who does not even know you, will go to sleep peacefully because you are a soldier of our army. You protect this kingdom, and you love it like nobody can."

The speech made Michael smile. And he was feeling confident. He could feel his worth again. Sir Light asked again, "Do you want to ask if I am afraid?"

"Are you, Sir?" Michael asked.

-"Not at all. Because, I have soldiers like you in my team."

It was Michael's first mission under the supervision of a King's Man. He was enthralled with the mission, despite being afraid himself, because of the chance to show his worth to the King's Men. Like everyone else on the team, he was also excited to look at the men wearing the cloaks with the Sword on the Circle, the King's Crest, in action. And like everyone else of the team, he was also hoping for a positivity towards being recruited as the next King's Man after a successful aftermath of the mission. Nevertheless, every one of the team came to an agreement that as soon as they face something unnatural within the forest, they would abort the mission right away and come back.

The mission started some hours prior to the time when the sun was on the pinnacle to allow maximum possible hours of sunlight for the rescue. Ten of the best horsemen of the nation with three King's Men including Sir Light in the front and seven soldiers from the seven regiments of the South Tower including Michael were in the team.

Although it was not advisable and any expert of both human anatomy and wines as well as an experienced and professional army chief would condemn this, Light and his team decided to stop for beers in the bar of the last village before the forest. It was not like a last supper before a mission impossible, rather it was more like a getting to know each other and a little enjoyment before a serious issue. Many people had assembled on the two sides of the road from the bar to the near of the Black Forest. As the soldiers passed them, they shouted out to cheer them with sanguine faces. The selfish motive of the amassing villagers was directed to the hope that the entirely dedicated soldiers would put on their lives in line to unravel the truth behind the dark curtain of the forest and thus the curse would be lifted. The more disturbing fact was that they cared less for the success of the rescue mission itself than to know of what lied beyond the trees of the forest that had killed thousands in different times. Young Junior basically was a cumbersome, spendthrift son of a man with affluence and avarice to them; both of the son and father were no close to the villagers.

Before leaving the seventh regiment of the South, Michael had met his friends - Daniel, Ben, Tim and some others. However, he intentionally had avoided Molly. It had been some months since James had gone missing in the forest. The only thing worse than the status of K.I.A. was a status of M.I.A. And manufacturing an ornate stone tablet in the regiment with their names engraved on gravestones would do no justice to them; it was only asking for forgiveness for everything from the lifeless stone. It had been days and nights for Molly and Michael to get accustomed to the instability related to the fate of James which was still an enigma to them. Again, it was uncertainty which troubled them. They had no idea of whether James was dead at all. And even if he was alive, they had no way to contact him or even know how he was. However, it was practically beyond any question that if James was alive he was in danger. But, they had no chance of aiding him. It was like James was behind a glass - a very rigid, opaque and almost non-transparent glass with light's distorted reflection. It was like they could feel or even see James, as if he was on the other side of the glass, however they had no way to have a possible communication. This uncertainty was unsettling because James could be alive but would not answer to their calls, or, he himself might be calling for help, or, might have left the world long ago. If they were to be candid and frank to themselves, Molly and Michael were hoping for the status of James to change from M.I.A. to K.I.A. This would be better for all of James and Molly, Michael who had been tired of waiting to get a call back from James.

Michael was sure that Molly had generated an antipathy towards the forest as it had taken away her loved ones in different times. And the news that Michael was going in there would obviously stupefy and petrify her. Not only because Michael himself was one favourite acquaintance to Molly and since James' departure from their lives, their relationship had quite ups with the sharing of common grief of loss, but also because Molly would be concerned if Michael could find James. And as finding James was definitely not a part of the mission and Michael was supposed to be attached to the only goal of the mission, this would force Molly not to share this request and suffer a suffocating condition.

Michael was in ambiguity about saving James. He almost did not believe that a chance of saving him would come up in the first place, successfully implementing that chance of saving him was even a more distant possibility. And as a professional, he was supposed to follow only what he had been assigned to, getting diverted from that might cause different problems; he might even be vindicated as rebellious for any unfriendly outcome. Again, there was no assurance on if James was alive. Having a biased assumption of it would do no help. Moreover, even if a chance would arise to save him and even if the entire team would follow to perform so, there was very least probability that they would be sufficient and successful. However, Michael knew that if such an opportunity would come, nothing could restrain him from taking the lower roads, no matter how deadly it would be. He knew that he would not stop himself from having this responsibility for his friend. That is why, underneath, there was a part of Michael himself who was not wanting to have this opportunity and was wishing for James' death.

As the soldiers entered the forest, they felt uneasy from the very beginning. It was due to the fear, of course. The first few meters into the forest were not uncommon; it was similar to a familiar environment with trees not creating much of a dense part. But as they moved more towards the core, the density rose and the cheers from the crowds got diminished gradually. Despite the time of the day, the brightness reduced as they went in because of the covers of leaves and bows of towering trees over their heads. Everything known to them was changing exponentially. The ambience was becoming wilder and they were going far away from the civilized society with every step of their horses.

Suddenly, there was an abrupt change of the surroundings - the density of the wild was high with unfamiliar trees, the quantity of dead leaves on the ground was significant, the sun was almost covered by the conspirers of the trees, the little light that could penetrate only made a disturbing interference with the shadows and the soldiers could no longer hear from the crowds outside. The diabolical nature of the forest was coming out as they moved further in. All of the soldiers, even the King's Men, were maintaining a low speed and were in a pack. They were surrounded and under the mercy of the tall trees around them. These trees were ancient, with their branches starting from low of their trunks to reach to the top of the crowns and kiss the sky. The trunks were thin, yet were strong to endure natural disasters through centuries. And leaves proliferated on each of their branches which aggregated to make a cover before the sunshine. The trees themselves seemed like spies; it was like they already had sent the news of the intruders to what lied in the depth of the forest. And it was like that they were watching the soldiers moving, it was like they were closely observing every footstep of the horses.

The air within, which had never gotten out to the free world, also was different from the one outside. This one was trapped with the curses within the Forest of Death, the Forbidden One for centuries. It was heavier yet pleasant, savage yet pristine. The soldiers were feeling an unnatural cold here than the outside and the random breeze of the air with sporadic winds and circulations was something supernatural.

The most problematic thing was that the entire place was like a maze with no trail or footprint of Young Junior or the aspirants who had gone to Young's rescue.

There was a strange silence in the place. The only sounds were from the wild birds singing on the boughs and the footsteps of the horses on the dead leaves. Some sudden sounds of wild animals were coming from unidentified locations.

Suddenly, there was one instantaneous change in the forest. The trees were coming closer to each other as the depth was increasing; it felt like the trees were on the verge of suffocating the intruders. The least of the sunlight that could pass through the impregnable cover of leaves was scattering randomly, creating patterns of shadows and light in places. The uneasiness and cold were more intense than ever. The familiar sounds of birds, animals and that from the horses' heels were changed drastically. The sounds of the living creatures were replaced by an abstract vacantness added to the already almost silent no man's land. And the familiar sounds of horses' heels were multiplied by some unrecognized footsteps. The rhythm of those unknown footsteps played like a symphony with that of the horses of the soldiers - they were balanced. With every footstep of the horses, the unknown were steadily coming closer. Michael felt that someone definitely was following him. He was suffering from the discomfort that some things were attentively watching him from the branches of the trees. And some things were running in parallel to Axilior far away in the dark horizon of the forest. He looked at the other soldiers. They were also as tensed as he was. He was periodically looking at the trees, from the bottommost branches to the top boughs, in search for something indistinguishable. They sometimes were turning their heads back to see if they were being followed. And they were also trying to cover the whole place within the limits of their sight by eyes. These assured Michael that he was not the only one to feel being followed, again, these also proved his fearful hypothesis that they were not the only ones there. Even the King's Men had abandoned their bigotry and were staying close to the team, without being hasty and braggart.

The unnatural silence was torn in a moment with a paranormal noise. It was a howling. It came from the core of the forest that the team was going towards. Presently, the soldiers including Michael definitely heard noises becoming louder with every passing second. These were the sounds generated by running horses on dead leaves. With every passing second, some things were coming closer to the team. The sounds also contained the one that generally was created by a predator big cat or dog family while on a hunt. After Michael had identified the sound, it reminded him of the deep wounds of big claws of the injured horse, the survivor of the forest, which had died that morning. Were these the hounds which guarded the gate of hell?

The soldiers stopped. The horses were panting with terror and agitation. Michael and the others were helplessly and restlessly looking at the surroundings and it was going in vain as they could find no one. All of them brought out their swords in preparation for an upcoming fight, or rather a defence. The horses were walking randomly and restively within a small region of perimeter.

The invisible hounds from hell were very close now. Michael could feel their insatiable wrath. He could see the dead leaves on the ground getting pressured down by the invisible paws. And with time, more and more leaves closer to him were getting pressured down. The hounds were getting closer. He also could hear and feel their exhaled warm breath. Some more howling was there from the deeper side of the forest.

The soldiers also heard of the approaching horses. This sound was coming from all over the place. Were they getting surrounded by the undead? The available perimeter for the horses of our soldiers was diminishing. They were forced to come closer and closer to each other. They formed a circle, with each of them facing outward with a prepared sword. Michael was recalling about the things he had heard from Molly and others about the unprecedented soldiers. However, they had seen them. But now, Michael could only feel being surrounded and almost getting compromised by some invisible horsemen. These definitely were not the unprecedented soldiers. These were different, probably deadlier. These definitely were the curses of the Forest of Death, the Forbidden One. These definitely were the dead soldiers of ages, awaking with the smell of blood.

For the past few moments, the soldiers had their undeviated concentration on their invisible and approaching enemies. After getting surrounded, they could not even realise the next disturbing event which was slowly grabbing them until it was too late. A dense blue mist covered the place. The trees were looking black and a distance of only a few meters was impossible to be perceived. The bluish field of darkness was everywhere; none could see the sky and the sun.

The temperature was near freezing. The soldiers could see the freezing breath as they were exhaling. A strong wind had just started blowing. The leaves and the branches were shaking heavily with the wind. The dead leaves from the ground were getting flown away with the storm.

The horses were shouting. Even they were sensing the unorthodox. The soldiers were frightened. "What are these?"

Some of them asked yelling in unison. But nobody had an answer to this question.

The undead and the hounds from Hell were very close now. Michael could feel their warm breath on his body. Judging by the awkward movements that Axilior was doing, he could assuredly do the intuition that Axilior was feeling them too.

Suddenly, Michael looked at the ground near Axilior's heels. There was something that he could never expect to find in such a place, especially not within the Forest of Death.

It was a miracle that at that very moment, the soldiers started to feel normal again. They did not feel being surrounded by the enemies anymore whom they could not see. The Forest also became normal again with the usual noises from wild animals and easy breeze. It was like in a moment, someone had driven the evils away from them. It was like the hounds of Hell were chained and taken away by an Angel. And after a long time, the soldiers could breathe comfortably again.

"Fall back," after checking the exhausting and the state not capable of withstanding more stressful journeys and fight from the fellow soldiers, Sir Light ordered.

It was a defeat. And it was shameful for all of them. Not only did they lose but they actually lost to something superficial. They could not even describe why, how and what they lost to. It was embarrassing as the mighty horsemen of the King were no different from the common people who had lost in the Forest.

However, for a certain thing, the soldiers were victorious at least more than the rest of the invaders in the past. The invaders in the past had not only lost their battle in the Forest of Death but also had lost their lives. But today, these soldiers were returning back alive, and that was the greatest victory as there is nothing more precious than being alive. Although according to the statistics from the previous incidents, the soldiers were not entirely out of the danger till the following sunrise, they were feeling livelier than ever. And they knew that there was no way they would die within the next few hours.

Their way back to the Castle from the Forest was another challenge. People had been eagerly waiting for them to get the news that they had been seeking for long. And to be honest, many people were surprised to see them back. They were aiming with mixed emotions at the returning soldiers. And it was becoming almost impossible to keep heads high by the soldiers through those questions.

"What did you see?", "What is in the forest?", "Where is Young, did you find him?", "Did you see the others?", "Is there a demon inside? What are all the noises from the forest?", "How are you alive?", "You will die before tomorrow morning", "Are you also the spies of the evil?" - and many more were the questions asked to the returning soldiers by the people making crowds.

Sir Light ordered to run horses faster to avoid the crowd. It was dangerous to stand in front of the running horses of the horsemen but people continued to make the crowd on the road and create a mess. And it was difficult for the soldiers to go through the crowd. The people knew that the soldiers would not run over them as it would put their priority under scrutiny and the King himself might step in if an accident were to occur. This was giving them the courage to block the running horses.

After a long time, the soldiers finally reached the castle to report.

A meeting was called on quickly. Each of the soldiers shared his experience. It was asked if they had seen the Undead - they surely had encountered something which they did not know what to call. It was asked if they had seen the Unprecedented Soldiers - from Molly's previous descriptions, they had to say that they had not. And all the possible consequences were discussed. The partial success of the mission had a bad part - from now on more people would like to take the challenge to go into the forest in order to prove his worth to the King. Many would do this with an urge to be selected as a member of the King's Men. The Order Bench, led by Walther, came up with a solution to this. It was decided to spread the news to the entire kingdom that the soldiers had failed to find Young Junior. And that the soldiers had encountered countless of enemies whom they were not confident about what to call - evil, undead, demons; and that the soldiers could not fight the enemies and had barely escaped. Keeping in mind the high status of all the soldiers of the kingdom and to save them from the stigma, it was also decided to spread that no living being could fight against those supernatural soldiers. And considering the possible instability of the citizens arising from their fear, it was suggested that no one would ever go inside the forest again and no one would get harmed by the evil inside anymore.

When Michael returned to his regiment, he found all the soldiers of the regiment waiting for him. All of them were glad to see Michael back alive. Young Tim became emotional and almost wept. Ben had to control him by saying that a soldier should always have control on his emotions. But finally, Michael started liking Tim.

Daniel brought a glass of good wine to Michael. And it worked as a panacea to his falling body.

Everybody was enthusiastically waiting, looking at Michael's face, to listen what he would say. They were prepared to hear everything, even if it was not related to his recent voyage - they were just waiting to hear anything coming from Michael's mouth. But after all, they were waiting to hear about what he had seen in there. Although they knew that first and foremost what Michael needed was a heavy meal followed by a refreshing sleep, they could not let him go before they could hear everything.

"I think many of you are surprised that I have come back in one piece," Michael started with a wit. But more surprisingly, or rather somehow expectedly, the amazed faces of his fellow soldiers' nodded to decline the truth.

"Come on," he continued, "history has been violated. The death tolls did not repeat this time. I am sure some of you are surprised, not even you, Tim?"

"Michael, I am so glad you came back," emotional Tim hugged Michael tight and started to weep. And some of the rest of the soldiers criticized his emotions, but not in a very harsh tone. Michael held Tim back and said, "I am glad I came back too."

Daniel shook hands with Michael and said, "We all are glad that you came back, my friend. We do not want to lose you too." It was a clear connection to the M.I.A. of James Wheeler and K.I.A. of Raphael and many other soldiers.

Michael looked at the faces of all his friends and fellow soldiers. There were the swordsmen-horsemen and the archers-horsemen. Even some of the blacksmiths from the armoires were there to listen to him.

"As we went into the forest, it was good at first," Michael started to share his experience. "There were birds singing, monkeys jumping. Everything was normal. Yet, each one of us knew of what we were going into. It was the Forest of Death, the Forbidden One. For years, it has devoured lives that came into its mouth. We knew that we might die too and soon. Every leaf and grass and tree were telling us to go back. Still, we went farther in. I knew there were soldiers among us who wanted to terminate it. I myself was thinking about it too. Suddenly we started to feel something different."

Michael's pause was something uncalled for the audience. They were getting impatient and at last one asked, "What happened then?"

-"We started to feel being followed. We could feel that someone was marking us. The singing of birds was long gone. The forest was becoming more impenetrable. And then we heard howling, more than once, from farther inside. And we heard footsteps of hounds and horses. We could feel their breath - warm and evil. We were getting surrounded. We were getting ready to fight and had swords in our hands. But we could not see anyone. However, there definitely was something, many things. Those were trying to attack and kill us. Only when we practically had given up and we only could swing the swords in thin air, there was something that happened. I am not absolutely certain of what it was. It was like more invisible horsemen came in to contest them and save us. And the hounds were gone too! In a moment, they were all gone! And as we returned, we did not face anyone else anymore. I do not apprehend what happened there exactly."

"What do you think who saved you?" someone asked the question which Michael already had answered. Michael answered to him again, "I don't know."

"Maybe they all were the undead. You know, as we hear - the dead soldiers from the past awaking to continue the war? May be the ones who attacked you were the evil ones and the ones to save you were the good ones. They are on our side," teen Tim came up with his own theory.

"I really don't know," Michael exhaled heavily.

"Tim, then how will you explain why many innocent citizens were killed? Why did not the good ghosts come to save them?" someone asked.

"Maybe because they were not soldiers, and the good ghosts only saved Michael and others as they were soldiers like them when they were alive," Tim tried to defend his theory.

"Could you feel anyone familiar in them? Could you feel James?" Ben asked the most obvious question. James was the only one they knew who had gone into the forest and never came back. Michael nodded to say no. However, underneath, he was questioning himself for not saying yes. There definitely was something that he had seen within the forest which was not wild. And somehow, it reminded him of James.

It was a while for Michael to be back in the regiment and still he was crowded by the audience. But right now, he noticed that Molly was not there.

"Where is Molly?" he asked.

Daniel and Ben looked at each other. And then Daniel said, "She left for an important mission this morning, only after you had left. She did not say, though, anything about the mission. But she did say that she would not be coming back for a while. She left me in charge. In her absence, right now I am the Commander of the seventh regiment of the South."

-"That is big news for you. I hope Molly comes back soon. But why do you look gloomy?"

The little silence from them drove Michael crazy. He yelled out, "Come on, do not tell me something bad has happened to her while I was gone!"

"No, it is not like that. Actually, she was looking upset. And she left without saying almost anything. I don't think it was because of the gravity of her mission. I think you should have talked to her before you went," Ben said.

-"That is ridiculous. I did not talk to her for her own good. And I was busy preparing for the mission. I think of all people she should understand the measure of a mission!"

-"Michael, you did talk to us before you went!"

Ben's talk completely shut Michael down. "Oh my God! Did I really do a bad thing? But I did for her own sake! What about her love for James?" Michael asked himself.

"One more thing," Daniel said. "All the other times she left before, she only asked me to take her place. But this time she asked someone to take my place too. Benjamin is the new Second-in-Command. It only raises the question of when she will come back. Or, if she will be back at all."

"Because otherwise there is no need to assign a second-in-command, right? As she would come back soon to take her position and you would go back to being second-in-command?" Michael clarified himself by asking.

-"Yes."

"Michael, I personally think you should be the second-in-command. You are the strongest of us all, maybe even stronger than Molly? If James were alive, no doubt he would become the second, or even the Commander. But in the absence of James and Molly, I think you should take the position. We are in a tough condition. Molly really handled well. And we do not know what lies ahead. I have no idea if we can resist another attack like the previous one now," Ben said.

Michael denied and talked contrary to him, "No, you are better than me. I believe you are as strong as me, if not stronger. And you do have more experience. Molly made the right choice," he said.

That night was very hard for Michael for many reasons. All the odds of the statistics were against him and he was supposed to die within a few hours. And the other nine soldiers who had gone with him into the forest were also under danger. Daniel had assigned soldiers to constantly supervise Michael's condition. And there were also soldiers looking after Axilior.

Michael was trying to sleep as it was way past midnight. However, after trying it a lot, he had given up. Something was bothering him. But he could not identify what it was. Was it the effect of the Forest? Was it only because of the exhaustion? Was he over thinking about something that had hampered with his sleep? Was it about what he had seen in the forest that rigorously was reminding him back about James? Or was it about Molly?

The experience of the forest, being followed, the attack of the invisible soldiers and hounds, being on the verge of death - these certainly were circling back within his head. And in his ears, he was still hearing the howling that he had heard in the forest.

And what about the thing that he had seen in there? And who had saved them all from the enemies? Were they the good Undead as Tim had been imagining about? Was James in them too? If he were in them, what was he thinking upon seeing him? Was not James dissatisfied as Michael never had tried to look for him?

Where did Molly go? Definitely she would not be coming back some time soon. But what did she go for? Was she angry with him as he had not talked exclusively with her?

How were the other soldiers feeling? Were they alive? Or were they dying because of the curse? He had to wait until the next day to know the answer. And he himself was not sure if he was going to survive the night.

However, quite surprising to himself, he was feeling completely okay and healthy. He was breathing normally, was not feeling any internal pain, ache or any kind of abnormality. His lack of sleep was nothing to be concerned about.

As at least one soldier, most of the time Tim, was observing him, he was pretending to be asleep. However, he was wide awake and thinking a lot of things. One of the things certainly was that he was wanting to go back into the forest.

The next day when Michael woke up, it was late. The sun was making a large angle with eyes but still was not at the pinnacle. Instead of feeling well after the sleep, he was feeling tired. He was not feeling his body and so decided to lie for some time more before getting up. And as he got up, wore the uniforms and came out of the empty tent, he found his fellow soldiers of the regiment in the training grounds. All of them, seeing Michael, stopped their trainings to wish him for the beautiful morning and congratulate for defeating death.

Daniel was supervising the session. Tim and Ben were involved in their fights. All of them came to Michael.

"A messenger from the King came a few hours back. The King himself wanted to be sure everyone of yesterday's mission is alive and well," Daniel informed.

It was a pleasure for Michael to be heard from the King himself. And he felt being closer to his dream. His only dream, to which everything else was irrelevant. He was feeling that the name Michael Chapman was well known now, to every single person of the kingdom. The members of the King's Men knew it, the King himself knew it. Now, he was closer to wear the cloak with the King's Crest - the Sword on the Circle. He was envisaging of becoming a member of the King's Men.

"Any news from the rest of the team?" he asked.

"Yes, we asked the messenger and he said he knew about four more of you. They are alive too," Tim replied.

It was reassuring to Michael. Not only the news let him partially be sure that his colleagues were alright but also encouraged him to believe that the curse was not working on the team of the mission.

"Commander Daniel, can I have a day off today? I need to go to the castle," Michael asked Daniel.

"I grant you. You certainly can have another day. Come back by tomorrow night. Have a good time," Daniel permitted.

Michael took Axilior and started towards the North, to the castle. And then he ran it as fast as it could so as to reach the castle as early as they could.

Upon reaching the fortress, Michael received a grand welcome from the gate keepers and the archers. Due to his duty on every Monday at the South Tower, he already had known every one of them. Josh, one young and promising archer who himself was from South Tower and had duties typically on every day other than Monday, came to receive Michael. Probably he had been waiting for Michael all day at the Gatehouse.

He greeted Michael, shook hands and said, "Happy to have you back, Brother Michael."

"Happy to be here, Brother Josh," said Michael.

-"Here to see the King, I presume?"

-"Yes, I am."

-"So, you go ahead. I'll take your horse to the stable."

-"Thank you brother. It will be good help. I already am a bit late."

As Josh took Axilior to the stable, Michael went into the Greathall. He rushed into it as he had so many questions to ask and so many answers to give.

When he reached at the King's, he found many people already in there. There were the King, the Queen, Commander Black, the Order as well as some of the members of the team of ten of the recent mission to the Forest of Death.

He walked to the centre of the Hall, bowed and said, "Pardon my delay, Your Majesty. My Lady."

"Rise and shine, Chapman," the King said.

The meeting today was actually a celebration. Although the mission to rescue Young Junior was a failure, the conclusion followed by no casualty was a sign of hope. As suggested by the Order, the messengers had spread the news of the mission throughout the kingdom. And the citizens had to abide by the laws. They were bound not to enter the forest. But, they were believing that the evil was finally satiating. And the curse was slowly and steadily getting lifted.

Michael was desperate to have an answer and he had to catch someone from the highest authorities who was directly in connection with the military. Fortunately, soon he found Commander Black. After the primary greetings, he asked him, "Commander, do you know of any mission, may be a classified one, that has been assigned to one or a few of the strongest and most experienced soldiers after I was gone to the last mission?"

"No, there is not. If there was, I would have known. But why are you asking?" Commander Black said.

The reason why Michael was asking this question was Molly. The few things she had said before she left indicated that she was going for a top secret mission. Otherwise, Michael could not see any other reason for someone as dedicated as her leaving her regiment in any time. No one knew when the next invasion might happen. Right now, the enemies could be plotting something destructive. Right now, the citizens of this kingdom themselves might form an ulterior. And the forest was still as mysterious, unknown and dangerous as ever.

"Nothing. Just a curiosity if I have missed anything," he lied.

Michael was getting very badly excited as he thought there was only one place that Molly could have gone to. And he tried getting out of the castle quickly. However, he was stopped by David Williams. Williams was from the sixth regiment of the South and was in the group of ten of the last mission too. Michael remembered him as the more than necessarily bold soldier who had been in the front row of the team in the mission all along.

Much later, Michael would know more about Williams. Williams also was from London. He was a son of a mass murderer and had been in a gang for long. He also had been convicted for a case of a big robbery. Most of his gang members were sentenced to death. But Williams had been bailed as he had played the role of the official witness and also presented alibi. He had been selected as a swordsman because of his exceptional talent. However, one must not forget that Williams had betrayed his comrades and had been a criminal. He had joined the sixth regiment of the South after the last invasion, which was after James had become M.I.A. And because of his similar skills and techniques, Williams had started to be called as the Second James Wheeler by many people. Williams himself was not delighted being called after one of the finest soldiers of the regiments. So, he had started to claim that James Wheeler had been the shadow of David Williams before the actual David Williams would come. This certainly had generated anger and hatred towards him from many people, especially from the soldiers of the seventh regiment of the South as they always believed that James had been the best of all.

Williams came with two glasses of wine, one for himself and one that he offered to Michael.

"So, I heard that they will recruit some more King's Men really soon. I bet they will keep members of our mission in mind."

Michael had no way of justifying if Williams' comment was correct or wrong or a lie. So, he remained honest himself instead of exaggerating. "I did not hear it. But I do think if they are looking for good candidates then our team certainly had some. There were seven of us of the seven regiments of the South. And there were the three King's Men."

-"And so the seven of us have the opportunity, am I right?"

-"I personally think so. I can't say if you are right."

Williams tried to play friendlier by putting his hand over Michael's shoulder. Michael did not like it as he was feeling that Williams had a bad intention. But he remained silent as Williams continued the conversation.

-"So, how many of us will they select? What do you think?"

"I don't know. They may select all seven of us or none at all!" Michael replied to Williams' question which he had found stupid.

-"And if they were to select only one of us, who do you think is suitable?"

For my readers, I need to inform something. When the authority required to recruit only one soldier from a team of many, and if each of the soldiers was found equally worthy by the authority, then the authority would ask the soldiers themselves to select the best out of them. This way they would be sure to be recruiting the one who had demonstrated true leadership and was the one most trustworthy.

Michael realised what Williams was trying for going towards. He wanted to have Michael's vote for himself for the possible election. Both of them were the youngest of the mission and were almost of the same age. And so, Williams might be thinking that Michael was not very ambitious and desperate for being a King's Man. And he was presuming that Michael might already know that Michael might not be selected because of lack of experience. And that was why he would not mind giving up his vote to Williams.

To his great surprise, Michael took the opposite way. "I think I will vote myself," he said.

"That is so great!" Williams exclaimed. "I also think you are suitable."

-"Thank you, Williams."

Williams squeezed Michael's shoulder a little bit in an endeavour to enhance his gesture of being a friend. "But do you think you are worthier than Scott from the first regiment? He has been in the army for about ten years! Do you genuinely think you are a better swordsman than any of us? Look at me. I have seen more deaths and blood than anyone else in this Hall. Only I have the courage and strength to confront anything!" he said.

Michael was fired up. And the fire was not one with heat and excitement. It was cold with calm and confidence. "Williams, I don't see anyone more suitable than me. Seeing the most blood doesn't make you the worthiest. If you insist, let us see who they choose," he said.

Then he quickly got away from Williams, got out of the castle after taking Axilior and started towards the South. For the last few hours, this was what he was waiting to do. Excitement had prevented his sleep the previous night. He knew if James was in there, it was the time to rescue him. And he could not stop until he was successful.

After some hours, Michael finally reached in front of the Forest of Death, the Forbidden One. It took him more than the standard time as he had to take a longer road in order to avoid the seventh regiment of the South. He did not want anyone in there to see him heading South.

Today he was alone in front of the forest. The wild breeze was coming out of it. The leaves were waving like the mane of a crazy lion. And the howling was there from inside - the howling from the hounds of Hell. The place was lonely. Only Michael and Axilior were there. And the forest was challenging them to confront.

The sun had crossed the peak. The cold of the day was increasing. The forest was becoming from wild to evil. Mysterious darkness was covering it all over. And the distant core was calling Michael through the mazes of trees.

Michael was listening to the howling closely. As soon as the seventh howling was heard, he started riding Axilior into the Forest of Death, the Forbidden One.

He rushed through the obstacles of trees. The cold and speedy breeze trapped inside the forest was hitting him and was resistive against his motion, but was not resistive to his determination. The boughs and leaves were all shaking and waving with the rhythm of the breeze. The sounds of the wild were changing every instant - at first it was the ones from birds and animals, then it was an unusual silence followed by the paranormal noises. And sporadic howling was there all along. The forest was becoming denser, the air was becoming heavier, the light was becoming dimmer.

Suddenly it was the moment what Michael had been waiting for. He felt the trail of hounds behind him. He felt being watched from the branches of the trees. And then he heard the sound of the invisible horsemen chasing him. The dead leaves on the ground were pressed down by Axilior and the invisible horses. The breeze had turned into a tempestuous storm. The trees or the spies of the wild were coming closer to suffocate him. The branches sometimes shook off roughly as if something had jumped out of them. And Michael was feeling the warm breath of the hounds. Their fierceness was reflected out by their chase, warmth and strength. And the invisible soldiers were starting to surround him. Without giving much attention to any of these, Michael continued to run towards the core.

The hounds were very close now. And the undead were too. Today, the good ghosts were not here to assist or save him. Axilior was feeling the foes too and was trying to run faster and faster. Still, the enemies were getting close, they were coming closer, and closer, and closer...

Michael found himself in somewhere else. No. He was not out of the forest. In fact, he was at the core. But it was not what one would expect from the Forest of Death. One would expect it to be the place of a demon, the Devil and something evil. One would expect it as the place where the plots to slay thousands had been proposed and planned. And it was supposed to be the densest of the entire forest.

Michael Chapman was standing in a garden, a wild one, of white roses. It was a field with hundreds of plants, isolated from the civilization by the forest which covered it along the circumference.

The breeze was normal again. The air was light again. And there was no evil within.

The roses, so many of them, were colouring the place with the peace of white. And the flowers themselves were spreading the odour of love. The petals and leaves were dancing with the breeze. And some free petals were flying with it. The pollen grains were also flying, playing with the rhythm of the air. And the sunlight was diffracting by them, making them shine brightly at the thin air. They reminded Michael of the Stardusts in the Starshine.

The petal of a rose that he had found the previous day at Axilior's feet had led him here. In the wild that petal was a difference. And the team was saved by something unexplainable. Was it James? Was it him who had left the petal for Michael to find, and chase to here? If James had died, Michael thought, this place must be it where that had happened. For a soldier like James Wheeler, only a place like this was worthy of being his burial ground.

Michael came down from Axilior and sat on the ground. He started watching at the wild garden for long. He forgot that he, in fact, was at the core of the Forest of Death. Evils were out there, waiting for him to get out of the wild beauty - the Eden on Earth in the heart of the Forest of Death, he said to himself. But he did not stand up so soon. He was reunited with James after a long time. And he could feel James' arm on his shoulder.

As if James was saying, "For me, it was destiny. Stop pulling it on yourself. Not you, nor Molly. So, let it go."

***

6
Rose Scarlett

It was one fine morning when Michael and Tim were called on in the castle. And they presumed that it was work, and they thought that it was something important - they were called in on an emergency basis. But they did not know what it exactly was.

Once they went there, they found that Williams and some other soldiers from different regiments of the North, East and West were already there. All of them assembled at the South Bailey of the fortress. One King's Man was there to instruct them about their mission.

It was some days since Michael had met Williams the last time. And that encounter did not end very friendly, although it had started with a fake attempt of forming a nexus from Williams. And today, they met again, once more for another mission together. Williams looked at Michael as Michael looked back at him too. The cruel eyes of Williams wanted to contest Michael in a gamble of swordsmanship. He wanted to prove himself as a better swordsman and horseman than Michael and show it to everyone else in the mission. And he also wanted to demonstrate to the world that he was better than James Wheeler. Finally, he wanted to prove himself as the best veteran ever.

It was quite fascinating how fast James had become a legend. And he was spoken of equally with the legends of the seven regiments of South who had fought bravely and sacrificed themselves about fifty-two years ago during the Great War. James was remembered as the most promising young soldier of his age and of this era and for his untimely demise, though his body was never found and his status still was M.I.A. People had heard of James' skills and knew that he had the potential to become the next King's Man, might be the best King's Man ever. And common people, wherever or whenever found someone like him, started to build hopes around him that this soldier would go on to defeat the evil of the Forest of Death.

The recent outcome of the mission in the forest to rescue Young Junior had enthralled them. They started to find another James from the team - another legend from the team. And they again started to hope around that soldier whom they had been seeking.

The names of Michael Chapman and David Williams were spoken frequently lately. People knew about them. They knew that Michael had been a long-time friend and companion of James and that Williams was very strong himself. "Who of these two will become the King's Man?" - they asked themselves. And they also argued with their answers. Some chose Michael as their favourite whereas some thought of Williams as the more suitable one. Speaking in favour of Michael had many reasons. One of them surely was that he was very similar to legend James Wheeler. And training together for a long time had made Michael learn a lot from James. Moreover, he was a genius of his own and was one of the most hardworking soldiers of the entire military. His focus, resilience and determination were praised by all. But, the only reason for not finding him as a suitable candidate was that people still looked at him under the shadow of James

Wheeler. They found him as the substitute of James who could never become as original as him. On the other hand, people talked in favour of Williams as he was fierce, without any fear of death and was unnaturally strong. People knew about his past and about how he had spent his entire time in illegal but robustly challenging activities. But they also knew about his background and how he had betrayed his comrades, making it hard for them to trust him.

In the recent past, Michael had met Walther to ask him about Williams. "What do you know of David Williams of the sixth regiment of the South, Walther?" he had asked. "David Williams, son of John Williams, one of the most criminal minds of this kingdom in the recent history. He was the mastermind and also directly involved in many crimes - from robbery to mass murders. He formed a gang that involved people from the dark world. And they lived in one nearby city. Within a very short time, they owned wealth worth thousands of gold coins, all of them were stolen or robbed. All the members of the gang were very strong swordsmen and horsemen. They needlessly assassinated many innocent citizens. Even many strong soldiers of the army died while trying to confront and arrest them. And they continued their ill doings, their malice. They became a menace to the entire kingdom and the then King had to order his King's Men to arrest them. Awards were offered on their heads. This resulted in some battles full of blood and murders. At last, all the members including John were killed. Many people of their families and friends were also arrested, hanged or sentenced for life as they had supported them in their crimes or hidden them from the law and statutory. But, David was out. He was in his childhood while his father was killed. Even at that age, he was in the red circle of the army; he was under scrutiny. He already had been involved in many small robberies and thefts. He was incarcerated sometimes but was later released due to lack of alibi or as he was underage. But he had the blood of his father going through his veins. He was as cruel, cunning and strong. Moreover, unlike his father, he was not very hasty. He did not commit any murder that would eventually make him be arrested and sentenced. But, he reformed the gang of his father from the ash. He built the castle out of the decimated kingdom. The gang became well known again. And members of the gang started to emulate their predecessors. They murdered, robbed, even raped. But Williams himself was very smart. He was out of any of the crimes and led others to do it. And their crimes were perfect in implementation, hard to prove their involvements. Williams was the brain child as I think. Then one day, they committed a serious crime. They attacked the house of the wealthiest businessman of the city. And there were murders. Later, they were arrested. And we could convince Williams to assist us to prove their guilt, which otherwise seemed impossible. The condition was that we would recruit him in the army, and his guilt would be forgiven. And thus, Williams worked as our witness," Walther had said. Michael then had asked the obvious, "How do you trust someone like him? How could you recruit him in the army, someone as criminal as him?" "Michael, it was not only me. Some people, including some from the Order, supported recruiting him. They said that the environment of the army would change him. And that someone as strong as him should be in the army, not behind the bars. Besides, it was the condition of his working as our witness in the trial of his comrades. But, I personally never supported this," Walther had replied.

It had been a while and Molly still had not come back. It worried Michael a lot. He felt responsible somehow and feared how James would have reacted to him at this point if he were here.

Since last time, Michael had been in the wild garden at the heart of the forest some more times. He used to go there, sit on the ground and watch the majestic view of the roses with the shinning pollen grains in the air reminding him of Stardusts in the Starshine that he used to enjoy during his watch at the South Tower every Monday night. And he also continued leaving a note for James every Monday night at that tower during his watch. There, he would inform about his week, any pertinent news of the kingdom that included from economics to social, about the seventh regiment, about his training, sometimes even about the last good meal he had had. He also would ask some questions, or answer some himself.

Today was a normal day to him and he was called on for a mission on an emergency basis. But it was not the first time it had happened, and so he did not think of any higher with the mission. Even in the past, he had been called on like this and the missions were an investigation or a common patrolling.

However, it is so magnificent that we do not know what our recent future holds for us that eventually becomes very important to us for our whole lives. Future is unpredictable, that is the beauty of it. Sometimes, there comes a day, started as usual, no different than any other day, but we end up facing something unique. And at the end of the day, our lives do not remain the same anymore. The unpredictable future grants us something that changes our lives forever. And that makes that particular day which started as normal and common a special one in our lives.

"We have a little emergency," the King's Man said, "we have a work. It is to escort some royal family members from the North. They will be coming from Cambridge. And some of our army and police from outside this Kingdom will escort them till the northernmost border of the Kingdom. Now, previously, we assigned some other soldiers to escort them from the border to the castle. However, they will not be available. Therefore, we require you to go to the border now and wait for the royal carriages to come. You will identify them easily as there will be a flag bearer. They will also identify us as we also will have a flag bearer with us."

It was decided that the King's Man himself would be the leader. Tim would be the flag bearer holding the flag with King's Crest, the Sword on the Circle.

Personally, Michael was a bit disappointed. He was hoping for something more challenging. He was not sure if he wanted to go, however, he was bound to go. But even if he were not, opting out of this work would become the biggest mistake of his life. Future cannot be foreseen, and we mostly assume that there lies nothing important. However, future proves us wrong over and over. And that is why we should never opt back from an option, as we do not know what lies ahead on the road of uncertainty. The destiny of our lives may be waiting for us at the destination.

At about noon, they reached the border. The King's Man was the leader, there were Michael and Williams, a few more of them and Tim was the flag bearer. And they started to wait for the royal carriages to reach from the other side.

After some time, a group of soldiers and police force arrived escorting five royal carriages. Michael and the others identified them as one of the soldiers was carrying the flag. On the other hand, the arriving team identified and became assured of their new companions after looking at the flag with Tim. And as they came, both the leaders had a little chat and then all of them, excluding the police force, started towards the castle.

There were nine of the royal family. There were King's uncle, from his mother's side, Mr. Neville, aunt Mrs. Neville and cousin brother Mr. Gary Neville. There was Gary's bride-to-be Ms. Jane Harley and her parents. There were Ms. Jane's siblings, a brother and a sister. And then, there was the Princess of the Kingdom - Ms. Rose Scarlett.

Ms. Scarlett was in the last carriage. And Michael looked at her. And his outlook of the world changed within a second. For all his life he had considered only his dream of becoming a King's Man, his trainings and missions as his only goals. But right now, he found new ways, paths and meanings of life. In her deep brown eyes he found new reasons worth living for. And her smiles forced him to forget everything that was going on beside him. Her golden hair undulating with the air made him realise that it was the most beautiful thing he had ever seen. For a moment, he knew he was going to hold her hands tight, look at her eyes, accompany with her smiles for centuries and would never get tired. The beauty of Rose enthralled him, fixated his eyes, retarded his breath, and accelerated his heartbeat. And at the very first sight, Michael knew he was going to love this woman as much as he could, as long as he could. He knew that if heaven were to give him the chance, he would befriend her, become her soulmate and spend time with her till eternity and beyond.

Michael slowed Axilior down to come at the back of the team and to stay at the closest to Ms. Scarlett's carriage. He tried to make her look at himself. And he pretended and acted as a devoted soldier only, who was not interested in anything else but was there to perform his duty. He also drove Axilior with skills - soft and smooth, which would make Ms. Rose get interested in him, as he was hoping for. Although he was pretending to act disinterested, he every now and often was looking at Ms. Rose to look at her eyes and smile, and to see if she was looking back. Most of the times, as expected, he was disappointed. But there were a very few times when it was not at all disheartening, rather the opposite; it was what he was expecting for. Ms. Rose looked at him back as he was looking at her, and there was a little smile of joy at the end of her lips.

Ms. Rose Scarlett had left her homeland and the Kingdom to go to Cambridge three years ago. In the University she had been studying Astronomy, Alchemy and Medicine. Now, as her study was over, she was returning back.

All the way Michael stayed close to Rose. And all the time he was thinking about her. He also was very concerned about his gestures and movements of hands, legs, etc. so as not to look abnormal in front of Rose. Even when this mission was very important to him like any other ones, all his concentrations were concentrated on Rose. And many times he was looking at her. He was loving riding beside her, and was loving to dream all the dreams he was having at the moment.

When they reached the fortress, they found the King and the Queen already waiting at the South Bailey, near the Gatehouse, to receive their daughter and the guests. And many soldiers - swordsmen and archers from the castle, the regiments, and King's Men were present too. The members of the royal family greeted each other with kisses and hugs. The King and the Queen were very happy to have their daughter back again after a long time, and Rose was happy to be back too. And Michael saw all of them go inside the Greathall together. He saw Rose go with them. Here his duty was over. And he had to return to the regiment. However, he was wanting to go into the Greathall and look at Rose for one more time; he was also wanting to go and talk to her. But he knew how impossible it was. He already had seen Mr. Gary, Ms. Jane and her siblings. He had seen their affluence, they were the royals. And Ms. Rose Scarlett was the Princess, the most beautiful girl in the Kingdom.

He blamed his fortune and asked Tim to accompany him to the regiment.

On their way back, Michael and Tim talked about the royal family. Young and enthusiastic Tim already had come to know about the people they had escorted. Mr. Neville the senior and uncle to the King was the owner of lands in Cambridge used in agriculture and living. He had the ownership of many inns, hotels and buildings used for different official works. He was one of the wealthiest people in the entire Great Island. Mr. Gary Neville was his heir. Ms. Jane was the eldest daughter of Mr. Harley, one successful merchant at international level. Mr. Harley definitely was the wealthiest person in the island after the King. Listening to these facts made Michael feel demotivated. He was imagining the affluence of these people, their big mansions, the big and beautiful gardens, their hundreds of personal soldiers and secretaries and maids and horses and carriages, their clothes and meals, their spending holidays in heavenly places. Tim informed him of the upcoming royal wedding between Mr. Gary Neville and Ms. Jane Harley. The ceremony would be organized in the castle.

Michael started to think about the possibility of Ms. Rose Scarlett marrying someone of this status someday - someone handsome and wealthy. And this made him hate that man although at this point he was completely imaginary.

At that night, Michael and Tim were in the tent with Daniel and Ben. Ebullient Tim was sharing the experience of his day with the other two; he sometimes was exaggerating too. Michael was sitting near the entrance of the tent and was looking at the North. He could see the summit of the South Tower from here. He was thinking about Ms. Rose. What was she doing right now? She might be enjoying a time with her family, or listening to an orchestra, having a grand dinner, or planning for the upcoming royal wedding. Was she thinking about him right now like the way he was thinking about her? Did she want to meet him? Could he meet her again?

There were a lot of such questions that Michael was silently asking himself while looking at the Tower in darkness. And then he felt a pain in his arm. Daniel had thrown something hard at him that had hit him at his arm.

"Ouch!" he exclaimed.

"Hey dreamer, are you with us or not?" Daniel asked.

-"Of course I am. Where else would I be?"

"Well, we don't know, the Greathall may be?" Ben bullied.

"What?" Michael was finding himself in an uncharted ocean.

"If you are with us then tell us what Tim just said," Daniel said.

"He is talking about the day," Michael tried.

"No, that moment is over," Ben said.

"I was just talking about how you have got a feeling for the Princess," Tim said. He sounded excited.

"What? No! Is that what you are thinking? It is wrong, you are wrong. And right now I am not thinking about her, I am thinking about tomorrow's training," Michael denied.

"Yes, we understand. But did we ever say you were thinking about the Princess?" Ben was quick to catch the flaw in Michael's speech and bullied again with it.

Michael stopped speaking. There was no point in talking anymore as he had been caught red-handed. And he was surprised himself on how foolish he was to reveal himself like that.

"So Tim, how is she? Beautiful? I am asking you instead of our dreamer as asking our dreamer at this time is just waste of time. He either will not answer or lie or say something biased," Daniel was judgemental.

"Yes, she is beautiful. She is very beautiful. In fact, she is the most beautiful girl I have ever seen!" Tim was excited still.

"And can our Chapman become her Prince Charming?" Ben witted.

"Yes! Why not? Our to-be Prince was looking at her all the time and Princess was looking at him too," Tim said.

"No! She did not look at me!" Michael denied instantly.

-"Yes, she did."

-"No, she did not."

And this went for a while. But deep down, Michael knew that there were times when she had looked at him. And he still was memorising the fraction of smile at the end of her lips when she was looking at him.

As the night progressed and the darkness deepened, Michael kept thinking about Rose. He was lying and trying to sleep. But all the thoughts were coming and making crowds at his brain. He was still thinking what Rose might be doing right now. Was she thinking about him? Was there some meaning behind the smile? Or, was there nothing at all? All these thoughts made Michael happy, sad and frightened at the same time. And all he wanted was to get up, take Axilior, run to the castle, enter into the Greathall and see her again right now. He wanted to know what Rose was doing and if she was thinking about him at all. He did not know what and why he was having these feelings. And he did not know what to call these feelings. Furthermore, why he was not thinking about the next day's training as he usually had used to - he did not know this either. But he did know that he had to meet that woman again as soon as he could.

The beauty of the uncertainty of future brought the chance to him very soon. It was the next Tuesday, the day after his next watch at the South Tower. During his watch on Monday night, he enjoyed the scene - the moon, the stars, the howling white owl, the darkness covering the entire place with the bluish wave on it and the dancing Stardusts. He wrote to James on a letter. There he mentioned about Rose for the first time. And I think it will be a better idea to write from the page for a while, verbatim, in Michael's tone rather than mine, to show the respect for him.

"Dear James,

How are you? I am fine. Daniel, Ben and Tim are fine too. I am sorry but we still did not hear from Molly. I do not know what mission is taking her so long. I hope she comes back soon. But do not worry, she surely is fine too. Nothing bad can touch her; of all people you know it, right? And God forbid, if something happens to her, we will know about it.

James, I think I should tell you something. A few days ago I went on a mission. It was an easy one - to escort some royal family members from the northern border to here. I must admit, I was not very much interested in it at the beginning. But I am glad I was wrong. And I thank the Great God out there, and I want to thank everyone in this world who made me get involved in that mission.

I met the Princess there. Yes, she was one of the people we were escorting.

James, I know you will find it abnormal and crazy to hear this from me. But, I cannot stop thinking about her since that day. Hey, is it bad that for the last few days I cannot concentrate efficiently enough in my trainings? Even during the sessions, I keep thinking about her. I know it is not good at all, and it may become a hindrance to me in my becoming a member of the King's Man. But right now, it is not my one and only goal, though I am confident of becoming one someday.

But right now, all I want is to meet her again and make her look at me with those beautiful eyes and smile like that, once more, even if it is the last time. I want to talk to her even if it is the first and last and only time. But if it is the last time, then I will make sure that it will never come to an end. I will make sure it will go on, me sitting by her side, looking at her eyes and talking to her - I will make it continue till the end of the day and the day will never end. That is how there will never be a last time.

James, am I going crazy? I never felt this way before. And I never thought I would too..."

On the next morning, after his watch of the week, Michael decided to stay for a little while in the castle ground to take a little rest, freshen up, have a meal and feed Axilior before leaving. He also got involved in a gossip with Josh and some other soldiers of the castle. And it all took him some hours before he could leave.

He was leaving the Gatehouse and heading towards the South when he heard something coming from behind. It was a royal carriage guarded by a few soldiers. And there were Ms. Rose and Ms. Jane in it. All of them left the castle territory and Michael had to take the road to South and the carriage had to take the one to the North. Fortunately, both the roads were superimposed on each other for about half a kilometre until they parted; the road to the South continued and the one to North took a right turn. I must remind my readers that the Gatehouse was at the southern side of the castle.

Michael slowed down a bit to let the carriage go in front. And he remained close to it.

The two ladies were wearing beautiful white gowns and long skirts of fine silk and velvet. They were wearing jewels with gems at their necks and there were gems at the different layers of their dresses too. However, they were not wearing any crown. The hair was tied at the back while having some curls at the front. And they were carrying light umbrellas with designs that Michael would describe as 'like the paintings on the glasses of the castle' in his letter.

The carriage had parts made of pure gold. Skilled carvers had drawn on them - pictures of natural and abstract beauties.

The old Coachman with a big moustache was wearing a dress made of silk and far that Michael could not afford. Now Michael was having the chance to notice all of these. His eyes were busy elsewhere the last time.

"I cannot believe so many things have changed! I hope I will be able to recognise the shop," Ms. Rose said to Ms. Jane.

"And the wedding dress you were talking about?" asked Ms. Jane.

-"Yes, I had seen it before I left for Cambridge. It was the most beautiful wedding dress ever. I was dreaming to wear it in my wedding, however, that is not any time soon."

-"Oh! You were thinking about that?"

-"Every girl thinks about her wedding since her childhood, right? She wants it perfect with the perfect man. I also was dreaming about that. And that he would propose me in a very romantic night. I would wear that dress in the wedding. The wedding would be in the castle. Many people would be there."

-"Looks like you have everything planned out!"

Ms. Rose laughed. And Ms. Jane continued, "If you love the dress so much why do you want me to have it in my wedding? You should have it on your own!"

"I don't even know if the dress is still there. It was three years ago when I saw it the last time. Someone might have bought it by now. It will definitely not be there by my wedding. So, if it is still in there then I want you to have it. And I am sure you also will love it," Ms. Rose replied.

For the rest of the road, they continued to talk about the dress, the shop, plans for the wedding, the invitees, the flowers and many more. Dukes and duchesses of different places, rich businessmen, merchants, landlords and even some Kings and their Queens of various kingdoms would be there. Michael enjoyed listening to them.

Although he was a little curious to see the dress which Rose had liked for her wedding, he was not that interested to go in the shopping. Besides, he needed to return to the regiment and he was not assigned to guard the carriage today. Following it would make him fall in troubles. But, he was a little disappointed and frightened and disheartened by hearing the wedding plans of Rose for her own wedding. Someone like him could never fulfil them in a million years.

When it came to be parted, the carriage took the right turn and Michael continued to head south. And he rode Axilior to run at its highest speed. He showed his own skills too to accelerate it within seconds and maintain the balance. Hence, he was hoping that Ms. Rose and Ms. Jane were watching him run this fast. He was hoping that they were talking about how skilfully fast he was moving.

"Hey, does she even know my name?" he asked himself as he was running fast.

That night, Michael told all about the day to his tentmates. He told them all about the twenty minutes travel Rose and he had had together, alongside the other people who frankly were irrelevant in the context. Daniel, Ben and Tim were very excited and happy to hear from him. And beyond doubt, young Tim was the happiest of them. He made sounds of bells to mimic a wedding bell. It was to indicate that Rose and Michael would be getting married like the way little Rose had planned. But Michael said that that would never be possible as someone like him did not have the wealth to have one wedding like that. And first of all, as he reminded, he did not even know if Rose liked him. His friends asked him when he was going to meet her next. And he said he was hoping it would be next Tuesday, just like that on-going day.

Thus, Michael started to wait for days to pass, and the week to pass. He was excited to meet Rose again and was rehearsing all by himself to try to talk to her. He made some long lists of speech for conversations that he could have with Rose. And he started to wear nice and look well. His tentmates started to make fun of these. A big part of him was tensed - what if he would not meet her the next week? Or, what if she would be with her own company making it impossible for him to talk to her? Therefore, a part of him was excited for the next week but another part was afraid. A part of him wanted to have the opportunity to meet her whereas another part wanted to never have that as he thought of having no possibility of being with her. And as a part of him wanted to continue to have these feelings, another part wanted to get over and run away.

The next Tuesday was not in his favour. After his watch, he waited at the South Bailey for long. He kept himself busy by taking care of Axilior to avoid any unnecessary attention from others. And at the same time, he kept himself clean and he looked at the entrance of the Greathall over and over again. He also looked at the big windows of the Hall with a hope that someone was looking from them. He had assumed that Ms. Rose typically went out at that particular time of that particular day of a week. Even if it were not like this, he wished that Ms. Rose had remembered meeting him exactly a week ago and so would come herself to meet him again.

Unfortunately, nobody showed up. And after a long time, he had to leave.

Daniel and the others were having their afternoon training when they saw Michael to come back. So far, they were having a speculation that Michael had been with the Princess. But they found a gloomy Michael returning. He left Axilior at its stable and went straight into his tent without talking to anyone.

So, Daniel, Ben and Tim finished their day quickly and went into the tent to meet Michael.

Michael was lying on his bed, covering himself. He was terribly exhausted and was sleeping. The hard work of the whole day, the sleepless watch of the previous night and the overthinking process associated with the probable meet with Ms. Rose had sucked all of his physical and mental strength out of him.

It would not have been a bad idea to let him sleep. However, Daniel decided to wake him up as he did not want him to sleep the long night that hungry. Yes, Michael had not had a good meal since the morning. As Michael woke up, he offered him some bread, meat and rum. And Ben, Tim and he joined Michael in the dinner.

Michael had not eaten anything since long. So, he was supposed to be hungry. But today, he did not feel like eating. He was feeling very sad about something, and he knew what the reason was. But, he was unwilling to accept it as the reason. "A soldier should not have any mortal feeling," he said to himself silently. But undoubtedly, Rose was the reason.

Michael was reluctant to eat anything. He just finished half a bread, a little meat and a glass of rum.

So far, everyone was silent. Ben talked the first, "What happened Michael, are you alright?"

"Yes, I am fine," Michael replied in a very low tone.

"Did you meet her?" Daniel asked.

"No, she was not there," Michael replied.

"So? What is the big deal? You did not meet her today, you can meet again!" Ben said.

This time Michael gave it up to himself and admitted that Rose was the reason behind his exhaustion and he betrayed that he definitely was having a strong mortal feeling despite being a devoted soldier.

"What is the big deal? Last week we met. Now, it may be true that she usually goes out on this day of the week at that particular time, or it may be false. But even if it were false, she could come to meet at the exact spot if she had wanted to," Michael said with disappointment.

"Michael," Daniel interrupted and stopped him, "your theory is wrong. She might be busy. With the wedding, or she might have had guests. Besides, does she know that you go to the castle every Monday? It may be true that she had waited for you in the previous week for days and thought that you would not come again and so gave up."

Michael thought for a moment. Yes, Daniel was right! Rose did not know that he used to go there every Monday. It could have been every day, or once a month, or even once a year. Coming to the conclusion and torturing, hurting and ruining himself so far were definitely some very bad ideas. But, did Rose wait for him to come in the previous week? Had she been waiting for days? Did she give up on her waiting as Michael did not come back? These questions again terrified him. But still, he direly wanted these to be true.

Tim talked for the first time, "I have heard that the wedding is within a month. There will come many people from the Great Island - many rich men and their sons. What if one aristocratically highborn becomes engaged to her? I mean, this happens at weddings. Furthermore, Ms. Scarlett herself may be looking forward to this day to meet new people."

Daniel stopped him by saying, "What are you talking about? Ms. Rose will not get engaged this soon! She still is young!"

But it did not fix the already broken. Tim also understood that he had done a mistake. And it was too late.

Michael thought of it for a moment in complete silence. Tim was right, he thought. Many respected people would come to get their sons engaged with Rose. And one should remember that it was the Princess they were talking about. Getting married to her meant to be the next King - many people would come with this thought in mind. And, Rose had come of her age too.

"Look brothers, there will never be anything between her and me. It is the Princess. Who am I? Tim is right. Even if not now or not in the wedding, she will someday become engaged with someone of her status. A Prince of a different nation may be. Besides, how can a soldier like me just go and talk to her in the first place? I should just forget her and live my life," he said.

There was an inevitable silence. Everyone was thinking about the same thing or rather the same person - a person who was bold but caring and smart enough to deal with such a situation with maturity. At last, Michael himself said out. "I wish Molly was here," said disheartened Michael. And then, after thinking for a moment, he added, "Daniel, can I have tomorrow's day off too? And I need Tim. I want to go in search for Molly."

The question was serious, definitely, for many reasons. It was long since any of them had seen Molly. After James had gone missing, Molly had started to change. From outside, anyone would make the mistake and state that she was the same Molly. But underneath, she had become introvert and self-centred. Fear of losing something had grasped her. And she always had tried to pretend as nothing had happened. She always had forced herself to emulate the former Molly to deceive and swindle others.

Why and where Molly had gone were two big mysteries. The last time one saw her, she had told Daniel that she was on a mission. And she had appointed Daniel as the Commander of the regiment with Ben as the Second in Command. Daniel always had been the second after Molly. However, who was the third in Molly's mind? Nobody knew that. Michael was a candidate in thoughts for sure, as he was the strongest after Molly. But Ben definitely was more mature, experienced and he knew the regiment far better. But choosing Ben over Michael by Molly had raised a dispute.

"Is there a clash between Molly and Michael? Is that why Molly chose Ben but did not choose Michael as the Second in Command?" Many people had asked this question. There could be no reason for such a clash - Michael always commented. Molly had been the partner to his brotherly James, and so she had been dear to him too. She also had been his supervisor in his special trainings. Yes, Michael himself always admitted that Molly had been unusually rough and sometimes heartless, but he equally always admired her. He always said that Molly had been the best Commander to him. And she, on top of that, had been like a sister.

The mistake that Michael had made was to avoid Molly before going for a critical mission. The amplitude of the mission could have made itself the last mission to Michael, yet, he had decided not to meet Molly before undertaking the mission. To exacerbate the already worsened condition, Michael had met every other soldier of the regiment. But, he definitely had one noble cause behind not meeting Molly - it was for her own good.

Daniel said after hearing Michael's plea, "Uh! Yes. You can go. And Tim can go too. But I don't know if you should. If Molly has gone on a mission, she will come back. And we should not interfere. Besides, you already have tried enough in search for her and James. How much more are you willing to do? It is badly affecting you. You seriously are looking a lot pale nowadays. You should be taking care of yourself."

Daniel's suggestion was genuine. For the last many days, Michael had been working like a machine. And he had been over thinking a lot. He already had tried enough to find or rescue James and Molly. He had been going into the forest alone in search for James. And he had investigated and interrogated well enough in search for Molly. But he always blamed himself for what had happened to James and what possibly had happened to Molly. So, he did not have the option to back off.

On the next day, Michael and Tim went on their horses. Michael knew the places where Molly had spent her childhood and significant times of her adulthood. Michael knew these places; Molly herself had shared her memories. And Michael assumed that these were the only places where Molly had spent most of her life. There could have been the possibility of the existence of other places where she had spent her past life in but had never shared it with him. However, Michael could not afford to accept this possibility. The criticality of the situation forced him to think biased; this was all he could do.

Michael and Tim visited those places - some in the villages in front of the forest, some in towns in the East and West. The whole day they just met with people and talked to them. They asked if those people personally knew Molly. The intention was clear as crystal. Many people knew Molly as the Commander of the seventh regiment of the South. And they knew Molly as one of the strongest soldiers in the military. But Michael needed someone who personally knew Molly - someone who could tell him about where Molly might have gone, someone who could tell something significant of Molly's history that could make Michael infer where she might have gone. There also was this possibility that Molly had been staying at someone else's house, maybe an old friend or family of hers. And Michael direly needed to find such a person.

Michael and Tim tried the entire day in search for that person whom Michael had been desiring to find. They had to skip every meal. And they had to travel a lot within the span of some hours. But at the end, it all went in vain. They could not find even a single person who personally knew Molly.

At night, Michael and Tim returned to the regiment. Michael was almost exhausted to death. For the last three days, he had been working way more than what a soldier could possibly do in the extreme and excess. And such hard works were deteriorating his health. He felt strong pain in the back of his head and in his back bones. He suffered intense head rushes. He almost fell over and threw up. It was like a malevolent hangover, only, it was even worse. He had to go through an unbearable headache. He even had difficulty sleeping. But once he slept, at last, he woke up very late, tired and pale.

For the next few days, Michael tried to concentrate only on his veteran duties. He tried to live his life like how he had used to before. And he tried to erase Rose completely off his mind. However, doing it was more difficult than saying. And trying harder than the limit was becoming heavier on him - a cumbersome burden. The more he tried to get her off his mind the more he was failing. This was why he tried to completely involve himself on different activities so that he would not even have the time to think about her. He also tried to be with people. But again, there were times when he was wanting to be entirely alone. And he also went into the wild garden of roses in the core of the Forest of Death, the Forbidden One. The wild roses were somehow reminding him of Ms. Rose Scarlett, but still he stayed there for long and liked being in there - like a silent lover. And the pollen grains dancing in air, diffracting light reminded him of Stardusts in the Starshine. He also remembered about James and Molly. He was missing Molly. She did not come back since she had gone. And it was a long while. If Molly were here now, she would be a good help as a company to Michael, to cheer him up, bring him back to the mainstream or even help him talk to Rose.

Future and fate are the two strangest things in the universe. They control everything, yet no one can control them. Every course of history is written so as to flow to a definite future and fate, yet no one can foresee her own future and fate. They are unpredictable, yet they define the past and present beforehand. And they are uncertain, yet if there is something that is meant to be, no one can terminate it from happening. No one can define future and fate, and it is absurd to search for defining moments, but the moments that define the present have already caught with the flow.

Michael did not know what lied down the road, even in the close ones. But his future was guiding his life to a definite destination.

A few days later of the same week, Michael had to go to the castle. He had to submit an official report to the Order from Commander Daniel. Both of Daniel and Ben, who were the Commander and Second in Command respectively, were occupied elsewhere and Michael, who unofficially was the next in the hierarchy, had to do it.

Michael submitted the report to Walther and came out of the Greathall to the South Bailey in order to take Axilior before leaving. And there he found some from the royal family. There were Mr. Gary, his bride to-be, her siblings and Ms. Rose Scarlett. And like the other days, Mr. Gary was not wearing a royal gown. But today he was in armours. And he was fighting friendly battles of swords with some soldiers of the castle. The others from the royal family were enjoying it.

Michael saw that Mr. Gary was fighting against some swordsmen, not anyone from the King's Men. And he definitely had impressive skills. He actually came out as victorious in some consecutive fights. Michael observed his movements and techniques for a while. Despite being from the royal family, Mr. Gary could easily become one commanding soldier. However, swords fight was his hobby; for Michael, it was life. And Michael knew that Mr. Gary, with all due respect, was nothing compared to a King's Man, and was nothing compared to him too.

Rose and the others were impressed with Mr. Gary. The amazement in her eyes could not conceal itself from Michael. They must have been thinking that Mr. Gary was stronger than almost all the soldiers; one could not blame them for this misunderstanding, Mr. Gary successfully had already defeated some of the soldiers of the castle. Mr. Gary himself was full with confidence. He was asking if there was anyone else who could challenge him - surely one good way to impress his bride to-be. And Michael could never let this opportunity go to waste from impressing his love. Moreover, he also could never back off from such a challenge.

He moved forward and bowed. His body was steady with determination, yet shaking with excitement.

"I, Michael Chapman, would like to accept your challenge," he said.

"Hello Michael, I am Gary Neville. Where are you from? I did not see you in the castle," Gary said.

-"I am from the seventh regiment of the South, Sir. But I sometimes come to the castle for different duties like today."

Gary was not very aware of the conditions of different regiments. So he asked, "Michael, I have defeated some very good soldiers of the castle. You are not even from the castle. What makes you think you can beat me?" Gary was thinking that the best soldiers were from the castle.

-"Sir, the soldiers of the seventh regiment of the South are the strongest of all after the King's Men. And you are looking at the strongest of all in the seventh regiment of the South. No soldier from the castle, except for the King's Men, is a contest to me. You are an amazing swords fighter. I can tell it that you have been fighting since long. But I have been fighting since always. I have performed duties successfully that almost no other soldier of the nation could. That is what makes me think I can beat you."

Gary was intrigued. He was inquisitive to find how candid Michael's speech was. Rose and the others from the royal family were interested in the fight too. And the soldiers present in there, who hitherto knew Michael, were captivated to see the fight.

The fight began. At first, Gary was overly confident. And was too aggressive, but Michael easily defended his offenses. Experienced Michael knew that if it went on like this, Gary soon would tire down and he could beat him in the next moment. Gary also, after many failed attempts of knocking Michael out with close combat aggression with which he had defeated the other soldiers so far, found that it was not working against Michael. Thus, he changed his strategy from total attack to defence. But this gave Michael the chance of counter attacks. His continuous blows started to become heavier every passing second on Gary. Michael himself was galvanized with Gary. He was tougher than what he had thought. Gary, so far, was successfully defending his best counterattacks. Now, Michael tried to take it slow.

"Tell me Sir. Have you heard of the Forest of Death?" he asked.

And he continued to fight.

"Yes I have, a little, but I do not know much about it," Gary replied while fighting.

-"People say it is haunted. Many soldiers and innocent people have died in there, fighting wars in various times. And they wake up at nights to continue their fights. And there are hounds from the hell, waiting for blood. If you go into it, you will not come back alive."

"What?" Gary showed scepticism, "I cannot believe it. It is just a story, some bedtime lullabies to some children. These ghosts, hounds - do you seriously believe in it?"

-"You should believe me too. And you will if you stay here for long as you will get to hear more, from more."

Gary stopped talking to concentrate on the fight. But he was getting curious. At last he asked, "Alright. I believe in you. But why are you telling about the forest all of a sudden?"

-"Because, I have gone in there, and come back alive. I have defeated the evil in there that many people never could." Michael was waiting for this moment. He slapped Gary's arm with the sword that caused Gary to lose his own sword. Gary sat down supporting his injured arm with the other hand. He was in agony. And his sword was lying on the ground some feet away.

Ms. Jane rushed towards him to assist him to stand up. And the rest of the family was amused, looking at Michael. The soldiers present were already expecting this outcome and were glad that someone finally could save the entire army from the stigma. And they were moved and influenced by the entire fight from Michael, especially how he had won it so easily.

Michael bowed and said, "It was a good fight, Sir. Thank you. And I beg for your apology. I hope the injury is not fatal."

Gary was a true gentleman. Although he was defeated in front of his family and by a soldier where he was a royal himself, he was not angry with Michael. He thanked Michael back for the fight and said that in future, they would fight again.

Michael was at the stable in the South Bailey where he had left Axilior. He was here to get it before heading for the regiment. And he was feeling quite satisfied. Winning the friendly battle against Gary was more than just a victory to him. For him, the significance of it was ineffable. And he was touched by Gary's behaviour - he was a nice man. As he had pictured Gary beforehand, he was supposed to be extrovert, egotist and arrogant. Michael had thought that Gary, because of his prosperity and luxury, would distance himself from the soldiers, however, in the training ground, Gary had behaved like a common soldier. It was very reassuring to Michael that Gary accepted his defeat as how it actually was, but not as an insult.

Michael was feeding Axilior when he heard a mellifluous voice from behind. He knew the voice; he had heard it for a very few times till now, but it was a voice that he could identify even from a roaring crowd. Although, at this point, he was quite surprised and he had to think a lot before turning back, as the voice was familiar but unexpected.

It was Ms. Rose Scarlett, standing behind him. And it was her voice calling for his attention.

"Hello," greeted Rose.

The situation still was unexpected to Michael. Most interestingly, he had been waiting for this moment for some days and he had been hoping copiously for this too. However, as the situation itself was here, he got nervous and could not speak. Rose felt the awkwardness in the situation. She realised how Michael was finding it difficult to talk to the Princess in an unknown context. So she herself took the initiative to ease the gravity.

"Mr. Chapman, I am Rose Scarlett," she said.

"Wow! What is going on? Am I dreaming? Why is she here? What does she want from someone like me? Should I say something? Yes, I should. But what?" terrified Michael said to himself.

His silence was increasing the awkwardness; he wanted to say something. But he was frozen. He felt being tied at the neck; he could not breathe. Every passing second was making it even harder for him to catch up with the context and join the conversation.

"Should I answer friendly? Or, should I act as if I do not care? How will she receive and react? The situation is getting embarrassing. I must say something, I cannot make her wait and portray myself as one crazy fellow. But, what should I say?" he kept asking himself.

At last, he could say, "Yes, I know who you are. You are the Princess."

"Yes, fine. It was a good one. Now, do not waste any such time to reply the next," he was thinking again.

"You surely took a lot of time to memorise that Mr. Chapman," Rose joked.

"Great! Now, even she is making fun of me," Michael kept thinking.

"What do you want from me, Ms. Scarlett?" he asked.

"What a great way to talk to your Princess, you idiot!" he castigated himself.

"The fight was quite impressive. Gary is strong. And he struggled against you. You defeated him very easily," Rose said.

"Thank you! It is such a pleasure being praised by you," Michael said in an exuberant pitch.

-"I need one favour to ask. But, I am hesitant. And, I am embarrassed too to ask as you surely will think ludicrous about me. If you can do it, only then I will ask."

"What is the favour? Is it something bad? Is it something good? Can I awe her by doing it?" Michael asked himself again. He truly was overly concerned about what he was speaking so, he was taking time before talking.

"Anything Ms. Scarlett," he said. And he kept thinking of what it probably would be. He could hear his own heart quivering.

"I want you to teach me swords fight," Rose surprised him.

"What?" Michael had thought of about a thousand of possibilities within a minute of the silence - from finding out her stolen necklace to even getting married and from informing her about the Forest of Death to even assassinate a foe of hers, but the actual favour was unexpected to him.

"Why do you want to learn it? What will you do with it?" Michael laughed.

-“Why? I am a woman so I should not fight?”

“No. No. That is not what I meant,” Michael was tensed because of being misunderstood, “I meant, you are the Princess. Why do you need to learn swords fight?”

“That is exactly why I want to learn it,” Rose was bold, “I don’t want people to look at me as the King’s daughter. I want them to respect me for who I am. I want to prove to them that even after my royalty I can be a good swordsman, like Gary. And people adore Gary as he is a strong fighter despite being a royal. I want people to look at me like that.”

-“But people respect you not as you are the King’s daughter. At least I respect you for who you are.”

-“Much appreciated. I mean it. But I still need to learn swords fight. I hope you can instruct me. Otherwise, I will have to find someone else.”

“No!” Michael was stubborn, “Please don’t find anyone else. I will do it. I will teach you.”

-“Alright then. So, when will we start?”

-“I must warn you, my Lady. It will be a tough work. You can do it, right?”

“Of course I can! I need to!” Rose was confident and she eagerly tried to convince Michael.

“Okay. I will meet you tomorrow at this hour at here. You may need to produce a camouflage. People should not recognize you, or it may promptly become a problem. And we will go to a nearby open field at the East to train,” Michael said.

“Done!” Rose confirmed. She was excited to start her first training. And she looked at Axilior, kept looking, then touched it at the forehead softly, saying, “She is beautiful.”

“If you are teaching me swords fight, I think I also should teach you something in sufficient return. Do you want to learn Astronomy?” Rose asked.

Michael honestly did not have any interest in learning about the sky and the heavenly bodies. But learning something from Rose would be allowing him some more time to spend with her, however small a span it might be. And he was unwilling to let this little span slip away. So, he approved.

Unlike the last few days, tonight Michael was cheerful. And his tentmates noticed that. But they were oblivious to the context and so they asked, "Michael, you look very happy tonight? Did something happen today?"

Michael told them everything. And asked if he could get a small time off from the training the next morning and probably on some more following mornings. This request was directed to Commander Daniel.

"I grant it, but do come back in time to join us in the training," Daniel said.

Michael was feeling nervous about the next morning. But, unlike most boys of his age of different periods of time - from ancient to modern, he did not have many options for clothes and shoes. His only option was to wear clean, new and shiny armour, to have one handsome-looking sword and to look nice himself. He went to the armoury that time of the night to get these - one new armour and one new sword.

The next day Michael got there earlier before the scheduled time. Still many questions were coming and gathering in his head – "what will happen if she does not show up", "what will happen if she finally gave up on learning swords fight", "what will happen if she found someone else, say from the King's Men who is more efficient as a fighter and as a teacher than me", "how is Rose as a human being", "what will happen if someone finds us", and many more. And thus, he waited. While waiting, he cleaned sweat off his face, fixed his hair some many times. At last, he saw a soldier, in full armours and helmet on the head - a pretty decent camouflage, coming towards him. Michael understood that it was Rose.

Without much of an introduction, Rose asked him to lead her to the training ground in the East. She did not want anyone to find out that she, the Princess, was going out of the castle alone with an ordinary soldier. And they headed towards the East after coming out of the castle. Both of them were riding their horses as Rose followed Michael.

As they were on their way, Michael was remembering what Tim had suggested him the previous day. Tim apparently was extraordinarily efficient, exuberant and ebullient on giving suggestions on such condition - going out with a girl. And one particular point that he had emphasized a lot reminded Michael to step up. He needed to ease the environment and stop it from becoming an awkward, unfriendly one with an uncooperative silence.

"How is everyone in your family?" he started.

"They are fine," Rose replied in succinct.

Michael recalled another of Tim's points - even if his endeavour was not working he needed to keep on trying. Hence, he asked again, "And how is the planning for the wedding going?"

"Good. Everyone is involved in there. It is going to be a big one," Rose's answer was short and quick once again.

Michael got demotivated on her answers and the fact that she herself did not ask anything to him. She barely had an interest in joining a conversation. As a result, Michael only concentrated on the road for the rest of the way.

They reached their destination about an hour later. It was one open field before a small town in the East of the castle and some kilometres away from it. Michael already had been here in the past and he knew that this place was quiet - without much external disturbances. The open field was not big itself, and there was a lake beside it. The lake was not large either, and it basically was a detached part of a river died long ago. Both of them were separated from the outside world by a wall of trees at the circumference of the field. All of these made this place perfect for training in solitude. The water of the lake was usually cold, the edge of the field with the lake was foggy because of the vapour and the grasses of the field were ruthlessly tall. Dew at the top of the grasses, even during that time of the day, were glistering. All the grasses were not green, but some of them were yellow, red, and? Some combinations of red and yellow, blue and green? Michael could not recognize. The water was pleasantly transparent, yet perfect reflections of the trees were forming at the surface.

Michael started to guide Rose by basics. There were fundamentals of how to hold a sword at the handle and to swing it freely in open air. The difficulty level then increased as the freely swinging of sword got more complicated. Now there was more swinging and footworks were added. Gradually, the movements of arm, legs and body got more involved and convoluted.

With time, Rose started to become friendlier. She started to call Michael by his first name rather than the Christian name. She asked Michael many things – "Michael, tell me about your regiment", "tell me about your friends", "tell me about your family" and more.

"My regiment is the seventh regiment of the South. It is the most dangerous regiment. There are many reasons behind it", "I have many friends. They are my fellow soldiers from my regiment and even outside my regiment. There are Tim, my current commander Daniel, and Ben. They also are my tentmates. I also had a friend, he was the closest person in my life, like my brother. His name was James. He was the strongest, stronger than everyone else. He got missing during a war and never returned. And I don't think he will return ever again. The Forest of Death has devoured his soul, like how it did for many others. I also had another friend, Molly, my previous commander. She was an amazing fighter. See, you asked yesterday that as you are a woman, you are not supposed to fight, was that what I thought. But, I myself had such a person in my life - a woman who was one wonderful soldier. I do not know what to think of her. She was a little tough and rude. But underneath, she was like my own sister. She also is gone. And I don't know when she will return", "I don't have a family. I never knew my father and my mother abandoned me when I was a kid. My regiment is my family now"- Michael replied to Rose's questions.

Rose also asked about the Forest of Death, told Michael about Astronomy that he carefully listened to, and smiled and laughed. And at the end of that day's training, she asked for forgiveness, "I am sorry I was a little rude in the morning. Actually, yesterday night I had a fight with my mother. Please do not ask what it was all about."

Michael was afraid for a certain reason and so he had to ask, "Did she find out about your training with me?"

"No, no. It was a personal reason. And don't worry. No one will find out about our training," Rose assured him.

-"Oh! But if it is personal then why should I bother asking? I do not even have the authority to ask what the Queen and the Princess were arguing about."

-"No. It is not like that. Besides, please do not treat me any special. I absolutely do not want you of all people to have a distance from me only because I am the Princess. And I have already told you. I am tired of being looked high because of my father, the King."

This particularly could have many possible hidden and inner meanings that Rose might want to convey. And Michael thought of almost all of them the rest of the day. And it deserves mention that they agreed to meet again the next same day of the next week.

7

THE ROYAL WEDDING

During the last few days, messengers from the King spread the news in the entire kingdom, and beyond. They also traversed miles of lands to visit neighbouring kingdoms of England, Scotland and Ireland. They travelled cities and villages, crossed lands and waters to send the words of the King. The other Kings and their Queens of the Great Island were invited. Many esteemed personalities such as landlords, merchants and businessmen were invited. It was the Royal Wedding.

I don't know if Gary was called Prince Gary. The reason behind this question was that he was not directly related to the bloodline of the King. However, he was the cousin brother of the King from his mother's side and people might call him a Prince to display the respect he deserved. I, therefore, will continue to call him Mr. Gary Neville or simply Gary, and I hope I will not be crossing any boundaries of courtesy.

It was the wedding between Gary and Ms. Jane. The odour of the wedding was everywhere. The air smelled like flowers. Everything was ornate to perform beautification. The castle itself was looking like a big aisle. The entire kingdom was decorated and rejuvenated on prior of the visits of the esteemed invitees. Lights were lit everywhere to brighten the kingdom even during the darkest nights of no moon.

It was a moment of high security. The entire military had to be aware. The army, along with the King's Men, was divided into two groups with a ratio of one to three. The first group was assigned to guard the castle and the second was to fortify the kingdom outside the castle. Michael and Tim were recruited in the first group whereas Daniel and Ben were in the second.

It was better for Michael as it would give him the chance to stay with Rose during the wedding as he was going to stay in the castle guarding it. And as always, Tim was very excited about Michael and Rose. Actually, Michael was speculating that it was Tim himself who had asked to recruit Michael in the first team. And Michael was silently thankful to him for this.

It had been five times already that Michael and Rose had met in the castle ground with Rose in disguise, and went to the open ground in the East to train swords fight. They typically met once a week, preferably every Tuesday. They used to train for about some hours, Michael taught her different techniques of swords fight - allout attack, defence, and counter; he taught her the correct combinations of movements of arms and legs. He also used to tell her stories about his missions, including the one where he had to go into the Forest of Death, the Forbidden One. He used to tell her about his days in London, about James, about how they had met the two King's Men. On the other hand, Rose used to tell him about her days in Cambridge, and teach him Astronomy, Alchemy and Medicine.

The last month had gone like a dream coming true for Michael. All the times with Rose were everything he could ask for. And even when he was not with her, all he could think was of the next day he was going to meet her. He waited for the Tuesdays to come. And he wanted to meet her every day, hold her arms, smell her hair, and look at her eyes. However, he knew that it was not possible to meet the Princess every day. He used to think what Rose might be thinking about him. Did she like him too? There were so many reasons to hope for the positive of this particular question. Many things had happened during their trainings. They talked, smiled and laughed. Michael held Rose's hand to teach her movements of arms with sword. Rose held Michael's arm to point at a definite direction at the sky to show what the position of a definite star was going to be in the following night. They also rode Axilior together as Michael wanted to show her how fast his horse could run. And Michael wanted to share everything with her, but he decided to skip telling her about the beautiful garden of white wild roses in the core of the forest. He also did not tell her that he secretly had been visiting the garden; it was for her own good, he did not want her to follow him to the Forest of Death.

And he never shared his feelings with her and it was for many reasons. First of all, she was after all the Princess and he thought loving her by someone as common as him was equivalent to crime. Secondly, he was afraid that everything would go wrong if she would deny, and he would lose the friend Rose Scarlett. Michael was afraid to love Rose, equally he was afraid to lose her. During the last month, every time they met, Rose asked him about his weeks, his health, consoled him for his past. Michael used to look at Rose's family, recall his past and sigh in grief. A suffocated pain from inside always tried to come out by tearing his throat, but he never allowed it to, never but one day. One day, they had been talking about their childhoods after that day's training. Rose's childhood had been in roses where Michael's had been in thorns. Rose's childhood had been happy, joy and gay. She had gotten costly toys and dresses, travelled heavenly places, had delicious meals, and even had her own maids. And Michael's childhood had finished before it could have started properly. He had seen the harsh truth and reality before he could have grown well enough to endure the pains. After a long time, on this day, Michael had remembered everything - how his mother had left him in his childhood, the treatments he had gotten from people because of the two apparently inclusive words of 'bastard' and 'leftover', how he had to strive to survive every day and work on fields where it was expected that someone like little Michael would be playing in the fields. Talking about these made Michael very emotional after a long time and he had teary eyes. That time, Rose had held his hands strong and had said, "Oh my God! Are you crying? Please don't do this. You are not alone here, Michael. You have your friends, they are your family now. Of course they are not James and Molly, but they are everything you have now. And if you like, you have me too. I will always be there for you." During these times, Michael had become friends with Rose. He had started loving the human Rose, her soul. Her presence was everything to him. And he was terrified of losing her.

Michael also had visited the forest and the garden within it some more times in the recent past. And every time he had come back alive. Nothing had happened before the next sunrise. Despite his apparent success of defeating the evil, he never stopped believing in the demon inside the forest. Even he used to hear the howling while he was inside. He thought that the good ghosts from Tim's theory were there to protect him from the undead and the hounds of Hell. And quite naturally, Michael never had told anyone else about his visits in here.

No one had heard or seen the unprecedented soldiers so far. It was like they had come from nothing and had gone to infinity. Mass destructions, murders and cruelty - the citizens had suffered a lot by them. They feared the unprecedented soldiers.

As it was the wedding's week, security was tightened to the extreme. Many volunteering soldiers from the citizens were recruited. Many were recruited as part-timers, and the part-time job at that time was exactly similar to today's - people used to work a small time of a day after their actual jobs and get paid which was some extra earning for them after their earnings from the actual jobs. New armours and swords were manufactured every day. The watchtowers of the stronghold and the regiments were made advanced and provided with extra equipment. The Order Bench frequently visited the regiments and the entire Kingdom. By this, they oversaw the conditions of security and suggested their valuable supervisions.

One day, Ben came to Michael with an old woman in her fifties.

"Brother, let me introduce you to Mrs. Brenda. I know her for a long time. She was a friend to my mother's," he said. Michael greeted. But he did not know what the point was to meet her.

Ben answered his silent query. "Mrs. Brenda is the personal maid of our Princess."

Michael was shocked at what she was doing in here. It could have been risky for all of them.

"Don't worry. She will not come again. Besides, she is just visiting her old friend's son in the regiment. Right, Mrs. Brenda?" Ben said.

"Yes, yes! I am so glad that you adore her, my dear," Mrs. Brenda was very happy, "she is such a charming and beautiful girl."

"But please don't tell her about this," Michael was concerned.

-"No, no! Not to worry. This old lady can keep secrets. All mouths shut!"

Michael was not convinced entirely, however, he decided to let it go and ask her the question he had pondered about for long. He remembered about the times when he had found Rose upset because of her personal life, and he specifically remembered about the first day they had gone for training. So, he asked Mrs. Brenda about it.

"Well," she thought for a while, "there is one reason that I can recall. It was some days ago. I was there in her room and she had a quarrel with the Queen."

Michael was exactly hoping for this one. So he responded instantly, "Yes! What is it?"

"Well," she again took a while, "it was about her marriage. The wedding is in this week and many good men will be coming. Rich and handsome. Even some Princes will come. The Queen wants the Princess to meet some of them. But the Princess does not. She does not want to get married now. Now, I don't know why that is. Many good men will be coming, you know."

Michael was glad to hear that Rose had turned down the suggestion of her mother. But, he at the same time, was down thinking about how her parents were looking for her possible groom already. And beyond doubt, they were never going to think about him in a million years.

"So, this is the reason behind that day! I wonder why she turned down that option. Is that because she likes someone else? Is that me? And is that the reason why she is spending so much time with me? I am almost certain that she doesn't spend this much of time with anyone else," Michael questioned himself silently, trying to cheer himself up with some possibly false ways of self-satisfaction.

After some more talks, Mrs. Brenda left bidding goodbye and Michael asked if he could meet her again. He assured her that their meetings would be confidential and no one would know anything about them. So, she needed not to worry about. And Mrs. Brenda agreed to him, it seemed like the noble lady was not afraid of getting caught as at her age, she, a widow and without any heir, did not have any reason to be afraid of anything.

Michael surprised himself that, at first, he himself was frightened that someone could find their meeting out and he would fall in a grave danger. But now, he himself was wanting to meet again, given the fact that if they were caught, this old lady would have to go through some of the worst times. He was ashamed of his selfishness. And he realised one quality of human beings - how we are willing to take risks if it is us to gain, and if it is for someone else's gain, we think a lot before getting involved in the danger. In this case, if it is us to gain, we think of taking the risk as worthy of taking, as we do not have anything to lose, but when the situation is opposite then the vice versa does not happen. After meeting with Mrs. Brenda and knowing her, Michael understood another property of human beings - their fear of death. We are afraid of death - the death of ours or of loved ones of ours, not because of the penultimate pains or the sorrow of losing someone. It is actually because we are afraid of being alone. We are afraid of dying as we are afraid of being alone for eternity in an unknown place of afterlife. And, we are afraid of losing someone when they die because, well again, we are afraid of being left alone; another consequence of human selfishness.

More days passed and now it was just the day before the wedding. Every preparation was at its final stage. Foods of the best quality were imported from different lands of the Great Island and from lands beyond the Great Seas. The best chefs were called on, the most skilled musicians were hired. And the rooms and halls of the Greathall of the fortress were decorated to depict the ethereal beauty of the wedding; anyone had to admit that these were the most beautiful places he had ever seen. Some of the eminent invitees were already here. The guestrooms, some of the most magnificent ones in the castle, were opened for them. These prosperous personalities, along with the Royals, were having delightful and irresistible dinners of best quality fruits, vegetables, cakes, aniseed, basil, bay, beefs, pork, rabbits, muttons, red wine, white wine and apple cider and finest cigars every day. There was music playing all the time. And there were dancing, singing and many more.

Michael and Rose mutually had decided to cancel that week's meeting as Rose had to be completely involved in the wedding. So, Michael, on that week's Tuesday which was the day before the wedding, decided to visit the garden in the forest. On some other week, today at this time, he would be waiting for Rose at the South Bailey. As the meeting was cancelled, he decided to spend the time with himself in the alluring garden of roses in the core of the Forest of Death, the Forbidden One.

It was an amazing day to sit and enjoy in the garden of roses. The time of the year was getting closer fast towards the coldest of days as the seasonal cycle rotated. And this time was the time when it was neither hot nor cold. The sun was shining brightly, yet its heat was pleasant. The breeze was neither too fast to create instability nor too resisted to cause suffocation. And like the weather, the breeze itself had one average temperature. Michael was sitting, and then lay in supine in the solitude. He could see the blue sky and the white clouds of cotton floating. The white roses smelt stunningly and their petals were waving at the rhythm of the air. It was like one Principal was conducting an orchestra and the roses were dancing, singing the violins, cellos, brasses and pianos. The entire forest surrounding this garden was the audience, enjoying this ephemeral beauty. And the bees bombinating at the roses were adding more romances of renaissance music to this orchestra concert. At last, the pollen grains flying with the breeze, diffracting sunlight were the Carole dancers to this concert - they were the Stardusts in the Starshine. One somnambulist could sleepwalk, following this concert and come to join the audience, in the Forest of Death, the Forbidden One.

Michael was thinking about many things. As usual, the place reminded him of James and Molly. Both of them did not return since they had gone. Although James' status was engraved in the stones in seventh regiment of South and in the National Memorial Ground as M.I.A., nobody knew anything of Molly. Michael had tried to ask some from the highest authorities about Molly. He had contacted the Order, Commander Black and many more. But no one could say anything. Even during his time with Daniel, Ben and Tim and of course with Rose Scarlett, Michael seldom felt alone because of James and Molly. He always thought of being responsible for their fates, although he did not know what had happened to Molly. He always thought that if he had not listened to Molly that day more than a year ago, had not gone to alert the other regiments and had joined the war from the very beginning, then James could be alive now. He had warned James not to go carried away, but still James had done it. If Michael were there, he could have stopped him.

"I should have talked to her. I could have talked to her. Before I left," he blamed himself for Molly. He always thought how selfish he was to forget these two most important persons of his life this easily and early. But did he really forget them?

"I almost have done nothing to find them out," he criticised himself again. He, so far, had met many people from the highest authorities, as mentioned earlier, to ask them about Molly, searched for the probable remnants of her family, but could not find a single person alive. And he frequently had visited this garden, within the Forest of Death, in search for

James. May be it was all he could do. But he was not satisfied. He always thought that he was not giving his all and as if there was a big lack, a big void in his dedication. Daniel and the others always rebuked him for taking this whole tough task of finding James and Molly out onto himself, but he never listened to them in this aspect.

Daniel and the others always told him that he had done enough already. It was time to let go. "You cannot hold them forever. James is gone. It has been more than a year! We all are sad for him, and for you. He was our best friend, such a good friend, such a good soldier. But he is gone. You cannot moan for him forever. You will go crazy. Do you think James would want that for his brother?" Daniel and the others always asked him.

Michael himself started to believe that James really was gone forever. But he could never stop searching for him. He blamed himself for James' death and stopping searching for him was not an option to him - in fact, it was a cruelty, selfishness in his eyes.

"It is not that I will not stop searching for him. Actually, I cannot stop searching for him," he always replied to Daniel and the others.

And Molly? Well, nobody knew what had happened to her.

Michael was thinking about his life. How it had changed its paths to come to where it was now.

All of a sudden, he heard something that made him stand up at once. And he took Axilior and hid on the other side of the forest than the one from where the sound was coming.

Was it the undead? Or the unprecedented soldiers? Or, was it another attack from the French and pirates? Michael was scared. But he was steady. He needed to check what it was.

The reality was nothing like what Michael had been expecting and worrying about. But it definitely was something to be concerned about.

It was some soldiers of his own kingdom. There were about twenty of them, from different regiments. Michael could identify some of them. There were soldiers from the regiments of North, East, West and even South. And most interestingly, there was Williams among them.

Michael did not come out from the hiding. Instead, he let them pass. At the same time, he asked himself what these soldiers had been doing in the forest, how long they had been in here, and most importantly, what they had been doing in the southernmost part of the forest. These soldiers had come from the side of the forest even Michael never had gone to. It was more in the south, beyond the garden. However, it must be mentioned that the soldiers did not pass through the garden, instead, they chose to pass through the trees - a way of hiding themselves from other eyes. And as they passed, Michael came out, took Axilior and started to follow them from a safe distance.

The soldiers were running fast as if they were in a great hurry. And they were talking amongst themselves that Michael could not hear from the distance. The soldiers also were confirmed with where they were going. They did not hesitate or spend unusual time in deciding the way even within the deep forest; it was a clear indication that they had been here before. However, as per Michael's knowledge, only Williams had been into the forest in the past and even he never had come this far.

The soldiers followed their way out of the forest and Michael followed them. After coming out of the forest, they continued to head towards the North for some kilometres and then turned to the left towards the West. Riding some more kilometres in this direction led them to an old house. It was a two-storied broken and abandoned house. The wooden board hanging at the front door entitled 'Charles Inn' and introducing the house to the world was hard to decipher because of the dirt and its age. The house must have had one glorified past in its hay day. However, now it was just a reminder of that history; now it looked like it had suffered consecutive hurricanes and earthquakes. The wooden windows had broken down long ago and now only the holes were present to represent the past. The walls once had been polished to show its luxury and to attract the richest of the travellers. Presently, all Michael could see against the fast approaching night was some crumbling walls which were some ghostly memories of their historical existence. The history was trapped within the house with the echoes of the prevailing and was reflecting from the walls and ceilings. The laughter, joy, fun of the people who once had stayed in here were lost in the oceans of solitude that the house had chosen for itself. And the only residents now in the abandoned spooky house were bats and insects.

Michael was wondering what might have led the soldiers into this house that contained the threat of getting relapsed to its age and collapsed. So, he decided to investigate. He left Axilior at a distance, and hid down under a window to listen to the soldiers.

The soldiers lit a candle to lighten up the darkness and started their discussion.

"So, postponing it was not a bad idea," someone said.

"But if we were to attack now, we could have made more massacre and chaos. Many kings will be coming tomorrow," another one said.

"But look at the security. It is very strong nowadays. Don't forget that the wedding will be for the Royals. The soldiers and the King's Men are not here to enjoy the wedding. They are going to be more alerted tomorrow," a third one reported.

"Yes, but we also have a large army. We could have made some decimating impact. And because of the people attending the wedding, chaos can be created very easily. That would really help us," added a fourth one.

"Everyone listen to me," Michael heard the familiar voice, "please don't forget our goal. Our goal is not to create a chaos or even kill the invitees. Only one King is in our red list," the cruel voice of Williams was heard.

Michael came out, still hiding, crouched to Axilior and rode it fast away from the house. He could have stayed there to listen to what the soldiers were discussing for more information. But he already had got the gist and it was all he needed. And staying there for more could have been a danger too. He was nothing against a team of twenty soldiers with someone like Williams with them.

They were certainly planning an ulterior; a conspiracy against the King. It was to overthrow him from the throne. The more disturbing fact was that they had one large army. Michael did not know what that army consisted. And then, he remembered finding the soldiers coming from the forest. The army must have consisted of the French and the pirates. And there were the scoundrels from the King's own military themselves who were going to betray their own King. And the unprecedented soldiers?

Michael was in a topsy-turvy condition. He did not know what to do next. It was a concerning news. He had to alert everyone. However, he did not want anyone to know that he had been in the forest too. Anyone would enlist him within the suspects. Anyone would interrogate him what he himself had been doing in the forest.

At long last, Michael fought against himself to decide to share everything with Commander Daniel. His status in the military would be an advantage to convince others. And so, he headed towards the seventh regiment of the South.

Michael was late. Most of the soldiers including Daniel and Ben had already left for their duty - an important duty because of the wedding. And they were not coming back until the next night. Only Tim was waiting for him at the tent. However, revealing everything to him was of no help or significance. Besides, the possible war, the raid, and the civil war were not going to occur on the wedding day. So, Michael decided not to speak of it until he saw Daniel again.

The next morning, Michael woke up before anyone else. From the stable, he took his old horse. Axilior was a famous horse and he needed to bypass any attention; he needed not to be recognised. So, he also did not wear the armour, instead, he wore his old dress and the black cloak to have a perfect disguise.

He rode to the ruined house of the previous day. Before entering the house, he investigated the adjacent places. No, there was no one in there and now he could safely enter. It was the room that Williams and the others had had the discussion where Michael wanted to enter.

The room was on the ground floor. It might have been the one where the guests had used to dine, drink and smoke in the past. It was a big, yet, completely desolate and empty room. There were only one round table and some chairs, which were relatively new with respect to the house. They might have been brought by Williams and the others. There was one burned down candlestick on top of the table. And there were some papers, which were the matter of Michael's interest.

The room was dark and not at all airy, despite having the holes in places of the broken windows. And it had been abandoned for long, was standing as a part of the entire skeleton, as a forgotten beauty of a long past. The walls could no longer keep the room and its mother safe against the tempestuous storm, rain and snow. The poignant condition of the ceilings, floors and the interiors of the walls were showing the unquestionable proof to it. And in its old age, the room, with its mother, was dying being left indifferent under the dust and dirt.

As Michael walked into the room, the floor made one ghostly squeaky noise and it looked like the whole house was shaking, on the verge of collapsing. It was like the floor had just sent the news of Michael's arrival to all the residents of the house - the bats, the insects and the souls, laughter and joys long forgotten in the wayward flow of time.

Michael had to hurry and so he did not bother worrying about the condition of the house. He walked straight to the table and looked down at the papers. Those were some maps of different parts of the Kingdom. Most of the maps had one common feature, a similarity - they started from the Forest of Death. There were some things written and drawn on the maps. This was a plan of a supervised attack starting from the forest and leading towards the castle. There was so much to remember, but Michael could not afford to take the maps with him. So, he took a while to memorise as much as he could.

Then he came out of the house. And he returned to his regiment. He already was getting late. So, he put his uniform on and went to the castle with Tim for the big day's duty.

The wedding ceremony started just before the evening. All the eminent invitees were already here. The Kings from Scotland and Northern Ireland had come only a few hours ago. The size of the army that had escorted them was not too large but was worthy of being noticed. Each of these soldiers could have been as powerful as a King's Man. And with the Kings, had come the Queens, the Princes and the Princesses.

The entire castle had been decorated with flowers and many more that Michael could not even name of. He had never seen such costly ornaments before. The ceremony was going on in the Hall on the ground floor, it was the biggest of all the halls in the castle. This Hall had been divided into some parts - one stage for the attendees and the place for the post wedding feast, in front of that was the second stage as the ballroom for dancing, one stage for the musicians and their instruments, the pathway in the middle of the Hall as the aisle and at last, the altar. There were dining tables in white cloth covers with foods and wines on them. Each table had a candlestick made of gold with ten lit candles on them. Hundreds of chefs were cooking thousands of cuisines - fruits, vegetables, meat, eggs, fishes, puddings, cakes, wine, beer and so many more. Many men were continuously serving them. There was a long table, the most decorated of all, for the Kings and their families including the bride and the groom.

Michael and Tim were standing by the door. They had been in the castle since the morning. As soon as Michael had returned from his confidential investigation to his regiment, they had gone out towards the castle. And now they were at the much-awaited wedding.

For my readers, I must say a few things about weddings in medieval century Europe. First of all, there are so many similarities between a wedding of that time period and one from now. The traditions of the Christian wedding did not change very much. A typical arranged marriage was more common at that time. The brides sometimes did not even know the groom until the wedding. And the brides did not have much of a saying to this. However, men were sometimes able to choose their brides. Marriage back then was not based on love; most marriages were political arrangements. Husbands and wives were generally strangers until they first met. If love was involved at all, it came after the couple had been married. Even if love did not develop through marriage, the couple generally developed a friendship of some sort. After the marriage was arranged, a wedding notice was posted on the door of the church. The traditions, as mentioned earlier, were very similar. There were best men and bride's maids. And there were the ring bearers as there was the tradition of ring exchange. The groom waited as the bride walked down the aisle; there were the wedding vows and one priest to conduct.

For a long time, Michael's eyes were searching for a certain someone. At last, he could find her; she was at the altar, as the bride's maid. She was wearing a beautiful red dress, a byzantine necklace and diamond earrings. Michael kept looking at Rose for some time and could not take his eyes off for that span. Gary was standing on the altar with the other maids and his men and with the old priest. He was wearing his suit with gold belts and buckles and a sword. A few moments later, Ms. Jane arrived in her white wedding gown, holding arms with her father, both walking down the aisle. Everyone stood up to show respect to the bride. When they reached at the altar, the father kissed his daughter at her head and left the stage.

The priest started, "We are here today to celebrate the love of God. To celebrate the love between a man and a woman, and to God there is nothing more beautiful than when two people are in love." The rings were exchanged and the vows were made. The priest came to the final part of the wedding, "Repeat after me - I, take you, to be my lawfully wedded wife (or husband), to have and to hold, from this day forward, for better and for worse, for richer and for poorer, in sickness and in health, to love and to cherish, until death do us part." Gary and Jane were standing on the altar, holding hands, facing each other, and looking at each other's eyes. After the vows, they kissed. And then they came on to the aisle to greet the attendees.

Michael and Tim had no interest in listening to the wedding vows. They had been looking at the roasted chickens and the red wine. As the feast started, they also joined in.

They had to hurry up as they needed to go to the South Tower to exchange the duty position with the soldiers in the Tower. Michael tried to talk to Rose, however, it was harder than he thought. Quite naturally, Rose was very busy. And on top of that, the Queen was always with her, introducing her to the sons of the other Kings. She was also suggesting them to dance. Michael was hating the Queen. He was also looking at Rose having the dances with the elegant and well-dressed Princes of the other kingdoms.

In a time of need, Michael could not find Tim. The boy was lost in the grand feast. For the first time of the night, now, Michael found Rose apparently alone. She was not with the Queen or any of the rich invitees. But she was with someone whom Michael hated the most; he basically was his archenemy and both of them had an antipathy towards each other. It was David Williams. He also had been assigned to guard the castle. Michael saw him for the first time in the night.

Michael approached towards them to interfere into their conversation. Till now, Williams had been talking about something which Rose had been listening to with great interest.

"Greetings Princess," Michael ignored Williams completely. He remembered that Williams had been also in the mission of escorting the Royal Carriages, more than a month ago, on which Rose and the others had come.

"Were they meeting secretly lately?" Michael asked himself.

He was angry with both of them. There were so many reasons behind his anger for Williams. And for Rose, there was only one. He falsely tried to convince himself that the reason, in fact, was not jealousy. His brain tried to concentrate on how sometimes he had asked Rose if they could meet more frequently. But Rose had denied. "It would be nice. But I am busy now. I hope you can understand," she had said. Michael was thinking that Rose had lied to him in order to meet Williams. However, only if he could think clearer, he would understand that there was no reason to think like that. Firstly, Rose had her own choice of whom to meet and whom not to. Secondly, Rose might have met Williams within the castle and might not have spent much time. Her statement of being busy might have been candid. And Michael underneath was reluctant to condone these.

We make mistakes a lot. And one common form of mistakes is to speak ill with our loved ones because of our emotions like anger, jealousy, our ego and abstract pride. We cannot control our emotions and end up saying and yelling ill. We realise, later, about our mistakes but sometimes it becomes too late to recover.

Rose showed courtesy. Moreover, she did not know that Michael and Williams knew each other. So, she introduced them to each other. But Michael could not help shouting at Williams, "You better get your butt out of this place."

Cunning Williams handled the situation very carefully, "Why? What is wrong, Michael?" He was acting surprised as if Michael's demeanour was completely unexpected to him.

Michael still was not very cool and easy about it, "I said get out of here!" He almost yelled.

Rose understood that the situation was not friendly and creation of a scene in such a ceremony would be an embarrassment. So, she tried to calm Michael down, "Michael stop! What are you saying?"

"Alright, fine," Williams was clever to back off. But thus, he lost the battle and won the war. "I am going. Besides, I need to go back to my duty. It is always a privilege meeting you my Lady," he kissed Rose on her hand.

As he was gone, Rose turned back at Michael and asked angrily, "What was that? Are you mental? Or, are you drunk?"

This is the moment when Michael committed his mistake. He had some expectations from Rose and he was angry by seeing them go wrong. That is why he ended up shouting at Rose. "No! I am not mental neither am I drunk! You better tell me what it was."

"Excuse me?" Rose was shocked and humiliated, "Can't I talk to someone? Do I need to listen to you as you are training me swords fight? Or are you my husband prohibiting me from talking to a stranger?"

-"That stranger..." Michael stopped himself. He was about to reveal Williams' identity. He calmed down a bit and said, "I am just asking you not to talk to him. You have no idea what bad a person he is."

But it failed to ameliorate the condition and mollify Rose. She still was humiliated and felt being insulted. She said, "I will decide whom to talk and whom not to. Please don't teach that to me. And please learn how to talk to your Princess."

She left in a hurry. It was obvious that Michael's demeanour had been demeaning to her. And she wanted to avoid him, get back to the wedding and meet her guests.

It took Michael some minutes to realise the consequences of his idiosyncratic behaviour. So far, still, he was angry with Rose. But now, he felt sorry for what he had done. But he did not have the chance to go to her and ask for forgiveness. He was feeling ashamed, and her reaction to his apology could be bitter. This time, at last, Michael felt tensed up. She, after all, was the Princess. His temper would throw him in front of arrays of problems followed by sufferings. The only way of escaping was to apologise to her and never see her again, which itself was terrible to him.

"Where on Earth is Tim?" Michael was becoming restless. If Tim was here, Michael could have asked him to talk to Rose in his place. And then he heard Williams calling him, "Hello Michael, I think you have screwed something up? Are you thinking of re-wielding the tainted armour?" It was a metaphor for fixing one's mistake. He thought that Williams was the reason behind all these. His fight with Rose, the possible consequences after yelling at the Princess - Williams was the reason behind them.

Williams was standing, smiling at him. It was a smile of victory, a smile of dominance, and to remind Michael forcefully by slapping him that he was losing.

Michael was supposed to keep the things he had known the previous day a secret. However, he could not keep it anymore. He was mentally devastated, and he could not take Williams' cruel smile lightly. He was thinking that if no one were here now, he would have penetrated his pointy sword through Williams' neck.

"I will kill you! I swear to Jesus, I am going to slaughter you," Michael was very excited. He was almost shouting even when the hall was filled with people, "I know about you, and your ulterior. I know what you and some others are trying to accomplish. You are with the French and pirates. You are here to take the throne from the King. I will kill you all before that!"

Williams was genuinely shocked. It was unexpected to him. They had been meticulously planning on the civil war for a long time. There were undoubtedly many reasons for him to go on to this extreme - to betray his own Kingdom. But, they had been very cautious about its secrecy. He had no clue how, all of a sudden, Michael knew about it. He did not indeed perceive who else knew about the upcoming war. But, Williams was as cool and stable as a glacier. He did not panic, even though Michael himself was too excited and was almost speaking aloud for anyone else to hear him clearly.

"Well, congratulations Michael. I am happy for you that you have found it. Listen," he placed his arm around Michael's shoulder, "there are many reasons for us to go on for an open war against the King. I will tell you everything. You will understand too. Just listen to me carefully. Do not be hasty. Choose carefully. The French are way better. Join hands with them. Help them over-throne the King. And both of us can become the highest in the King's Men."

Williams was trying to lure Michael in. He knew that Michael was an asset, a strong fighter. Moreover, Michael knew about their plan. However, Michael could find out the inner intention from Williams' talk.

"Are you really thinking you can make me a fool like that? I am never going to betray my nation. That is as absolute as the Sun and Moon," he was dedicated.

Williams exhaled with a fake disappointment. It was as if Michael had made a mistake by choosing the wrong side. It was as if Williams himself had tried hard to save Michael as he was Michael's true and faithful friend.

"Then, my friend, I do not have any other option," his voice hardened now, "with everyone else, I will have to eradicate you. I and my army will annihilate the entire Kingdom. The French will take the throne, and I will be the commander of the new King's Men. We will form a new King's Men as all of them will die. The King and the Queen will die. And I will marry the Princess, we will have kids together." He stopped for a second to think something, then continued, "No. I think I will keep you alive to see me with your beloved Rose. I will be having sex with her every night, and you will be behind the bars."

Michael tried very hard to control his fists and temptation of not punching Williams. He just left into the crowds and now he found Tim.

"Tim! Where were you?" he asked. But he did not let Tim reply. He knew that Williams' comrades were here, might be closely observing them right now. Before the previous day, he had no intuition that there had been so many traitors in the military. Even now, he did not know how many more were there from or outside of the military. He did not know how many people of this Hall itself were involved in the planning of the treason. Any wrong move could make Tim's life to fall in danger. They were already very close to the slope of the cliff.

"Listen, Tim. Listen to me very carefully. And don't ask any questions," he started. He knew he did not have much time, so, he tried to make it short but clear, "war is upon us. It is a civil war, a treachery. The French and the pirates will attack too. I am seeing you probably for the last time now. Or, maybe we will meet in the front. I am going away. You need to perform a mission that I am assigning. Go and meet Walther, Daniel and Commander Black. No one else. And tell them to keep it a secret. Many soldiers from the army are going to join forces against us. And David Williams from the sixth regiment of the South is their leader."

He said this very quickly and left into the crowds. He did not want to spend much time with Tim as the more he would spend the more it would be a risk to Tim. And Tim was surprised and shocked to hear from Michael and to see him getting lost in the crowd, probably for the last time. But, Tim quickly got himself back; he went to meet Walther and Commander Black who were there somewhere in the castle. Despite being the youngest and most inexperienced soldier in the military, Tim was fitting fine in the army. He had quality. Now, he was showing his worth in the army by going to contact Walther, Black and later Daniel along with saving himself from evil eyes.

Michael got out of the castle. He had needed to hide for the next few hours before the ceremonies were over and everyone was back. But, he knew that the opposition was in search for him. They had to kill him as he knew everything about them.

On the other hand, Michael also could not reveal everything to just anyone. There were a lot of reasons behind this and one definitely was that the person whom he would reveal could himself be from the opposition.

He reached the South Bailey and found Williams, with two other soldiers. They might just be waiting for him. Michael knew the other two soldiers. He had seen them, on the previous day, coming out of the Forest of Death and having the confidential meeting in the old inn. They were also involved in the upcoming civil war.

Michael brought his sword out when Williams said, "There is no need for us to get violent, Michael Chapman! We have decided to leave the army and officially join the French. That is how we will not betray this Kingdom. I realised your concern and I understood that it is so low for my nature. So, we will leave tomorrow morning. We will fight - you as a soldier of this Kingdom and me as a soldier of the French. We will meet soon. So, why don't we drink for a last time together?"

He poured two glasses with red wine that he had taken from the ceremony. And he gave one to Michael while keeping one for himself.

"Cheers," he drank and so did Michael.

Michael drank from the glass after Williams. He did not say anything, but was observing them and trying to anticipate their intentions meticulously. He knew that Williams had his pride. Was he really thinking of leaving only as Michael had called him a traitor? Was he really going to abandon such an opportunity to decimate the Kingdom from inside? And, although he was having the perfect opportunity to kill Michael right now, as Michael clearly was outnumbered, he was having wine with Michael.

"Why don't we go to the North Bailey? There is a beautiful garden there. And there is a beautiful statue there too, of

I think Madonna? Or, of a guardian angel? In comparison to the North Bailey, this South one looks lifeless," Williams offered.

Michael had no idea what Williams was thinking. Was he thinking of killing him in the North Bailey? As most of the stables and barracks were in the South Bailey, the North one was relatively quiet. It was a better place to kill someone in there without getting caught. And Michael was the spine to their almost perfect plan of taking over. It surely was a good idea to eradicate Michael.

Williams could read Michael's mind. He laughed, "Are you afraid that we are going to kill you? No! There are so many soldiers here in the castle tonight. Maybe we are under surveillance right now by the archers on the walls and the towers. I am not a fool to take this risk. So, will you join us now?" he asked.

"Alright! Let's go have a drink for the last time," Michael agreed.

8

The Trial for Epiphany

Michael woke up. He was exhausted and was under unimaginably intense pain. And the pain was unnatural. He felt an ache in the back of his head, neck and backbone. His stomach was hurting badly and so were the interiors of his neck and chest. He was lying on a cold hard floor, which definitely was not the soft bed in his tent. Michael opened his eyes and took some time to adjust them with the brightness of the ambience. No, the ambience was not bright at all, rather it was dark. However, his eyes had been closed for a long time and even this barely bright ambience was heavy on them. He also tried to lift his head up and turn himself around to catch a glimpse of the place. But his exhaustion did not let him do this. So, he decided not to overdo it and lie down for more. In the meantime, he tried to think.

"Where am I? What happened to me?" These were the first questions he asked himself.

After some time, he sat up. Now he could have a better perception of his surroundings.

It was a small room with only one door, locked from outside. There was only one window, high enough for him to not even bother to try to climb up and look outside. The room was made of stones and was extremely cold. There was one foul smell in the place and the source of it was unknown to Michael. Probably, it was because of the confined air and water as the room had been locked for a long time before someone put Michael in it. Or probably, it was as the room was heinously dirty. There was carbon dust all over the walls. Once painted walls were these. But now, they had blackened due to the dust. And there was one fluid on the floor. Was it water? No. It was not transparent. It was red and had one fierce smell. Was it blood? Whose blood was it? His own?

Michael started to cough roughly. And the cough continued for long enough for him to be concerned. And every time he was coughing, his aches in stomach, neck and chest were magnified by multiple times. He tried to control his cough, but this worsened the situation. He threw up blood.

Michael tried to calm down. It was direly needed. He stopped thinking anything for a minute. And he only inhaled and exhaled as much air as he could despite the foul smell.

"Where am I?" he started to think again. This place was completely unknown to him. He could not even imagine how the room would look like from outside. He had never been in here.

Now, he tried to remember anything he could; what had happened to him the last? He could remember something - it was something to do with Rose, and Tim, and Williams. There had been many people. Yes! It was the wedding. And, anything else? There was something to be concerned about. What? He could remember Williams' face, his cruel smile and cunning brain. Why was he remembering him? And now, he started to recall the Forest of Death, the Forbidden One. Why? Was not the King in danger? And the Kingdom too? Who was going to kill the King? Who was going to annihilate him? Who was going to destroy the Kingdom? Was it someone from behind the forest? Was it the French and the pirates? Or was it the undead, hounds of hell, the unprecedented soldiers? Was not there a treason going on? And were not there twenty soldiers who had gone into the forest? Was not Williams with them? Yes! And the last thing he could remember, he had told Williams that he had known of everything. And later, he had been having a drink with him in the North Bailey.

"Where am I?" he started to rethink it again in the better perspective.

"Am I abducted? Am I a prisoner of the opposition? Am I a prisoner of war? Did the war occur? Did it end? What is the result? Did we lose?"

He stood up. His legs were shaking badly. And he had to put force on a wall by hands to support himself to stand. But, he did not even try to walk. He was having enormous head rushes.

"Was I poisoned? Yes, I can remember that I had wine with Williams. But, he also drank from the same bottle. Would he take the risk to poison himself? Then is it that he was not poisoned but only I was? How is it possible?" he was confused.

Michael tried to look up. The room had one impressive height. Darkness had clotted at the roof like blood, concealing the roof from Michael's weary eyes. The length and width of the room were small whereas the height was big - one could vehemently and confidently conclude that Michael was a prisoner.

Michael now paid attention again on himself, particularly what he was wearing. He was not wearing the armours, but still was wearing the uniform that he had used to wear underneath the armours. And he already had felt that the uniform was wet at the chest. Now he concentrated on what it was - it was blood. So, the source of the blood on the floor was he himself! But what was the reason behind his bleeding?

He still was feeling extreme pains in his stomach, interiors of neck and chest. Michael found that he was missing his sword. What happened to Axilior?

At last, the door was opened. Someone came in. The person was someone Michael could never even imagine to find in a place like this. It was Commander Daniel, commander of the seventh regiment of the South.

This forced Michael to rethink about almost everything he had been thinking so far after getting awake. What was Daniel doing here? Was he a prisoner too? Or was there something that Michael was missing? Could he trust Daniel? Was he also working with Williams against the King?

Daniel was wearing his armours and had his sword with him. This indicated that he was not a prisoner.

Michael took a moment to think about Daniel and his relationship with Daniel. What kind of a person had Daniel been so far?

Daniel surely had been an amazing and trustworthy friend. He had been a very good fighter. He had been for Michael in his happiness and sorrow. He also had been an efficient commander of the strongest but most dangerous regiment. Michael had never questioned his patriotism and dedication. But, could he actually trust him? So, everything that Daniel had done so far was just to pretend to be a friend? So, Daniel had played one seemingly perfect act so far and shown his true face before the civil war?

Michael wished if he could break the mask of each one of these traitors and show the face hiding underneath to the world.

Why was Daniel here? Was he here to interrogate him, given the fact that Michael knew everything? Michael was wishing if James were here, and Molly. Where was Molly? Did Daniel kill her as, beyond doubt, Molly had been perfectly dedicated to her regiment and her nation? Where was Ben? Could he trust him too? And where was Tim? Yes, he remembered something more. He had told Tim about the possible treachery and had asked him to contact Daniel, Walther and Black. Could he trust Tim? Was he also involved with the opposition? And what about Walther and his Order? And Black and his King's Men?

Michael sat on a relatively neat place on the floor. Daniel sat beside him.

"How are you feeling now?" Daniel asked.

"Not good," Michael was succinct.

-"Can you remember anything? What happened?"

"Is he interrogating me? Should I answer to this question? I think I should not. But, again, they already know that I have all the information. Hiding anything anymore will not help too. So, I think I also should strike back," Michael thought. He was in a dilemma.

"The last thing I can remember I did was to have a drink with Williams of the sixth regiment of the South in the North Bailey, at the wedding night," Michael stated.

-"Can you remember anything that happened later?"

-"No. Everything afterwards is foggy."

Daniel was disappointed. He had been hoping to hear something better and more useful from Michael. So, he tried to force a little, "Michael, I want you to remember. It is very important!"

"Why? Why is it so important? I cannot remember a thing. I don't even know which day it is. And what is this place? Why am I here?" Michael got furious instantly.

Daniel realised that Michael was not in his usual cool. So, he stopped being forceful. Instead, without being fixated on the abstracts, he came to the main topic. He asked, "Michael, do you know why you are here?"

"No!" Michael was curious.

-"You have been arrested. You are charged with a case of murders. Right now, you are in custody of the army."

"What?" Michael could not help expressing his surprise. "Murders? Whom did I murder?" He was completely within a maze and was taking the wrong ways over and over again. He could not find the way out. He was lost.

It was not very surprising to Daniel to see Michael not able to remember anything.

"Let me tell you everything I know," he started. "After the wedding, Tim met me. He told me about the war that we are going to face. He also told me that there are some soldiers amongst us who are going to betray us. The French and the pirates will attack and these soldiers will assist them. This is what you had asked Tim to inform me and Walther Livingston and Commander Black. No one knows if what you have said is true. Even I don't know. But I believe you, with all my heart. After hearing all of these from Tim at the night after the ceremony, I did not waste a second. I went with him to contact Walther Livingston and Commander Black. We came back to the castle and we faced another problem. We found that there had been a clash in the North Bailey. Although I was going to find you too before meeting Walther and Commander Black, I did not expect to find you that soon. We saw that you had been arrested for killing two of the gardeners of the North Bailey. Tim had no authority but I had. So, I sent him to meet Walther and Black and I went to see you. And I found you here. You were acting totally crazy, no, I should say you were acting like you were being possessed by a demon. You were dangerous to everyone, and so they put you here in this isolated cell. Your health condition was very poor. You were throwing up blood. Doctors were called in. They diagnosed that you had been in drugs. And they prescribed something to let you go to sleep. Today is the second day you were sleeping continuously. In the meantime, I took the news. Two soldiers had found you killing the two gardeners. You were caught red handed."

Michael could not feel anything; he could not feel being in there, on Earth, anymore. He was feeling being gradually getting erased from the lively world to a vacuous continuum of infinite emptiness. It seemed that there was an epidemic of apocalypse, within his body, which was destroying him by every organ. He did not know how to believe what he just had heard. The most frustrating part was that he still could not remember anything.

"Wait!" Michael suddenly got a clue, "you just said that two soldiers had caught me. Who were they? And where was Williams?" From Daniel's description of the two soldiers, Michael came to the definite conclusion that they were the two soldiers with Williams. And no one had seen Williams since that night. But no one also had found him at the crime scene.

Suddenly, Michael remembered something. And he shared that with Daniel, "I just recalled something. On that night in the North Bailey, only Williams and I had the drink. The two companions of him did not have. So far I was thinking that the drink must have been innocuous as otherwise it would equally harm Williams. But now I think there were drugs in the drink. Williams also was equally affected. However, he had the two soldiers to assist him getting out. I did not have. I had already sent Tim to you. I think when Williams and I were wasted, the soldiers themselves killed the two gardeners and falsely charged me. And they got Williams out of the place safely."

Daniel thought of this possibility. And he agreed, "I think you are right. It does make sense. However," he changed the context, "right now, we need to deal with something more important. It is night already. And tomorrow is your trial - a trial for epiphany. I am fighting for you. If all of your information is true then we need you. I need to free you and I need to do it as soon as I can."

"My trail?" Michael was afraid to face the even bitter reality.

-"Yes. So far the fact is, you were in drugs, got into a fight with two innocent civilians and beheaded them. If I can't prove this wrong, they will hang you for this despicable act."

A silence dominated the ghostly place for the next few minutes. Michael could hear his own heartbeats. He was frightened. The hanging floor was flashing at his sights. He could not say anything. He felt unnatural coldness, like a flow of freezing air was flowing through his veins. And he felt like he was lacking enough blood for usual physical activities to go on within his body; he was pale. He forgot about the aches in his stomach, neck, chest and back he had been having so far. But now, he had a different kind of pain in the left part of his chest: a pain of fear in the heart.

Daniel gave him courage and said, "We cannot prove the possible civil war right now. So, I have decided to go with something else. You will say that you were under attack by the two gardeners. You were drunk but not in drugs. And to protect yourself, you had to kill them. I already have contacted some of the soldiers who saw you in such condition at the crime scene and they have promised me to be on our side. Your friend Josh, the archer, was also there. He also helped me to convince those soldiers."

"And Walther and Black?" Michael asked.

"We could not contact them. And right now, it is not possible for me to contact anymore. They are in the jury. And I am fighting for you," Daniel said at last.

Daniel left for the day. And Michael was taken to a better cell. He also was given food.

It was midnight now. Michael was lying on the cold bed to energise his feeble and falling body. He was getting ready for the next day - his trial. Any wrong step, from now on, could put his life in danger and his head through the hanging rope. But Michael was not afraid anymore.

Now Michael could remember everything. And he was feeling embarrassed. He was hating himself. Daniel was such a good friend to him, he always had been such a great person. And here he had been doubting Daniel's trust. Daniel was there after Michael had lost James. Daniel was there to help him train. Daniel was there for his silly issues of love with Rose. And what about Rose? She had been such a great support to Michael. She had told him that he was not alone when he had been thinking that he had lost everything. She was the one to hold his hands tight when he had been thinking that he had no family. Yet, he had talked to her like that. And Molly?

"It is over. I am done hurting the most valuable persons in my life. I am done hurting them. I almost have lost each one of them. But not anymore. Now, it is my turn to save them. I will give my life to protect them, they are my family. This kingdom is my family."

Michael thought about Williams. That loathsome swine surely had successfully played his trump card. He definitely was in the vantage by deleting every important piece in Michael's chess board. This was Williams' strategy, it always had been so. Williams himself was in a safe place, so far away from this havoc and from the hands of law. But his cunning plan had worked perfectly so far. His King was safe under castled by his Rook. Whereas, Michael's King's position was weakened by perpetual checks. It was almost the end game and Michael only had one pawn where Daniel had the Rook, aiming for the checkmate. But the game was not over, as

Michael thought. His pawn was a passed pawn, waiting for the perfect next move to be converted to the almighty Queen.

The next morning, Michael went to the courthouse on the scheduled time. He was accompanied there from the cell by Josh and a few more soldiers of the castle that Michael knew. All of them encouraged Michael and promised that everything was going to be just fine.

Michael reached the courthouse. His hands were tied with chains.

The courthouse was a big hall in the castle. There were more courthouses in the kingdom outside the castle, but this particular one was for cases like this where a soldier was involved. The greater part of the Hall was for the audience - the common civilians and soldiers. Today also many people were here to witness the judgement. At a glance, Michael saw them. There were so many of them. Everyone knew Michael as one of the most promising soldiers, the gem from the seventh regiment of the South, the companion of James Wheeler and one of the ones who had tricked death in the Forest of Death, the Forbidden One. But Michael knew a very few of them. There were the innkeepers of some inns he usually visited, some local villagers and Mrs. Brenda. At the centre of the Hall, there was a cubical construction of wood for the convicted to stand in - the Suspect Stand. On two opposite sides of the Hall, there were the seats for the members of the jury. And on one side, there was the Judge - the King.

Not Walther but Ray was the leader of the jury because of his long-term experience serving this Kingdom. Commander Black and a few more King's Men were also in the jury. Finally, there was one messenger, two attorneys and their witnesses and supports. Of the two attorneys, there was Daniel fighting for Michael. He was the Defendant. He had Tim, Ben, Josh and a few more in his team. And the other attorney was Gabriel

Malcolm, well known in this profession in the Kingdom, who probably had been hired by Williams using a lot of his father's mugged wealth. Malcolm was the claimant. As expected, he had the two companion soldiers of Williams, a few more that Michael had seen in the forest, and a few more that Michael did not know in his team.

As Michael arrived and took his position, the messenger announced to introduce him.

"Michael Chapman, swordsman-horseman from the seventh regiment of the South Tower, convicted for murders of Jim Cook and Charles Hooper, the two gardeners of the garden in the North Bailey of the stronghold, on 15th September night," he announced.

Till now, Michael had been thinking, or rather hoping, that all these just were a part of a very bad dream - a nightmare. But, he totally realised the reality now. Everyone in this large hall was paying undeviated attention to him. A part of them was here to see him get a release or at least a conditional bail. But, a big part was here to see him getting incarcerated for life or even worse, getting a death penalty. But, this still was not the worst part.

During the medieval century England, there were many methods of death penalty common in the society. These methods varied with myriad techniques involved. Some of these were used to assassinate a convicted witch, some were used to kill a mass murderer, some were for a rapist and many more. One common feature of all of these methods of death penalty, or should I just call them different types of murders, was that they all were inhuman and involved with unbearable torture. For example, one method involved wiping out nails of fingers and toes before cutting them off. This method was used to kill a witch or someone who was possessed by a demon. Another method of torture involved gutting the convicted on flame when he or she still was alive. All of these had resulted in from superstitions and lack of education. Although, most of these inhuman practices had been abolished during the previous King's reign, some of them still were present in the darkest of the poorest sides of the society. And some citizens still were proponent of these practices and of bringing the abolished ones back. There were such kinds of people in Michael Chapman's trial as well.

Daniel started. He gave a brief introduction of himself and then said, "Your Majesty, I know Michael for almost two years. I have seen his dedication to his Kingdom. I have seen him putting his life in the line for all of us. He has been on critical missions, may be for more number of times than most of the soldiers of your military. He had gladly accepted a seemingly suicidal mission to the Forest of Death. He cannot just kill two citizens of the Kingdom he is born to serve. I, as the Commander of one of your regiments, strongly and confidently state to release Michael Chapman, unconditionally."

"Not so fast, Commander," Daniel was interrupted by Malcolm. Now, he took the position of the stage, "Michael Chapman was found red-handed with the beheaded poor Mr. Cook and Mr. Hooper. Diagnosis by eminent physicians has proved that Michael Chapman was in drugs. That happened from having excessive alcohol and smoking. It was the wedding night. Michael Chapman was assigned duty in the wedding hall. He surely had those drinks there. And after leaving the castle, he went to the North Bailey, got into a verbal disagreement with the two poor men. And then he killed those unarmed men."

-"It is a total lie, Your Majesty!" Daniel was not willing to give space to his counterpart. He said, "Michael had drinks, excessively might be. But that was not the reason behind the murders. We, the soldiers, frequently have much stronger rum.

Michael also is used to them. During the wedding night, we had costly wines. They were weak as drinks. They were not strong enough to cause any hangover to Michael."

"So why do you think Mr. Chapman killed the poor men?" Malcolm talked to Daniel like he was laughing at his amateur counterpart for speaking something totally rubbish. But Daniel was smart to reply back.

"Michael was attacked by Mr. Cook and Mr. Hooper. Apparently, they had thought that Michael had something costly with him as he was returning from the wedding. And Michael's horse was in the South Bailey. The only way to escape the situation unscathed was to kill them," he said.

"And what was Michael doing in the North Bailey when his horse was in South?" Malcolm asked.

Now it was Daniel's turn to undermine Malcolm. He laughed and said, "Why? Is there a rule that Michael Chapman cannot go to the North Bailey?"

Malcolm did not lose his cool. The end of the judgement was a long way to go. He was, therefore, calm and was slowly pulling the thread to catch its end.

"So, what do you think, Commander? What was the reason behind Mr. Chapman's unusual behaviour when he was caught? And again when he was under custody? If he was not in hangover, why was he sick and acting like he was crazy?" Malcolm asked.

-"Michael is a devoted soldier. He had wine excessively but it was not strong enough to cause hangover to him. On that night, unfortunately, Michael had to kill two citizens. He took it like a shock which triggered the hangover and sickened his health."

Now it was the time to bring the witnesses and support for their statements. Malcolm's first witness was a physician who had tested Michael. He gave his alibi on why and how much Michael had been intoxicated.

Daniel asked for permission to question this witness. And the permission was granted.

"Doctor, how critical do you think Michael's condition was?" he asked.

"Very critical," the witness replied.

-"And what is your status? How good are you as a doctor?"

-"What do you mean? I am not good enough to test and treat such a critical condition? Do you need to see proof of my qualifications?" the witness was angry after being insulted in front of everyone.

"Have you ever treated someone suffering from a cold?" Daniel was calm.

-"Yes, I have. Many times."

"Tell me. What is the only cause by which one can get a cold?" Daniel asked.

-"Only cause? There are so many causes. Getting a cold in the cold weather, getting a cold by getting wet in rain or sweat in hot weather. There are more."

-"So according to you, there are so many causes behind a simple case of getting cold but only one for getting such a condition like what Michael had?"

It was totally unexpected for the physician to be questioned like that by a mere soldier. It also was insulting for him to be questioned from the domain he himself had mastered in. Daniel said again, "Can you deny that a little alcohol and a lot of mental shock can also cause such a trauma?" The witness had to answer.

Malcolm came to his witness's rescue. He said, "So, Mr. Chapman is a strong soldier who even has gone into the Forest of Death. Still, he got such traumatized by seeing two dead bodies where I am sure that he has seen many during his missions."

"Your Majesty, Mr. Malcolm is unnecessarily interrupting when I am talking to the witnesses," Daniel expressed his annoyance. It basically was a strategy of gaining advantage in the house. And he was successful. "Mr. Malcolm, you will have your time," said the King forbidding him from interrupting.

Now Malcolm asked for permission to ask questions directly to Michael.

"Mr. Chapman," he started, "on that night, we went to the North Bailey. But your horse was on South Bailey. Why?"

"I have heard that there is a beautiful garden with a statue of a guardian angel in there. I went to behold it in the night," said Michael. As directed by Daniel, he did not say anything about his meeting with Williams. Proving the possible treason was impossible at this stage and trying to do so would make them lose the ground under their feet on the case.

-"But you had duty on the South Bailey. You are a devoted soldier. Still, you went to enjoy the scenery instead of going to your duty."

-"I had some time to spare."

-"That is suspicious. If you were devoted to your duties, you would have spent the time performing your duties. May be in the wedding hall or in the South Bailey."

"Are you trying to question my professionalism?" Michael got fired up. He said, "I have joined the army almost two years ago. Since then, I have performed many duties, many missions. More than the person who has paid for you. I have been to the Forest of Death. I have faced things in there that you cannot even imagine." Michael turned to the audience and continued, "Death is easy. It is a way of escaping. Many soldiers die in missions. People die every day. We all see someone dying at least once a year since our birth that it becomes a common phenomenon in our lives. Still, we fear for it. This is because we fear for what comes before death. The pain, and when we see the grim reapers. When I was in the forest, I saw the grim reapers, thousands of them. The hounds which were there to snatch me to the other side of Hell's Gate, to the Purgatory. I was experiencing death with every step forward. Still, I did not abandon my duty, my comrades. That is my patriotism."

There was a strange environment created within the house with Michael's speech. People were silent and also discussing loudly amongst themselves on what they had just heard from the convicted.

Malcolm said in Michael's context, "You keep on saying about your fake patriotism. But we all know that you are not from here. You are, by birth from a far north, and have spent majority of your time in London."

Now, Michael had no answer to it and Daniel had to come to his assistance, "My Lord, Mr. Malcolm is asking my client too many personal questions." It worked a little for the time being as the King warned Malcolm.

One of the two companion soldiers of Williams came this time for his statement. He stated that they had found Michael, on that night, in the garden of the North Bailey with the two dead bodies. Daniel asked permission to ask him questions.

"What were you doing in the North Bailey?" he asked.

"I had duty on the castle ground. And I guess you know that the North Bailey is a part of it," the soldier replied.

Daniel understood that interrogating him was not going to be an easy job. He was going to defend himself and hide information. So, Daniel decided to go rough, "So, you found Michael with the two dead bodies. Right?"

-"Correct!"

-"So, it is also true that you did not see him murdering them. Correct?"

-"There was no one else. Who else could it be?"

-"Anyone else could have been! It could have been someone else and Michael just was the first one to find the victims when you arrived. Or, as we are saying, there could have been a clash and Michael had to kill them to save himself."

-"We saw blood on his sword. And he definitely was in hangover."

-"That is because he killed them as a self-defence and the shock traumatised him."

Josh came next to give his statement. He stated that he and some other soldiers had seen Michael and his condition had not been that serious. The statements regarding Michael's condition had been exaggerated, he said.

Malcolm got the permission of interrogation. "You just said that when you saw Mr. Chapman, it was about an hour from the murders. Can you deny it that even a strong hangover can lose its strength by then?" he asked. He strategically used the word 'murders' and tried to prove the Michael had been under drugs while killing.

"Look, there is no point in answering this question. Michael was not in drugs," Josh was stubborn.

But Malcolm was not a person to give up. He was someone who would cut the flesh with a blunt knife to get to the bones.

"Commander Daniel is saying that the seemingly hangover-like condition that Mr. Chapman suffered was due to trauma. You certainly have seen that condition as you were one of the firsts to notice him. How could you differentiate between intoxicated Michael Chapman and Michael Chapman in a trauma?" Malcolm asked.

It was a very tough question to Josh. It was something related to medical science and even if Michael were in a trauma, Josh in reality would not have figured out whether he had been in hangover or something else.

"I understood it as Michael still was conscious. He was talking, a bit vague though. And he was upset with the killings," Josh tried something that was not good enough.

Malcolm witted offensively, "Each of them a property of a headless drunk!"

The trail ended for that day without a proper result. It was postponed to the next day. Michael went back to his cell and Daniel went with him. Tim and Ben also wanted to go but they were not allowed to.

"You were really great out there," Michael praised Daniel thankfully.

"And do not forget, it was only my first time," Daniel took the pride.

-"You could have a good career even in law."

"What do you think? How did today go? Advantage on our side? Or theirs?" asked Daniel.

"I think today was equal for both the sides," Michael was unbiased although it was natural for him to get inclined, at least to hope, to say that they had the vantage.

"Let me tell you about our strategy for tomorrow. Tomorrow, I will bring on Tim as a witness. And Ben and some others as our supporters. Tim is the one who had seen you the last before you left on the wedding night. He is our trump card," Daniel was ambitious.

On that night, Michael brought up some time, in the lonely cell, to think about his present situation and recent past. He was thinking about what his friends were doing in order to save him. He already had thanked Daniel and asked to convey gratefulness to the others. Daniel, however, had thanked him instead by saying, "It is you who should be thanked. You have risked your life to find out about the upcoming war. Even right now, it is you who is suffering. It is again because you have risked your life to find the news of the war. You have done enough already. Now it is our duty to save you. And I promise, I swear, I will save you."

For the first time in a while, Michael thought of Rose. He had done something terrible to her. And he called himself her friend. He had not even apologised. Now, he was wanting to leave this confining cell, probably by breaking out from here, run towards the Greathall of the castle, and to Rose's room, knock at the door and as she would open, hug and hold her so tight under arms that she could not break free, and tell, "Never leave me."

"I wish I had a cigar now," he thought.

On the next day, the trial continued at the scheduled time. Tim came to give his statement at the first.

Tim said that Michael had been with him before leaving the wedding hall. He also said that Michael had been in a perfectly normal condition, without any trace of high intoxication. He argued that after leaving, Michael had gone to the castle grounds for his later duties. And he had not taken any more liquor to get more wasted. Thus, Tim supported, as a witness, that the cause of the strong hangover certainly had been the well discussed shock.

Malcolm took over to question Tim. He asked, "Tim, as per I have heard, you also had the duty together with Michael in the castle grounds. So, what were you doing? Why did you not join Michael?"

"Because I was hungry and I was eating," Tim answered to Malcolm's face, keeping unblinking eye contact, with laudable confident.

"You were eating?" Malcolm almost shouted. And said, "It was an important day and you were wasting time by eating, leaving your duties?" He then turned back to the King and continued, "I am sorry Your Majesty, but I don't think Tim is eligible to pay a statement here at this stage."

"Why?" Tim was not willing to give up. "That day, Michael and I were performing back to back duties since the morning. It is natural to get that hungry and take a break. Let us see if today's trial goes till night. And we will see how devoted you are. Let us see if you can perform your duty by not taking a break and having a meal," he said while emphasizing different parts of his own speech.

The audience liked his speech. Someone as young as Tim was successful to defend Malcolm's offense and perform a perfect counterattack. Even Malcolm could not reply to this. And the audience laughed at Malcolm.

The humiliation triggered Malcolm. He quickly brought up many paper works and a team of some villagers from the audience. This was going to be his trump card. This was going to be his final and deadliest strategy. It was almost the end game of the chess. And at last, Malcolm had attained the pieces formation he had been wanting to have. He had the full control of the centre now, the most crucial and delicate position of the board. And all of his pieces had the tempo or single move advantage to attack the opposite King.

The villagers, who were brought up to the stage, mostly were women; some of them were old, some were young.

Malcolm started to introduce them to the rest of the people in the hall, "Your Majesty, respected juries, my fellow attorney and everyone else in this courthouse," Malcolm was shouting in excitement. "The two poor men killed during the unfortunate incident were from a squalor village at the South-East. These are the families of them."

And then he handed those paper works to Daniel, his counterpart, and said again, "And these are the names, ages, occupations and addresses of all the people in the village and even in outskirts who think that Mr. Cook and Mr. Hooper could never attack anyone, specially a soldier of their country.

They were true gentlemen, and devoted citizens. Yes, they were poor. But they could never do a nefarious job like that! Today, I have their families with me. And a list of about two hundred other villagers on support of me. I have collected these data only yesterday. So, think about it, if I had a time span of a week, how many more of these citizens would be here with me? Please allow these poor wives, sisters and daughters to speak!"

One by one, each of the women went in front of the King, bowed and gave her statement. They recently had lost their husband, brother or father and the moments were very daunting to them. They tried not to break down in front of the audience, but some of them failed miserably. And others had to go to comfort them. The entire hall was stunned and speechless, listening to these women with undeviated concentration. And at the end of their statements, Michael, Daniel and their team had no idea on how to tackle the power of true love and honesty.

One speech that the people liked a lot came from Mr. Cook's eldest daughter. She talked stories from her own life and she talked about the times she had spent with her father.

"My father was poor. But that never forced him to commit evils. Neither did it stop him from loving us, his family. On last Christmas, we had a fancy day with Christmas Tree, presents and delicious meals. My father bought dresses for everyone in the family, except for himself. And for that, to earn the sufficient money, he had to work hard for two months. After his job in here, he worked overtime in mills. My father loved people and was loved by people. Although we had a small family with the parents and three daughters, our small house was almost always filled with people. That is because my father liked inviting people over to our house, for a meal or drink or a game. The occasions in our house were simple, but lovely.

My father had a little number of clothes, shoes and only one hat. This was not due to poverty, but as my father was a very simple man with no high desire for himself. However, he had high hopes with his three daughters. And so he never let any financial or social drawback to come in the way of his daughters' happiness. But, after all, he never considered theft or robbery as ways of earning. My father was a true Christian. He worshipped God. He feared God. Heinous undergoing are crimes by law to people, but for him they were forbidden by God. I don't personally know this convicted soldier who murdered my father. I feel grudge against him now. But, I also am a true Christian, at least I try to be so. And that is why, I will not think or wish bad of this man, even though he has killed my father. My family will never be the same again. The loss is overwhelming to us. But, still I will oppose the death penalty of this man. All I want to say is, he is lying. My father did not attack him for money or anything else."

The entire courthouse was in a pin drop silence after the speech. The loquacious audience was silent. Daniel was shut up. And Michael was wanting to run back to the Forest of Death and let the hounds to catch him, tear him apart, break his bones with their sharp teeth and strong jaws, and take him to hell. He was standing within the confined wooden chamber with his head down. For the moment, he forgot that it was not him who had killed Mr. Cook and his friend. He was thinking he was the one culpable and so he deserved the penalty.

Daniel was in delusion. He had no idea what to speak. He looked at the King and the juries. Their faces were not tale-telling much. But, they were not looking satisfied with Michael and him too. With every passing second, they were losing the ground underneath. And he had to speak something to turn the heat around. However, his head was completely blank, and he could not think clearly. Yet, he had to talk anything before it was too late.

"We still don't know if Mr. Cook and Mr. Hooper were intoxicated," he gave an aimless try.

"Why don't you admit that Mr. Chapman was the one intoxicated!" Malcolm shouted at Daniel this time.

"Please keep the calm," the King himself said. "I almost am close to giving the judgement. Now, I need to hear what the jury team talks," he said.

The jury was in its discussion to construe the judgement to their final decision. They were about to speak but Michael himself was the one to speak first.

Michael understood the possible fate. He realised their mistakes. For the last couple of days, Daniel, Michael and the others had tried it all to penetrate into the opposition's territory. But, during the time, they had remained oblivious to the fact that their own King's position was under threat. Their ignorance had resulted in the next perpetual checks to their King and a possible checkmate in recent future. Right now, they had to perform sacrifices to save the King, even if it meant to sacrifice the mighty Queen. But, Michael remembered that he also had a final Jack in his hands - his final trump card. He remembered about his passed pawn on the board and he could convert it to a mightier piece. He could not save the game anymore, but could surely go for a stalemate.

He knew it was the time to say. And he knew that people might not believe in him. But he did not stammer nor did he go faint.

"You do not know the entire picture. Almost nobody in this house knows. What you are seeing is only the corner of the entire portrait. And it is only the river, but what you are not seeing is the vast ocean which is connected to the river. When I am in my tent in my regiment at night, looking at the North sky, I can only see the summit of the South Tower. But what I cannot see is how gigantic this whole stronghold is. I cannot see the other three Towers. I cannot see the tall walls protecting what is inside from outside for years. Neither can I see the castle grounds, nor the Greathall. But they are here. They exist, and their existence does not care about my ability to perceive it. The case against me is the same today. You are looking at me as the murderer. If I have killed Mr. Cook and Mr. Hooper. But did I really? What if they were killed by someone else? Can you assure me, each one of you who are proposing for my final penalty, that you can go to sleep knowing that you did not send one innocent person to the hanging floor while the true convict is out there in the fresh air? Can you assure me that this case is only about murders and nothing more convoluted is involved? If you ask me, I will say that this thread is long, longer than what you think, and the other end of it is buried in commendable depth under the ground. And now, I am going to address a certain somebody who is afraid of being present in this very courthouse. Your disgusting plan will never work. Because, you can pass a jungle when the pack of wolves is sleeping. But, you cannot even dare to enter if you hear a howling. I, hereby, promise you, that right now you are hearing this howling. Do not enter into the jungle. Do not start it. Because if you start it, all of you will die. We will kill you, I swear to Jesus. We will jeopardize your very existence."

Michael said it with confidence and accentuating with articulation while attempting to attack Williams who was not present in the house like the previous day.

A few of the many people present in the hall knew what Michael was referring to. And all of them took this differently. For example, Daniel was thinking of stopping Michael. Revealing everything was not their intention for two big reasons. One, almost nobody was going to believe that the soldiers themselves were going to commit treason and so it would not be fruitful to reveal. Second, by not revealing everything, they were hoping to give the soldiers, still within this Kingdom and involved in the treachery, the time of escaping. Thus, the Kingdom itself would get some minimum time to prepare itself against the inevitable war.

Malcolm took Michael's speech differently. He already knew about the upcoming war and he needed to stop Michael from revealing everything. Malcolm did not care much about the war and the Kingdom. His job was to sue Michael and bring him down. Williams already had paid a lot to him and was going to pay more later. As soon as Michael was going to get the death penalty, Malcolm was willing to take his wealth and run away to far North before the war would emerge. Thus, this very moment was troublesome to him for his own sake. And he needed to stop Michael. So, he made a desperate attempt by saying, "Mr. Chapman, we are already at the end of the trial. Your attorney cannot put any stronger alibi to save you. Now it is the time to listen to the judgement from the juries and the final judgment from His Majesty. So, I beg you, please stop saying anymore nonsense."

"Shut up, you scoundrel!" Michael yelled at Malcolm. He was impervious to the opponent attorney. "I am telling you what nonsense is."

Malcolm turned towards the King and appealed, "Your Majesty, I request you to give us the final judgment."

"Wait, Mr. Malcolm," Ray and Walther said in unison. "Let him say."

"No!" Malcolm knew the risk and so he became more desperate, "It is over for him. Hence, he is going to talk nonsense. I, as an experienced attorney, suggest you not to listen to him."

"Stop, Mr. Malcolm," this time Black said out. Black was also in the jury. "Tell us what you want to say, Michael," he said. He definitely had found something important hidden in Michael's speech.

Michael was going to say it. Daniel, Ben, Tim, Josh and the others in favour of Michael also knew that he had no other way of escaping the penalty.

All of them had to stop talking.

Two women were there who had stood up from the audience. They were wearing black cloaks and hoods all over their bodies. They came forward at the centre of the Hall, close to Michael. Daniel and other soldiers brought out their swords and alerted them.

Even Black ordered, "Show yourselves and get away from the convicted. Do not force us to attack you. You are surrounded by soldiers and King's Men."

"That will not be necessary, Commander," one of the two women said. It was a familiar voice to Michael that he was hearing after a long time. She opened the hood, and so did her companion. It was Molly, and the other one was Rose.

"I would like to give my statement as the only witness present in there when the incident happened," Rose said.

Malcolm and his team did not like it. They were afraid that Rose was going to disclose the reality. So, they protested by saying that no team had previously accounted her as a witness.

"Mr. Malcolm, are you afraid of the reality?" Molly's voice was cold.

"No. I am not afraid of the reality. The reality is already here in front of us. And she is the Princess. It was the wedding night. She did not go to the North Bailey leaving the wedding," Malcolm said.

"Are you inferring that your Princess is a liar?" Rose asked him. Malcolm had no more way of interfering.

The entire hall of audience, soldiers, attorneys, witnesses, supporters, juries, the King and Michael himself were surprised. They did not know what was going to happen next. The audience were baffled to find that the Princess herself had been sitting beside them in disguise. And they did not know what she was going to state.

Michael had many questions amassing and making crowds within his head. What was going on? When did Molly come back? Where had she gone? And why was she with the Princess? As per Michael knew, these two women had never met each other. Did Rose really know the reality? But why was she here to save him after what he had done to her?

"We have been here since the morning and we have heard what everyone has spoken. I can guess what the bench is going to state as its final judgment and I must predict that it is unfair," Rose said.

Both of Michael and Malcolm could not believe their ears. Michael was silent but Malcolm tried to protest again.

"Mr. Malcolm, you can try to interrupt and waste all of our time. But the final judgment will not be announced until the Princess gives her statement," Molly was clear to Malcolm.

Rose continued as Malcolm realised that all of his further endeavours were going to go in vain.

"I was in there when the incident occurred. I saw Mr. Chapman in the North Bailey. And the dead bodies of Mr. Cook and Mr. Hooper were there too. And Mr. Chapman was wasted. So far what I just said is not different from what Mr. Malcolm has been saying. The big difference comes now as I am going to say it. Mr. Cook and Mr. Hooper were already killed when Mr. Chapman and I reached at the place of crime. Mr. Chapman was intoxicated but he got aware of what was in front of him. And so he started to find out the culprit.

Unfortunately, at that moment, two more soldiers came. And they misunderstood the entire situation," Rose said.

A silence dominated the hall for a long time. All the surprised faces were looking at Rose and Molly. And everyone, especially the family members of the deceased, was in opaque delusion.

The King himself broke the long pause. He asked his daughter, "Do you know who killed the two men?"

"No father, I do not know that. I was not there to witness the assassinations," Rose replied.

"Then how do you know that it was not Mr. Chapman?" Malcolm asked as a form of interrogation.

"Because I had followed him from the wedding hall to the North Bailey. I needed to talk to him," she replied.

-"Why did you need to meet a soldier like him, my Lady?"

-"I don't think I am forced to say that. But I am glad that you asked. I was going to ask him if he could teach me horse riding."

-"Don't you think it was not an appropriate time for the question? And why would you want to learn horse riding?"

"Mr. Malcolm, you are again implying that your Princess is a liar. And why I want to learn it is none of your business," Rose was rough. And Malcolm acknowledged defeat by stopping further questioning.

"Then can someone tell me why a confident and commendable soldier like Mr. Chapman was acting crazy upon seeing the dead bodies? I think he was too drunk to be on duty. I think he should be prosecuted anyway for such irresponsibility," one of the two fellow soldiers of Williams broke the code of conduct and asked the last question despite not being an attorney.

There was a small verbal war amongst the people present, including Daniel and Malcolm. They were fighting on if this question was valid to be asked as it had not come from any of the defendant and claimant attorneys.

"I think I must answer," Molly said as Rose left her position for Molly. She continued while looking at the jury, "I am the commander and coach of Michael for almost two years. And I have seen the strongest as well as the weakest Michael. I, as his coach, know what troubles him the most at a warfront. And, I am not going to reveal it. But, I request you to believe in me. I, Commander Molly Pivot Wheeler, request you to believe in one of your soldiers who has been serving you for about seven years. Michael's craziness was some aftermath of his weakness and it was very natural. However, I also request you not to ask anything about the weakness and I want you to understand that I will never betray his weak points in front of probable enemies." She had a cold glare at Malcolm and his team.

The jury took its time now. At the end of the members' discussion, Ray gave their statement.

"We declare Michael Chapman as innocent. And we also appeal for thorough investigation to find out the actual culprits," Ray said.

The judgement ended in favour of Michael. The King, Rose and the jury left the place with the King's Men. Then vast audience also started to leave. In the entropy, Michael could not find Molly.

"She must have left with Rose," he thought.

He wanted to meet both of them, ask for forgiveness and thank them for everything.

Daniel and the others escorted Michael out of the house. A big part of the citizens not satisfied with the judgement were yelling and firing slangs at them. They kept shouting and cursing the soldiers while the soldiers were leaving the place. One big reason behind their disappointment was not caused by the judgement but was due to the lack of fulfilment of their expectations from the military. Most of these people believed in superstitions and were believers of the fallacy that all of their social and financial insecurities were caused by the curses of the Forest of Death. For a long time, these people and also their ancestors had believed that the military was going to defeat the evil inside the forest and win them their wheat and corn that were being snatched away from them for more than half a century. Without being aware of the status of other kingdoms and independent states of the Great Island, these people had assumed that they had been suffering unnecessarily for long only because of the forest. And they had expected that their mighty soldiers should have won against the forest by that present time. So, this was the time when they started to question the progress of the war against the forest and also why the soldiers were wasting so much time on useless and even malicious stuff like getting involved in murders of Mr. Cook and Mr. Hooper.

When Michael returned to the seventh regiment of the South, at first he went to Molly's tent. Then he went to the other nearby places where she could have been. The places included the training grounds, the armouries and the army memorial grounds where stones had been carved with the names of fallen and lost soldiers from many periods of time. But he could not find her. Now, Michael was sure that something was odd.

"Molly is here within the kingdom. She may be here for sufficiently long time. But why is she not in the regiment?" he asked himself.

"Has she resigned? Is it really because of something that I have done? Or, is there something else?" he asked more.

After all, he did not know what had happened. And he did not know where to find her. So far since Molly had gone,

Michael could mitigate his restive mind by thinking that Molly had been on a mission. He had thought that it was not something that he had done. But now, he was not sure of his thought anymore. And he could hardly try to convince himself anymore by thinking on these lines.

On the next few days, Michael, along with Daniel, met and tried to meet some important people in the authorities. They did not have much time to spare. They could see in front of their own eyes that some soldiers of the military were going missing. Certainly, these soldiers were leaving the Kingdom to join the army of the opposition. Fortunately, none of these traitors was from the seventh regiment of the South.

The days became very arduous to spend for Michael and his friends. They had to escape away from the cursing eyes of many civilians and the stigma that had been caused. Moreover, they had to win the trust of the authorities before informing them of the news that was hard to believe in the first place. Even someone who found Michael trustworthy would ask for how genuine the information was and had to verify if it was not one ingenious and vicious plan of Michael himself. Anyone could call Michael and his friends rebellious by misunderstanding them.

On the next Monday, Michael returned to the castle as a free man to his duty. And he did not know that it was going to be his last duty in the South Tower before the long warfare. It was the last time in a while when Michael enjoyed the night sky and the ambience from the peak of the tower.

The night sky was different tonight and it reminded Michael that winter was close. There were clouds in the sky, covering the moon and the millions of stars. Michael had to wait for them to clear away to get the glimpse of the extra-terrestrial beauties again, and to watch the Stardusts in the Starshine. His old friend, the white owl was also less frequent tonight. It might be ignoring the meets with Michael like most of the civilians of the villages. Or, it simply might be foraging more in the Forest of Death, the Forbidden One.

Michael thought of Rose. *"Can I meet her again? Will everything become normal again for us? If the Almighty gives me another chance of meeting her, and if she gives me another chance by accepting me, I will make everything alright once again. But, do I deserve to get the chances?"*

And he wrote:

The warmth of air and arms was broken, torn apart
By the intruders from the northern rocks, invading the land
That we belonged to, once; the fate of time has played
Its ultimatum, when the time has stopped for me.
The inundating wind calling the capricious, accompanying
Followed the snow, that faded the road to you
The leaves have left so long ago from the Tree,
And the mistletoe? It is no more...

Looking back to the days and night, I don't regret anymore
'Cause waking up by your side - they aren't just the memories,
And the memories of your voice, the touch of your arms
That I still feel now, they aren't any surreal imaginations,
I am holding the sublimes, and these are holding my
Ephemeral time; Again, I am not letting them slip away,
Again; Now, if you say Goodbye, that will be okay,
'Cause I will be waiting for you, anyway.

The rocks beneath the Northern Sky will make the pass again
For the wind, that will bring us the news of Christmas,
The snow will answer again, making the bridge - my credence
And my road to you - that I will take and run and run
I will never stop, until I get to you, and your arms
No turning back, until the Tree, where mistletoe will proliferate again.

The lesson that the past passed upon me, lessens my strength -
Irresolution, but, when you hold my hand, rewind the time, I will walk
Through the isles that the trees, snows and falling leaves make
"Close your eyes, because I am just a kiss away".
Your smile placates, mollifies all animosity I've gained
So, don't say Goodbye, because I'm waiting to be by you, again...

9

"I Want You to be the King's Man"

The meeting was confidential. And it had been going on for a long time. Only a few people were present in this not-so-much explored room of the Greathall in the stronghold. There were the King, Commander Black and Walther. And there were the commanders of all the twenty-two regiments including Commander Daniel from the seventh regiment of the South. And there were Michael and Molly.

The room was situated at one corner of the Greathall and was restricted from being accessed by anyone else. Unlike the other rooms and halls of the Greathall, this room was small and had not many reasons to attract interest from others. And unlike other rooms and halls, this one was not decorated at all. One could easily misunderstand this room with a temporary shelter of a hunter. It was not in any usage for a long span and thus had become dark and wet. There was only one big table in here and the people present were sitting around it.

The agenda of the meeting, that is, the reason for calling it in a sudden notice by confirming and performing the acts to keep the secrecy was clear to everyone present. And it was like an explosion. At first nobody believed in it.

It is hard for us humans to accept a harsh truth that we do not like. And we force ourselves not to believe in it. We force ourselves to think that no, it is not happening. We try to postpone the inevitable final point when we have no other choice but to accept the fact from which we were running away. But with time, things get more and more inundating. And we need to force ourselves more than before just to keep running away from the omen of truth. And thus, when we will have to accept it, it already will have become insufferable - the tiny tumour will have become a life-threatening cancer.

The commanders of the different regiments were unwilling to accept Michael's information for mainly two reasons. Firstly, they were trying not to accept that some of their own soldiers had betrayed them, the Kingdom and the King. The soldiers of the regiments were always thought to be patriotic who could sacrifice their lives in the blink of an eye for their King. More than fifty years ago, many soldiers had sacrificed themselves to save the future of this Kingdom and their legacy was supposed to be flowing like boiling lava to this course of time. Unfortunately, the fact was something different and anyone would try to run away from it. The treason of these soldiers had shaken the entire foundation of the soldiers' oath. Secondly, the joining of these soldiers with the enemies was dangerous. Not only this was going to be strengthening the enemies but also was going to supply much top secret information about this Kingdom's forte and fear. But this was something that the commanders could not run away from, as the proof was already in front of them.

"A total of a hundred soldiers have gone missing till now for the last three days. And today only, this number was more than thirty," Molly informed.

"So the number is increasing day by day," a commander from the North expressed his concern.

"How many do you think will go tomorrow? Fifty?" another one from the East asked.

"If this continues, we will run out of soldiers. Will only the commanders and the King's Men fight?" another one from the West said.

"Speaking about the King's Men, has anyone from them gone missing?" asked the commander of the first regiment of the South.

"No," Molly and Black said in unison.

"They will not," Michael said. Everyone turned to Michael.

"Are you sure?" the King asked.

"Yes," Michael was confident.

"Look son, we all understand that the King's Men are the strongest, most dedicated and are sworn to protect the King. But that doesn't mean every one of them is fully trustworthy. And besides, look at what is going on beside us. Our own brothers are joining the enemies. In this circumstance, how can you be so sure about that?" another commander of the East asked.

-"Can you remember who the mastermind behind this civil war is?"

"Yes. It is David Williams of the sixth regiment of the South," the commander of the sixth regiment of the South himself admitted his failure.

-"When I was almost fighting against him on the wedding night, he told me something that I can remember very clearly. He was offering me to join him and said that we would be decimating the entire King's Men army and reform it from the beginning. And I know he was not bluffing. This only means that the King's Men are not with him."

"Then it is very reassuring. The King's Men are not only the strongest but they share the darkest secrets of this castle, including all the secret passages of escaping or counterattack.

They also are aware of many confidential policies and laws of the Kingdom," Walther said for the first time.

"What is our total strength?" the King asked.

"About eleven hundred soldiers from the twenty-two regiments, about a hundred soldiers in the castle, fifty King's Men, and about five hundred more in the cities," Walther presented the data.

"Subtract the summation by hundred of the ones who have left," Molly reminded.

"So, it gives us a little more than fifteen hundred," Daniel said.

"What is the estimated strength of the enemy?" the King asked.

"I think it is fair to assume that the unprecedented soldiers will be there too. There are thousands of them. Then there will be at least five or six hundred of the French and pirates. Then there are hundreds of our soldiers with them," Molly said.

"There can be even more of them. This time they are going for an all-out attack," Michael said.

"One big concern. Do you people think that more of our soldiers will leave us soon? Or, even worse, will they betray us from being inside the system?" a commander of one regiment of West asked.

"I do not think any more of them will leave. The number of them escaping today was high and alerting. Thus, the army is getting aware. An endeavour of leaving the army can be caught red handed now. I do not think the opposite side is this fool to take the risk. However, I am not sure what to say about your second question," Walther said.

"How many days do you think we have left?" a commander from the North asked.

"A couple. As I just said, I don't think any more soldiers will escape. The thirty of them who escaped today will need a whole day to reach the end of the forest. And tomorrow, they will take a break and then start attacking on the next day," Walther said.

"What happened to your opposite attorney, Michael?" another commander asked.

"Mr. Malcolm. He has fled away. I tried to find him but I couldn't," Michael replied.

"We need more soldiers, don't we?" the King was pragmatic and concerned.

"Yes. Five hundred more. And I request you to recruit from the personal soldiers of the rich men of the cities and from the eligible lads and men," Molly suggested.

"I am not going to recruit common citizens. I don't want to make the same mistake as King Phillip V," the King said.

-"My Lord, you do know that King Phillip V also had no other way than recruiting from the common citizens. And you need to do it too. Otherwise, it is over for all of us."

-"How can some common citizens make a difference in the war?"

-"As we say the phrase - every blood counts."

"But how can we recruit five hundred soldiers in two days? And we cannot even ask for help from our friend nations," asked a commander.

"I want you people to leave the recruitment process to Daniel and me. We will head to the cities right now for it. And yes, we cannot ask for help from other nations. Our messenger will need at least a week to reach to our closest neighbour. We don't have that much time," Molly said. Molly had not talked with Daniel about it beforehand. But she, although was not the commander of him anymore, had full right to command him. So, Daniel accepted the duty without a second thought.

"Michael, if I can't make it before the war begins, Ben and you will guide our soldiers of the regiment to the war. Talk to Ben about it," Daniel asked Michael. And thus Michael became the Second in Command of the seventh regiment of the South.

"How is our evacuation going on?" Walther asked.

"Fine, Sir. Our soldiers of the seven regiments of the South are working day and night," informed the commander of the fourth regiment of the South.

The meeting ended here. The people returned to their jobs with an emergency notice. Some went to gather their soldiers, some went to evacuate the citizens of the villages, some went to recruit and some went to armouries as they needed to make at least five hundred good quality armours by the next day. At first, Michael tried to catch Molly and talk to her. He needed to ask her why she had been avoiding him lately. But Molly was in a hurry. So she just said, "Michael, I will talk to you when I come back." And then she left with Daniel.

Michael did not know what was going on in Molly's mind. He wanted to call her mental. And he was a little angry with her as well. But, he did not have much time to worry about these now.

On the other side, Tim and many other soldiers of the regiments of the South were involved in evacuation of the citizens of the villages in front of the Forest of Death, the Forbidden One. They had to make it quick. And so they only allowed the villagers to take clothes and a little food. They constantly requested them to leave their ornaments. The villagers were abandoning their homes. They were frightened. They knew that a storm was coming and this calm was the indication of it. But they did not know what the storm exactly was going to be. Many of them were taking shelter in the cities and many were taking shelter within the stronghold. Aids of food, clothes and medicines were arranged from the King's authority.

Long queues could be seen even from a long distance. One could see the poor villagers, men and women and children, walking towards the north. They were frightened and hungry. But they were almost silent. Only the children were crying. Their clothes were dirty. Their pots were empty. Their feet were bare. But, these could arise no concern to them. They were running away to survive. And sometimes, they were looking at the sky to predict if the rain was coming. The scene generated a flashback in Michael's eyes: the time when he had lived at the slum of London and had to leave the slum with the other poor residents during monsoons and winters.

As Michael returned to his regiment, he talked to Ben. He told him about the meeting. He also told him that Molly and Daniel had gone to the job and so Ben was the new commander now. After updating him, Michael went into the workshop in the seventh regiment of the South. It had been a long time. Actually, his last time was years ago, during his days in London. And tonight, he was back to his old job. Tonight he picked up a hammer, not a sword. They had to make at least fifty armours and swords before the next night.

The picture of the next day was no different. The whole Kingdom had heard of the upcoming war. There were talks about it amongst people. Some were afraid that it was the end of their lives. Some were hopeful that the soldiers were going to save them. But everyone was sure that it was going to cost many lives and a lot of blood. They also had heard of the civil war. They specially were dissatisfied with it. The King had tried to limit the spread of news. But, like a river at its strongest flow, no dam could create enough obstacle to stop the spreading of such news. One more thing that the King had to think of was panic creation amongst citizens. He tried his best to convince them not to worry about the war. Another thing was a possible junta followed by anarchy.

This time, the King had to step up literally with sharpened steel to control them.

The recruitment from the common citizens was a massacre. The military had to recruit at least three hundred of the most suitable men and lads. However, it was a lot harder than what they had expected, or rather, hoped. Most of the citizens were not only unskilled but also were unfit. They were frightened to go in a war against the unprecedented soldiers, and probably also against the undead.

Michael was there with Ben when a recruitment was undergoing. This recruitment was going on in the last village. The recruiting soldiers and commanders were trying to motivate the men and lads by saying that in the war the soldiers were ready to die alongside them for the Kingdom. But it was not helping at all. That was because a motivational speech could not enhance the skills and powers of the common citizens to fight against the mighty enemies of unprecedented soldiers. However, the motivational speeches were successfully inspiring many of the villagers, especially the young ones.

Michael saw young lads getting recruited. They were given the armours and swords. These lads were the sons of farmers, hunters, innkeepers, and shopkeepers. They had been living under the shadow of fear regarding the forest since their birth. By now, they had seen the soldiers fighting. They had made the soldiers their idols. They always had imagined how it would be like to lift a sword or wear an armour. They had played swordfight since their childhood. But today, they were given actual swords made of steel, not of wood. And it was not feeling right to them to leave their loved ones, even when they were going to do the work they always had wanted to do themselves - to fight for the nation and be heroes. They knew that it might be their last goodbye.

"Look at them. They can't fight against the thousands of unprecedented soldiers," said Ben who previously had faced those mysterious enemies.

"They just are the unfortunate decoys. The pawns born to die. However," Michael deliberately did not complete his sentence.

"Yes, however, we have no other choice. Every blood counts," Ben finished Michael's sentence.

"I think we will be outnumbered. And each of the unprecedented soldiers is equivalent to a King's Man. How can we win?" Michael said.

"We just have to win. For our fallen friends. For James and Raphael," Ben was determined.

That night, Michael slept in his tent, thinking that it was his last night in here. There were Ben and Tim with him. Daniel, with Molly, was yet to return. Before going to sleep for probably one last time, these three friends talked a lot. They talked about their childhoods, their previous lives, their motivations to join the force, etc. They also talked about their future plans which might not be going to be a reality. They even talked about their love lives. The context of Rose Scarlett was brought up. It had been days since Michael had talked to her. He was wanting to talk to her for probably one last time.

"Why did not you meet her today? I am sure she would forgive you for everything. After all, you are going to the war. And God forbid, it could be your last time seeing her," Ben said.

Michael also had wanted to meet her, for probably one last time. The whole day he was thinking about it. He had considered and reconsidered the same dilemma many times already - whether or not to meet her. But still he did not have the courage to confront her.

"We all were busy today, right? And besides, if she wanted to meet, she could have come," Michael tried to act hard to be placated.

"You are insane, brother. She is the Princess. It is the time of war. How could she come out of the castle?" Ben asked.

Michael was a little upset. He definitely had to meet her. And he was wanting to meet her right now. He was wanting to talk to her, for probably one last time, say thank you for everything and ask for forgiveness.

"I am sure we are going to win the war. And we all will survive. Our Michael will become the King's Man for his unquestionable contribution, and he and she will be back together," young Tim was enthusiastic.

Michael looked at the beautiful young face of the youngest soldier of all the military. He, for a moment, tried to remember everything that he had shared with him. At first, after James' M.I.A., when Tim had come, Michael had not been very flexible with Tim. He had been having difficulties to adapt with Tim, who certainly had not been in there to take over James' position. But the conditions had gotten better very soon. Tim had become his younger brother, where James had been the older. They had shared the tent, training sessions, and even lots of talks - personal and professional. Tim had been there in Michael's broken situations. He had been there to protect him during the trial. And obviously, he had been an amazing soldier, despite the age.

Before sleeping, Michael thought of some more things, probably for one last time. He thought about the days in this regiment, in London and in his first homeland. He thought about James and Molly. He thought about Rose. He thought about the training sessions he had together with Rose. And he said to himself, as if he was talking to her, "I will not be here for any longer. So, I will not be here anymore to help you with your swords fight. I will not be here anymore to ask you the reasons when you are upset. I need to leave and I cannot try to cheer you up anymore. So, you have to do these all by yourself. Finally, I want you to remember something important. You are the most beautiful and most wonderful girl I have ever seen."

He lit a cigar. The smoke from it was buoyancing up over his head. And it was making shapes - the shapes of the figures Michael was thinking in his head.

At last, Michael looked outside to watch the peak of the South Tower. And probably for one last time, he thought about the Stardusts in the Starshine.

The next morning, at first, Michael fed his and James' old horses. Along with the other soldiers of the regiment, then he visited the army memorial grounds. They maintained a moment of silence in there.

It was a beautiful place to sit and look at the trees, green grass and the blue sky. And the place had one spiritual touch that could heal a festering wound of mind. The friendly breeze was reminding the soldiers of their origin - Mother Nature herself. And the bees playing at the flowers were enchanting purity at the soldiers' ears.

There were shinning stones buried in the grounds with their heads up on the ground. They bore the memories of the fallen and missing soldiers since more than half a century. The names and heroic tales of these legends were carved on these well-maintained stones of memories. These handsome-looking stones were the only ones to depict to the generations to come the stories, myths and legends of the soldiers who themselves had become ideology. But, unfortunately, these stones also were humiliation; the Kingdom's worthless endeavour to ask for forgiveness from the lost and almost forgotten children of hers through the medium of lifeless stones.

All of the soldiers paying respect there were ready to be an integrated part of this land; they knew that many of them were going to be just some more names carved on some more stones at the end of the day. However, they were ready to be with their predecessors, who in their times had sacrificed everything for a peaceful future.

After returning to the regiment, they put on their armours. They talked and laughed, and smiled, probably for the last time. They helped each other to put on the armours, shared their swords and bows, gave motivational speeches and wished luck to everyone else, probably for the last time, before the deadliest war that was fast approaching and almost was knocking at the door.

Then they joined the other forces at the front, almost one kilometre in front of the Forest of Death, the Forbidden One.

The sun was not over the heads yet. And about two thousand soldiers were on their horses, prepared with sharp swords and pointy arrows. There were the soldiers from the regiments, the cities and the castle. There were the mighty King's Men and the inexperienced common men recruited. And there were the King and Mr. Gary themselves. All of them were there to protect their land from the foreign intruders.

Since last night the lives of different soldiers in here had been different. For someone like Michael, the night was not much different from any other nights. For the soldiers from the cities, the night and this day were real challenges, much more difficult than their common docile activities. For the King's Men, it was to prove why they were called the strongest. For the common men, it was almost the last dinner with the family - wife and kids or parents. And for the King himself, and also for Gary, it was to die alongside their soldiers for the citizens. But after all, they all had one thing common - they were here to sacrifice themselves to win the war. And they believed in the phrase - Every Blood Counts.

All the soldiers formed three rows - in the first row, there were the strongest swordsmen-horsemen including the King's Men and the King. In the second row, there were more swordsmen-horsemen, who were not as strong as the ones in the first row. The common citizens were in this row. And in the last row, there were the archers-horsemen.

Michael was in the first row. Axilior was standing at a position where there was no soldier he personally knew beside him. He could see Sir Light only, still, so far away from him. But this was the war - a stage to fight shoulder-to-shoulder with soldiers from different places, ages and races.

"Are Molly and Daniel back yet?" Michael thought, *"No, they are not. Otherwise, where are the large pack of personal soldiers of the rich men from the cities?"* Molly and Daniel were getting late to join. And the Kingdom direly needed them with more soldiers - the reinforcements.

"Has Molly run away, like before?" the question arose at Michael's back of the head.

"No!" he got furious at himself, *"I know her. And I know Daniel. They know about their importance in this battle. And they know how much we are requiring reinforcements. I believe in them. They will join us in no time."*

After about half an hour, they saw their enemies approaching from the horizon. At the beginning, it was like thousands of black dots coming from the horizon but as they came closer, the soldiers could see them clearly. There were more than two thousand of them - one quarter of which were the French and the pirates. Michael knew them and had previously fought against them. But the majority of them were different, Michael had never seen them. The French and the pirates were in armours, where the French had more advanced ones, and all of them were riding on trained horses. But the rest were wild; they were not wearing armours, rather, they were almost naked. And their monstrous bodies were covered in blood. It seemed that they had been worshipping their Gods and the blood had belonged to the animals used in sacrifices during the ritual. And instead of swords, they had axes and spears.

The enemies were approaching fast. By some blinks of eyes, they came within the combat distance.

The King was in front of everyone. He was riding his horse to reach each of his soldiers standing in the first row.

"The time has come, my men! The time to give everything you have, to show everything you are capable of. The time to prove everyone wrong, every prophecy wrong which predicted that you are nobody. This is the time to show everyone that you are somebody. You are over searching for defining moments. This is the moment which is going to be defining you for years to come. Today, you are going to fight, not for yourself, not for a single someone else. Today, you will fight for everyone in your Kingdom who is afraid and suffocating, but still is believing in you. You will fight for them who are waiting for a good news. The mothers, the children, the incapable, the crippled, the old - everyone is believing in you. Your King is believing in you. And your Kingdom is looking at you. Show the world. Follow the legends made by our predecessors. Remember, every blood counts!" the King motivated his soldiers.

He clicked his sword with that of his soldiers in the front row to form an eternal brotherhood. Then he raised his sword over his head to address and convey his faith to the soldiers of the other two rows.

The enemies were almost here; they were approaching fast, shouting in excitement - the excitement of mass destruction. Commander Black shouted in address to every soldier of his side, "Every blood counts!"

"Every blood counts!" all the soldiers responded, shouting in unison.

Warcries from both the sides were heard.

Hundreds of arrows were aimed from the third row and they formed a perfect projectile to go over the heads of the soldiers of the defending side and to hit hundreds of the incoming villains. Many of the soldiers and horses of that side, who were hit and penetrated by the arrows, were killed on the spot. However, those who survived kept moving forward. Very soon, they came within the space difference of two swords. And the war began. The King, the King's Men and all the other soldiers jumped into the flames of war with their sharpened swords.

The much frequently used phrase of 'every blood counts' meant in depth that if sacrificing someone's blood resulted in victory in favour of the Kingdom then the cost was meant to be. During the war the phrase was becoming a truth, but partially. Many lives were taken but victory still was a mirage. For most of the soldiers of the defending side, the war was savage, deadlier than what they had expected. Within some time since the beginning of the war, almost one out of five soldiers was dead from both the sides. And as Michael had predicted, the common men and lads only were the pawns born to die. The French and the pirates were tough as opponents. But one could surely wish to fight against three of them at once than facing one of the unprecedented soldiers without a helping hand with a sword.

The unprecedented soldiers were no normal humans, or if they were humans at all. The difference between civilized and savage was clearly visible. The French and even the pirates were, after all, a little merciful to their enemies, unlike the unprecedented demons who were targeting for cutting the heads half with their serrated and wild weapons. And their brutality was enough to engender coldness within the vines, which was equivalent to almost losing the war before even facing the bloodthirsty demons in human bodies.

The soldiers of the front row typically chose to face the unprecedented soldiers, leaving the French and the pirates for rest of the soldiers. As a soldier of the front row, Michael was facing the reapers of the Devil too. He could feel their inhuman strength whenever his sword clashed with the spear of one of them. And he had to give his best to keep on fighting. He could see that the King's Men were accepting the burden of extra duties. They not only were facing the unprecedented soldiers but were also trying to fill the void created by the death of a common man or lad by facing the French and the pirates. Michael, born with the will of becoming a King's Man as he used to say to himself, therefore, followed the King's Men. From now on, he had to be even more effective with efficient skills and time management. He did not have the chance to think about how Tim, Ben and the others were doing or if they were alive at all. He could only see Sir Light of all the soldiers he knew beside him. The man was fighting with praiseworthy expertise as expected. Michael and he sometimes were fighting alongside each other, by forming a team of duo and performing combo attacks and defences. There were times too when one of them was aggressive and the other was defensive.

The war had been going on for hours like this and the sun had travelled its way from the pinnacle to the inclined angle at the western sky. Almost one of the three soldiers was killed already from both the sides and almost all, even the unprecedented soldiers, were panting because of exhaustion of such a long and intense war.

Suddenly, there was the first turning point of the war. Michael saw that more soldiers of the intruding enemies were coming to join the fight. These were about a hundred of more French soldiers and the hundred traitors of the defending side. But Michael did not have the time to look at them right now as he had to concentrate on his current opponents. He, with Sir Light, currently was facing two humongous soldiers from the unprecedented army. And Michael and Light were losing. The opponents were so powerful that one blow of clash of sword and spear forced Michael to lose his grip and his sword fell down on the ground. And he could only stand there for the next second to witness the war, probably for the last time.

A young boy just fell down. He already had lost his horse and had been fighting, standing on the ground and being surrounded by enemy horsemen, for some time. At last, he got slayed by a French soldier. The exuberant young body became silent in a moment. And the livelihood became a soulless vacuous chamber. He might have had a dream. He surely had a family - old father and mother and a younger sister. The old mother would not even see her dead son. The father, who already had envisaged and forecasted the tragedy and had been trying to accept the cruel fact, would go senseless upon facing the reality. And the sister, for the first time, would go to sleep without his brother singing lullabies. The boy also might have a love. Unlike anyone else, she might still be in her room, looking outside through the window, singing almost silently while waiting for him to return. And she would wait more, for days, until her tears would dry up. A soldier from the city fell down. The spear of an unprecedented soldier had pierced through his heart. He might have gotten married recently. The wife might be expecting. The about-to-be born daughter would never see her loving father. And the soldier himself would never feel the joy of being called by his daughter. He would never again return to his house after a long day and lay down on his wife's lap and have a break.

Michael found himself back in the next second after seeing the disaster. The spear of the second unprecedented enemy that Light and he were facing had penetrated through Light's neck. Light's body fell from his horse as he acknowledged defeat for the first and last time.

The memories flashbacked in Michael's eyes. He remembered his times in London at the workshop. He remembered the day when Sir Light and Commander Black had visited their workshop and James and he had a friendly fight against them. Sir Light and Commander Black were the first ones to encourage James and him to join the force.

Michael looked at the merciless faces of those two soldiers. Then he quickly grabbed the sword from the hand of Light's falling body and stuck it in the chest of Light's murderer in a time quicker than that needed for a leaf to drop from a tree in static air. He again picked out the sword and got engaged with the battle against the first of those two soldiers. This time Michael was aware not to get involved in a physical fight as he did not want to lose his sword again. Rather, he relied on his brain. At last, his new techniques succeeded in defeating the mighty enemy.

The reinforcements of the intruders were already here. So far already, the defending side had been outnumbered. And the reinforcements of the opposition were more than what they could take.

"Fall back!" the King had no other option. And his soldiers followed him towards the castle.

Some of the soldiers could outrun the enemies, yet, many were not so fortunate. So, they had to get back into the war and they lost their lives. Many King's Men took the responsibility of resisting the enemy force and to allow sufficient time to their comrades to fall back. Some King's Men died during this clash too.

It was almost night when the soldiers with the King reached the castle. The Gatehouse was opened for them and was quickly dropped before the chasing enemies could enter. The archers at once took their positions on the walls and at the South Tower. Michael himself went at the top of the South Tower with Josh. Hundreds of arrows from the bows were aimed. They had perfect projectiles and hit many of the enemies successfully. The enemies also reacted with arrows gutted in flame and explosives. Those almost completely decimated the South Bailey and parts of the southern wall, and burned down many stables and barracks. Some unfortunate soldiers were also burned alive.

The two sides of the South Wall were burning. The barracks, armouries and the other warehouses at its north were under flames. Sometimes, flammable components used in the armouries and workshops such as coals, oils, etc. were coming in contact with the flames and causing mass explosions. The explosions were triggering the fire to spread towards the Greathall. Smoke was dominating the South Bailey and also was going up high in the sky. The suffocation was becoming harder for the soldiers with every passing moment, where a moment itself felt like an interminable span of sufferings. One could hear the cries of the dying soldiers, the shouts from the ordering commanders, the neighs from the clasped horses and the screams from the refugees of the other side of the Greathall.

The grasslands on the other side of the South Wall were also burning. The strong wind was being the catalyst to spread it everywhere. Yet, the enemies were tenacious to break in through the flames. The unprecedented soldiers did not care how much the fire was burning their skins. About ten of them were carrying a huge trunk of a dead tree. It had a pointy end. They were running towards the iron gate while carrying it and hitting the gate with it. After each hit, they went back, started to run again, got the momentum and hit the gate again. "Heave, heave," they were shouting - their warcries. And with each hit at the gatehouse, the entire South Wall was shaking. The soldiers inside the walls were trying to gather forces on the other side of the gate in order to prevent it from breaking down. With each hit at the gate by the enemies, the impact generated was throwing the soldiers, exerting force on the other side of the gate, away from the gate. But, the soldiers stood up again and came back to continue to push the force to save the gate.

"Defend the gate!" one could hear the King.

"Archers, the gate!" Commander Black from somewhere in the front ordered the archers to target the most concerning enemies of the moment.

Michael and the archers started to target the unprecedented soldiers who were hitting the gatehouse. They were getting success. Their arrows were reacting to the attack by penetrating into the enemies' bodies. The inhuman enemies were not bothering even when an arrow pierced through their arms and legs. However, their lifeless bodies were falling down when an arrow was perfectly hitting them at the head or chest. Unfortunately, another one of them came forward right the next second to take the position and continue the attack.

A crack at the door was seen. And it was getting dangerously wider. Would it break the gate down? Three, two, one...

This part of the war continued past midnight. This was a battle of cooler nerve, better leadership and teamwork. Where the attackers were trying to break down the walls to make a path into the stronghold for themselves, the defenders were trying to protect the walls, kill their enemies as well as save all the lives within the fortress. I must remind my readers that many villagers had taken shelter in the castle grounds.

Many soldiers of the defending army now were trying to mollify the flame and damage control of the wall by putting stones and wood at the cracks. Thus, they were trying to make a quick heal.

At about dawn, the war saw its second turning point.

Suddenly, the enemies stopped hitting the gate. Some of them fell down with some arrows on their heads, chests and necks. These were the arrows which were not aimed by any soldier within the walls. For the moment, the enemies stopped shouting warcries. They became alert, and might be for the first time, they were frightened because of the unwelcomed counterattack. They turned their heads from the castle to the south.

This was the second time a large force had arrived. This time it was led by Molly and Daniel. And the force of about three hundred soldiers started to dominate over the enemies. Every last soldier from the city was in this team. These were the personal soldiers of the rich men in the cities. Of course, they were not as skilled and experienced as the best soldiers and the King's Men of the military. But right now, the defending team was in standing at the end of an endless cliff. Even a minimum pull to assist it to come up was highly needed.

The intruders diverted their attention from breaking the walls of the castle to the ones by whom they were under attack. The soldiers defending from inside the castle also got sufficient time to clear the mess up and make a counterstrike. And now, the intruders had to fall back towards the Forest of Death. The army of the defending side, with the newly arrived reinforcements, chased them. They knew that they had to kill the last one of the enemy. Otherwise, the enemies would rejuvenate, evolve and broaden to strike back in future.

"Chase them down!" Molly was heard.

"Kill them all, we don't want any prisoner!" another commander shouted.

Michael and the others got up on their horses and started chasing. They were running faster than the wind. And one could only hear the loud steps of the running horses.

The army of the defending side tried hard to catch up with the intruders before the forest. The forest was a place of terror to them. For more than half a century, people of the Kingdom had been nurturing superstitions and fear about this forest. There had been a significant number of incidents around the forest that had caused death to people of the Kingdom and had risen the horror amongst them. On the other hand, the opposition was familiar with the environment of the forest. After all, the forest itself was the land of the unprecedented soldiers.

Unfortunately, the army of the defending side failed to catch up with the pace of most of the enemies. It deserves mention that they were able to catch up with a big part of the soldiers, most of whom were the French and the pirates, before the forest. However, the second big part, most of which consisted of the unprecedented soldiers and the traitors, could safely run away into the forest.

The army of the defending side got divided into two parts - the first part stayed in front of the forest to fight against the enemies they had caught up with, and the second part continued chasing the enemies trying to escape. Michael, Molly, Tim and many others were in the second part whereas the King, Commander Black, Daniel, Ben and the rest were in the first group. It was obvious that the second group was going to face tougher job than the first, and so it had more skilled soldiers. Most of the King's Men were in the second group, however, their commander himself was in the first. And it had a definite reason. Commander Black, right now, was facing someone that only he could face in a mortal combat. It was the leader of the unprecedented soldiers.

During the chaos of the war, Michael did not have a chance to observe how others were fighting. But this soldier had been easily noticeable. He was the only one from the unprecedented army who was wearing a necklace and bracelets made out of shiny stones, indicating the difference of his status from the others of his army. Like anyone from his army, he also was monstrous, cruel and merciless. And he had been fighting unlike a human, always taking on more than one opponent at once and killing them. Certainly he had the maximum amount of blood at his weapons and he was the final thorn to the defending side in their endeavour of saving their throne. The few times Michael had the opportunity to watch him fight, it had seemed to Michael that this evil had been fighting, killing and vanishing away all of his opponents within seconds; it had seemed to Michael as if it had been a screenplay, not an actual war!

Michael had to follow the others into the Forest of Death, the Forbidden One. And so, he could no longer watch Commander Black taking it on against the strongest soldier from the opposition.

Unlike anyone from his team, Michael, with his horse, had been into the forest several times. Thus, he could rely on his instincts on where to go and how to go. Contrary to the normal, he did not get over confident.

It was dawn already. While they were chasing, they were facing opponents whom they were catching up with. Brief battles were following every now and then during this act of running and chasing. Unfortunately, even Michael and the opposition, who had fair experience with the forest, had forgotten their unnatural threat. Something gave them an ultimatum and final reminder of this ghostly threat very soon. When all the soldiers were involved and concentrated on running and chasing, they heard a long and continuous howling that reminded them of death approaching, and the approaching demon from the core of the forest.

The brightness of the sun suddenly had a decline. The breeze became stagnant. The temperature became inundating and cold. And the forest became silent, yet noisy. And all of them heard of running hounds and horsemen - the undead, approaching towards them.

The soldiers from the defending side suddenly heard the screaming from the intruders they had been chasing after; death had caught up with them faster than the army of the defending side. And the army of the defending side itself felt being watched, chased and targeted. The hounds from the hell and the awakened dead were after them too.

"It is the undead!" Michael warned the others.

"They are coming from that side. We need to run to the opposite side," Molly said after pointing at one certain part of the forest's core.

"It is no use. They will catch us in no time!" a soldier said.

"All of you go towards that opposite side. Try to go out of the forest. And also try to catch and kill as many of the enemies as you can. I will stop here as a decoy. Now hurry!" Molly ordered to the others.

Standing as a decoy means standing on the ground in front of the enemies and letting her allies to escape. One may confront the enemies or lure them to a different direction. The goal is not to let them catch up with the allies. However, there is a serious drawback to this ancient strategy of battles. The soldier standing as the decoy inevitably gets killed.

Michael did not know what Molly was thinking. Was she thinking about sacrificing herself in order to save the others? Or did she have another plan?

"No! What are you going to do alone?" he asked her.

"You know what a decoy means right?" Molly's question verified Michael's agitation and distress.

"I am not letting you do this," Michael blocked Molly's way.

"Michael, why don't you understand? Why are you so stubborn? You cannot save everyone. Look, the other soldiers are already running towards the safer place," she shouted at him.

Michael saw that most of their comrades already had run towards the safer place as directed by Molly. Only a few, including Tim, were still waiting for them.

Michael came down from his horse, and Molly did the same.

"Why did you leave us? Tell me, Molly. You were gone for months. Is it because I did not speak to you before heading for my mission in the forest? And then all of a sudden, you were back to save me during my trial. How did you even know of the trial? Were you here in the Kingdom the whole time? And I did not ask for your help during my trial, did I? Tell me, Molly. Tell me the truth. You were thinking that I would not be able to save James, right? And you were so angry with me that you left, right? Don't you trust me?" Michael asked in one breath.

Quite surprisingly, Molly did not get angry anymore, which was an aberration from normal Molly.

"There is one reason why I left the regiment," she said in a low voice while tears rolled down from her eyes, "after James' death, it took me long to get over the shock and return to my mundane life. I needed to concentrate on the fact that invasions like that would surely happen again, causing more deaths. But, the day you went on the mission in the forest, it reminded me of that night over and over again. It shattered the sand castle I was in a hurry to build. I became aware of the fact I had been trying to run away from. I could never get over

James' death. And to be in the lead of the strongest regiment at that time with that mentality? No! So, I resigned and left. I needed a break. And I returned by the Royal Wedding. And I had to save you from the trial. You know the rest."

The environment had been intensified even more than before. Strong wind was blowing, badly shaking the branches and leaves of the trees. The intensity of the brightness of the sun declined even further. The clouds, hard to be glimpsed at by penetrating the webs of leaves and boughs, might have covered the sky. Finally, the ghostly sounds of the fast approaching hell hounds and the undead were getting even louder.

Michael was silent and was looking at Molly's teary eyes. Molly, at first, tried to clean her eyes and face, but later, she gave up. She allowed her emotions to flow. She embraced her true self - a soldier with mortal feelings. And for the last time in her ephemeral life, she became an ethereal beauty - a complete human.

"Michael," she said for the last time, "I am proud of you. And I am so sorry that I could not be a good commander. But, I hope, I became a good friend to all of you." She came closer to Michael, stood in front of him, and continued, "You have become strong. You have surpassed me, you have surpassed James. Now, all you need to do is one last thing." She came even closer, pulled her neck up to reach Michael's forehead, kissed him, and said, "I want you to be the King's Man."

When Michael was leaving with Tim, he turned his head to look at Molly for one last time. And he saw the best, bravest commander ever, a very best friend and an amazing person who always had been misunderstood as one heartless soldier. Michael saw Molly, standing on her ground against the invisible, invincible enemies of the dead.

Michael was leading Tim and a few more soldiers towards the garden at the core of the forest. He knew that nothing violent would occur at that heavenly place. He was sure that the garden was secured, from the rest of the forest, by guardian angels and the free spirits of the dead soldiers, including that of James Wheeler. However, as long as they were not into the garden yet, death was after them as destiny. And it happened. Michael was riding beside Tim when he saw Tim, all in a sudden, fall down from his horse.

An arrow had hit Tim's horse at the neck, killing it instantly and throwing it down on the ground. Tim also had fallen down badly and had broken his leg. He was screaming in agony. But the archer still was somewhere in hiding and Tim had to move to get away from the target spot. Unfortunately, he could not even stand up.

Michael had already come to cover Tim. His eyes were searching all over for the archer. The other soldiers who were with them also had stopped. They also had come to defend their injured companion. And they also were searching with sharp eyes for their enemy.

The next arrow came about a minute later and hit Tim at the chest. The penetrated arrow was stopped by the weak mortal resistances from Tim's chest and it stopped Tim's scream itself. The other soldiers were quick enough to spot the location of the archer and chased in that direction. Only Michael stayed.

Michael sat down beside Tim lying on the ground as blood from his chest was wetting it. Michael held his hands but could not say a thing. He only kept looking at the eyes of his dying brother as the eyes were trying to say many things. Those eyes were dropping last few drops of tears as they slowly were losing motion and coming to an eternal static. And the mumbling lips betrayed him as they stopped before betraying the last unfinished words.

The motionless hands of the lifeless body of Tim tried to hold Michael's hands for the final time. At last, he shook hands with the man in black robe and hood on a pale horse - his companion towards Hades' Gate.

Michael tried to close his eyes and pray. And he was successful in doing the first one, but failed to follow to the second. Teardrops were falling down from his eyes too, but he forgot the reason of this sorrow. For a moment, death seemed so natural to him that he denied to himself the very existence of Him. For a moment, he embraced death, sorrow, grief, agony and heartbreak as his old companions. He forgot the meaning and need of his own existence; he thought he had failed everyone in everything.

Michael closed Tim's eyes, washed his face and chest, let Tim's hands hold his sword tight, and stood up. He did not sing a eulogy. He got up on Axilior and started towards the core of the forest.

"James, Raphael, Molly and Tim."

Who said that? Oh! It was Michael himself within his head reminding himself of his failures.

When Michael was almost at the garden, he was blocked by his final opponent of the war. The man was in familiar armours, with a familiar sword and on a familiar horse. He was waiting for Michael and also had chosen him as his last opponent. His eyes revealed cruelty and jealousy. And his body depicted determination to annihilate Michael that he had been wanting to achieve for a long time.

It was David Williams.

Without spending any word on each other, they got involved in their fight till death. It was a fight between two old rivals who held not only antipathy but also grudge against each other. It was the fight between good and bad, love and hate, loyalty and betrayal. Michael was on it to take revenge for what Williams had done to him and his Kingdom, Molly and Tim. On the other hand, Williams was there to eradicate the person he hated the most and win the battle of this already lost war.

The two equal strengths stroke against each other and it continued for long. The only sounds were from the clashing swords and the neigh of the horses. Until at last, Williams talked.

"How does it feel to lose everyone you love, Chapman?"

Michael did not reply.

Williams provoked him, "How does it feel to look at that friend of yours with the arrow at his chest? Was he crying? Was he in agony? Did you feel the sorrow? Or are you just too heartless to feel it?"

"Don't you dare talk about Tim like that! And who are you to talk about heart and love?" Michael shouted in anger.

-"Yes, I am, Chapman! So are you just assuming David Williams never loved anyone?"

-"It's not an assumption, nor an intuition. It's a fact. You have killed so many innocent lives. Can you even guess the number of casualties of this war that you have started?"

-"I don't even care. All I want is to kill you all. And kill that worthless King. For what he has done to me."

Michael was in a maze now. He did not know what Williams was talking about. And he had to ask, "What did the King do to you?"

-"Are you thinking that I am talking about that bitch princess? Yes I liked her, she is beautiful. It would have been amazing to have her in my bed. But I always found her to have a special affection towards you. But I did not care. As from my childhood, I have had only one specific goal. That is my only goal in life, my only desire, my only source of all efforts. A long time ago, this Kingdom killed my father. I had nobody besides him. He was the whole world to me. And they took him away from me. They made me an orphan! They took everything from me! On that day, I lost the fear to die. I lost the will to love again. I lost any feelings. And I became a monster in a human's body. From those days, I have been working and waiting to see this day when I can have the head of the King like how this Kingdom had my father's. Now tell me, Chapman, how does it feel to be alone, completely alone in this cruel world, forever?"

Emotional Williams said while continuing his fight. And Michael took a moment before replying.

-"You are wrong about me from the very beginning. I already have felt how it feels to be alone in this broken and twisted world. I am glad that your father loved you, despite being a criminal, yes that was him. Do you want to be shocked? I have never seen my father. I don't know what kind of a person he was. I don't know how he looked. I don't know what he did for a living, a farmer, soldier, fisherman? I don't even know if he is still alive. In my life I have lost many people. And their places can never be replaced. But surely I could find other people whose places in my life and heart became as irreplaceable. I have lost my mother and found James. Then I met Molly. I lost James but I found Tim. And Williams, you are so relapsed that you are forgetting something.

Yes, I have lost Molly and Tim today. But still I am not alone in this world. I still have got friends for whom I will continue to live and fight."

Michael's sword gave a hard blow that Williams fell down on the ground, still holding his sword.

"They killed my father. And I never found anyone else as important as him in my life. I have never found. You and I are different. We are just two dissimilar persons. You were so lucky to find your friends. I was not."

Michael stepped down from his horse. He walked towards Williams as he was almost declaring defeat. Michael walked really close to him with his sword at his hand. But he threw away his sword.

"What are you waiting for, Chapman? Kill me! This is your only chance. Or, I will come back to avenge my father again. And this time, capricious will follow for sure. And in the heap of dead, I will find my pleasure. The dead will be my compassion; they will take the next special place after my father!" Williams was shouting.

Michael came and kicked him, forcing him to withdraw his sword. But, he did not kill him. Instead of ripping Williams' chest with the sharp steel, he moved his hand towards him.

"It is never too late, David. You still can have friends and even a family. And the Kingdom can still accept you as a loyal soldier of the army. Take my hand and let us go back home," he proposed to the defeated enemy.

"What!" Williams was shocked, "Are you making fun of me? I am warning you, Chapman."

-"David, you and I are not that dissimilar as you think. The state you are currently in, I could have been there unless I had met my friends. They have saved me from the infinite darkness. And they have saved the soft heart in the cruel world. They pulled me out when I was drowning deep down in the endless ocean. Without them, right now, I could have been with you fighting against this nation. Yes, maybe you are unfortunate, David. But, you still can change everything. Take my hands and let us go back home. The war will end soon and we will win."

Williams did not take the hand. Neither did he strike back at unarmed Michael. He stayed on the ground for a moment. And said, "My father was a criminal. But are not all of us criminals in some way? Today I have killed so many innocent lives. I have tried to trick and kill you. I have betrayed the nation which adopted this orphan of me. How can you forgive me?"

-"David, I just forgive and forget all that you have done. Because, I know that you still can make all the bad to good. I believe in you brother, and I believe in humanity."

Williams did not stand up for a while. Michael looked at his face which was trying to betray something- a word or probably thousands of words. He was trying to say something that he had been keeping within himself like the amassed blood under the festering wound. He was wishing if he could convey a miles long message in a single short sentence. He made his fists, the chin got hardened, the throat dried out and the thoughts became turbulent as he was about to say it. Yet he could not. Finally he was done criticising the Kingdom and was about to speak against himself. However, the unwavering pride like the burnt skin over the wound did not let the blood out. At last, he moved and Michael knew that he was about to do something.

Williams stood up. He took up the sword. He got up on his horse. And he said, "Goodbye, Michael. There still are colonies of the French on the other side of the forest. I am going to confront and prevent them from coming. But I will not survive. After this war, come back with force and kill them. Thank you for accepting me. Thank you for your forgiveness and for everything else. I am sorry for what I have done. And, Michael Chapman, you have acquired a special place in my life."

He rode towards the deeper from the deepest of the forest, all alone, and Michael saw his so-called eternal enemy for the last time. And thus ended the fight between the lucky and the unfortunate, the loved and the hated, the accepted and the misjudged.

Michael and Rose had been sitting in the garden at the core of the Forest of Death for quite some time. Michael had just found her following him, in the same unrevealing armours that she had used during her trainings. They were sitting in the beautiful garden of white roses. The war might have ended already. Peace might have been achieved. But this place was without violence and with love, as always. And they were looking at the grains from the roses, dancing with the breeze, diffracting the sunlight, and reminding Michael of the Stardusts in the Starshine.

It was a long time since Michael had properly talked to Rose. And now he was unable to rationalise how he had spent so many days without talking to the person he loved that much. He was unable to think how he had thought of her during these days. But, he was unwilling to remember the time any more. Right now, he was sitting beside Rose, in the Garden of Eden, and he was hoping if this moment would never come to an end.

"Michael, why were you shouting at me when you found me in this forest?" Rose asked.

"This is the Forest of Death, my Lady. Many people have died in here. Only today I have lost my elder sister and younger brother. I already have lost my elder brother in here. I do not want to lose you too," Michael did not hesitate to express his feelings.

Rose smiled and said, "Call me Rose."

They went back to enjoying the environment. The breeze, the songbirds, the sunlight - everything was assuring them that they were guarded by angels sent from the heaven in this Garden of earthling Eden.

Rose asked again, "Why do you keep coming here? Are not you afraid of losing yourself?"

Before replying to her, Michael remembered about Mrs Brenda and Williams. They had said something to him that he could not forget.

"We all are selfish, Rose. We are not afraid of death because it takes our loved ones away from us. We fear it as it makes ourselves alone. We fear to die not because of others, we fear to die only for ourselves. We are afraid of afterlives as inevitable loneliness awaits us there. Once we are done with these feelings and fears and once we don't have someone whom we are afraid of losing, we just stop being afraid of death anymore."

Rose did not like his response. She misunderstood from what Michael had tried to convey. So, she asked, "Don't you have anyone whom you are afraid of losing?"

Michael turned the eyes at her from the surroundings. He smiled and asked, "Do you think I have that person?"

"As a matter of fact, I do. You still have your friends. The citizens of the Kingdom, the King and the Queen," Rose gave an intentional pause.

Michael caught up with that interval. "What about you?" he asked.

"What about me?" Rose played dumb.

–"Let me say this in another way. Will you be sad if I die?"

"I will definitely miss you. You are an amazing person and wonderful friend. You have done a lot for me and for the Kingdom," Rose again was deliberate to suppress herself.

Michael did not question her against her own reply. He just placed his head against hers, smelled her hair as her hair had joined the pollen grains, the leaves and the petals in the dance with the breeze. He closed his eyes and so did she. Now they could smell the enthralling odour of the garden even more. They forgot, for the moment, about the war and about any more threats.

They did not speak for that moment until when Michael said, "You have made me what I am now. Thank you for everything."

★★★

10

The Sword on the Circle

Michael woke up very late in the morning. It was not like he had been working hard or had a mental pressure that would have exhausted him. The truth was, he had been in the hospital for a week.

The war had ended resulting the defending side as victorious. Although the casualty report was a satire to the Kingdom, a successful defending of the Kingdom and the stronghold against the strong nexus of enemies was absolutely praiseworthy.

During the last few days, many people, soldiers and common men, women and children had come to visit Michael. He had become a hero to the entire nation. Even the people who had wanted Michael's death penalty for the murders of Mr. Cook and Mr. Hooper, which Michael had been accused falsely, were celebrating Michael's heroism and wishing for his good health. Commander Daniel, Commander of the seventh regiment of the South Tower, and Ben, Second in Command of the same, were the most frequent visitors. They used to come early in the morning, have lunches together, and stay up to dinner. They had talked a lot during these days by which they had actually direly tried to fill the voids that had been created from the deaths of their fellow soldiers, especially that of Molly and Tim. Daniel and Ben had told Michael about what had been going on outside of the hospital. The Kingdom had been coming to the normal and peaceful state of herself. People had been going out, interacting, having beer and rum again. New recruitment of soldiers had also started. And this was the first time in his life that Daniel had to do it without martyr and former Commander Molly of the seventh regiment of the South. Daniel had also shared about how Molly and he had convinced the rich men of the towns to donate money and soldiers before the war. They all had to acknowledge that without Molly's contribution, the war would have been far from a victory.

Yesterday, the Kingdom had organised a mourning party for the martyrs. All the soldiers, many citizens, the King, the Order and the King's Men had assembled in the memorial grounds where the dead had been buried. Most unfortunate had been the ones whose bodies had never been found. However, everyone's name had been written in the stones of the grounds - the names of Sir Light, Commander Molly, Soldier Tim and that of many others. In a part of the grounds, there was a stone with the name of soldier James Wheeler too.

Michael, Daniel and Ben had spent a great amount of time in there. Michael also had found Rose in the party, in the company of her father. All the attendees had been wearing blacks, had sung eulogies and had paid a moment of silence in order to convey respect to the brave martyrs.

At the end of the party when everyone was leaving, Michael, Daniel and Ben had stayed. They had not talked but only watched. They had been watching the stones and imagining looking at their friends. They had thanked them silently. And after all of these, Michael saw a beautiful child girl, who might have come with her parents, running and playing on the fields, sometimes even lying down on the comfortable grasses. She was a sanguine girl, ever smiling one. Her laughter was compassionate to the deaths. She did not know what grief was. But, she was the symbol of resilience.

When I was reading this part from Michael Chapman's diary, I found an almost torn page at the next. That page was difficult to read and it was hard to make out the meanings. However, I had to spend an entire day on it as I found it very important to my life at that point. It was the third and last poem by Michael Chapman. And I am writing it, only by changing it to Modern English, for my readers and am asking them to find out the meaning of it as well as the significance of it in their lives:

The showers is not raining the joyous from heaven anymore
The true colours of the sky has changed a lot
Since last summer; the tempestuous storm tempting to
Call on capricious and impress satire upon the livings.
Heaven doesn't know, as the clouds have faded the mortals
Respite of angels alluding it, alleviating the sufferings
Of their wings; no one outside as if it's the last day
Or maybe it will last for eternity and forever.

Down in the Downtown, in the Downing Street,
Where the roads are drowning, and so is the town,
Little Nancy returns from the chronic day, taking the high road
Her non-muddy shoes being compassionate to the wet uniform
The temptation - to jump over the drowning road, and
Get the skirt dirty - a sumptuous situation that she can't afford.
The warmth and dry have been drained in rain, so long ago
And because of the umbrella - that she can't afford.

The veils of clouds will be torn apart, once more,
And the colours of rainbows will bring the news from the heaven
The angels will watch the roads crowded like never before
With the never ending laughter, that will break the silence.
Nancy will throw the umbrella she couldn't afford
And run to where she cares more, the muddy shoes - she cares the less
Because she believes that the sun will rise again, recalling the warmth
And I believe that you believe it too, my friend,
You will terminate the interminable pain of despise
Because the faith of overcoming is what the sufferings can never afford.

When I was reading this poem by Michael Chapman, I was struggling with my thesis and was worried thinking about my future. I had seen how my past had betrayed my trust, and I was losing my faith over my future as my present was cheating on me. However, somewhere deep down, I knew that things would never continue like this. I knew that someday, I would see the first light of a new day. A day would come when I would be laughing at my past, proud of my present and waiting for embracing my future. Back then, I did not know why Michael Chapman had written the poem. What had been going on in his head? "May be I will find later as I read his letters," I used to tell myself.

Today, although Michael had woken up late, he did not have the option to waste any more time. The King had called on a celebration party for the victory in the castle and Michael was a distinguished invitee. Besides, the doctors had already declared Michael as fit to go.

Although the party had begun early in the morning, the most important session was in the evening. And I am skipping right to it because of the depth of its significance. And Michael, Daniel and Ben attended it.

The ceremony was going on in the GreatHall of the castle. At first, the King thanked all the martyrs and the soldiers who had survived the claws of the war. I must remind that many common citizens also had participated in the war. Michael saw so many soldiers and citizens in the hall, most of whom he had seen only before the war, but not during it. He saw Gary, who also had taken a role in the war. Michael did not know how the war had been presented to the other soldiers, and if the other soldiers had lost someone very precious like him. But it was true that they all had given their best in the war for the sake of their lands, and so, all of them deserved the victory.

The King thanked the people who had taken part in the war from outside of the front. These people were the members of the Order who had directed the war from outside, the workers of the armouries who had worked hard to make hundreds of armours overnight at a sudden notice, and the villagers for their sacrifices.

There were tables of delicious foods and wine in the hall. Music was being played and people were dancing. But all of these parts of the ceremony had to stop as the King had something important to convey.

On one side of the hall, the King was there on his throne, with the Queen and the Princess by his sides.

The King called on Commander Black and the commanders of all the regiments. All of them were awarded for their contributions and leadership in the war. Commander Daniel was specially awarded for his special contributions in the war. He was the one who, along with Molly, had found reinforcements in a crucial time.

At last, Michael was called. He went in front of the King and kneeled down. A messenger arrived with a cloth and a sword on a beautiful tray.

Michael had been the one who, after a solo investigation, had found out about the war and the treachery. He was the one who had put his life on the edge to confirm it. And he always had been active during the war.

The King held the sword just over Michael's head.

"State your name, soldier," the King asked.

"I am Michael Chapman, from the seventh regiment of the South, your Majesty," Michael replied.

-"State your oath."

-"I, Michael Chapman, do hereby affirm that I will defend the lands of my Kingdom and the people of the same, against any power - natural or unnatural, mortal or immortal, domestic or foreign. My soul and sword are devoted for my Kingdom and for my King, and I will protect the trust and faith that my citizens have put upon me. May the Great Lord offer me the strength to bear my responsibilities even during the darkest hours. Finally, I will be ready to sacrifice myself for the sake of my comrades, my King, my Kingdom and my citizens. I, hereby, affirm that I will abide by my oath, by the laws and by the name of the Great Lord, till the end of my life."

-"Who do you obey?"

-"I obey my King and my Commander."

-"For how long will you obey?"

-"From now till the end of my breath."

The King was satisfied. He touched the sword on Michael's right shoulder, and then on his left shoulder, followed by his top of the head.

"Rise and shine, Sir Michael Chapman," he announced.

Michael stood up. Two women, who were standing by him, took the cloth from the messenger and helped Michael put it on. This was not any ordinary cloth, in fact, it was special. Wearing it was a dream for every soldier of the Kingdom. Michael himself had dreamed of it since his days in London.

Michael wore it with pride. And he let the black cloak of the cloth to undulate like waves, with unwavering resolution. He was honoured to find everyone looking at him with respect, esteem, admiration and approval. And he turned his head so that he could see the back of the cloak that he always had wanted to look at like this; in the swinging cloak, one part was constant and clear - it was the King's Crest, the Sword on a Circle. Michael closed his eyes for a moment, exhaled deeply with self-gratification and gratitude to the people for whom he was standing here today. And next, he opened his eyes, he was Sir Michael Chapman, the King's Man.

The next part of the ceremony was all about dancing, singing and having delightful meals. Michael talked a lot with his fellow soldiers and he loved being congratulated by all of them. May the Great Lord offer and grant. And he provided special time and space to Daniel and Ben. He talked with them, drank with them and laughed so hard with them.

Michael thought of his times in the farm. After twelve hours of hard work, he had used to get only bread and spinach. Today, the hunter style pork, sausages, liver and kidney beans, roasted beef, etc were announcing his victory over the struggles.

Life starts from a microscopic level. And at this period, it has many antagonists who always try to call on satire of nemesis upon the primitive life form. Sometimes, they become successful in aggravating and deteriorating the period. Sometimes, they even kill the weak and rudimentary cell. However, if life survives, it grows. It reproduces, evolves and expands. And thus, it spreads its influence over the world. It lets the world know of its existence by proliferating its roots down by tearing the earth's heart. And the roots advance more and more, like chains and like webs, deep down into the earth like veins of a parasite or an alien. Even now, it has so many adversaries; in fact the foes become more harmful than ever and so the struggle continues. The tiny leaves give the adapting life new hopes of a better tomorrow. They give it strength to fight in the cruel and cursed world. After a long time of struggle and sacrifice, the fundamental life form reaches the limiting sky. It becomes a gigantic tree, the Queen of the forest. All the enemies now stand at its feet, kissing the feet for mercy and looking up with an endeavour to behold its head with respect.

Michael had started from somewhere where he did not have the courage to dream, or even to envisage the future - bright or dark. He had everything which had been against his odds.

The situations and people always had tried to bring him down to his knees. And there had been times when he had fallen down; there had been times when he had got lost and blind and senseless. But he had continued to stand up; he had continued to find the lost path of his. The path had been very narrow. It had led to the destination; however, there had been cliffs at its edges. Thus, one could either walk through the narrow path successfully, or he could fall down into the darkness by missing the cliffs. In the darkness, there had lied the uncharted and uncertain ocean of flames. The dead had been screaming and throwing their hands up from there in order to catch and pull the passengers of the narrow path down towards themselves. Underneath the ocean of flames and the dead, there had lied Inferno. Michael had continued to cross the path. And there had been thousands of times when he almost had fallen down by missing the cliffs. And there had been hundreds of times when the dead from the Inferno almost had caught him by throwing their hands up at him while he had been crossing through the path. But Michael had been saved, unlike many others. In times, James had caught him, Molly had caught him, and Daniel, Ben, Tim, and the others of the Kingdom, and of course Rose had caught him when Michael had gone lost. They had pulled him up and helped him stand steadily again on the path. They also had given a gentle push from behind to let Michael continue his voyage again. But tonight, Michael had reached his destination. He had crossed the path. Tonight, he was like the tree. All his enemies were beneath.

In all of our lives, we face situations when we have two paths in front of us, both of which are equally predilected by us. But the two paths differ in respect to their time-form to us. One of the paths is familiar to us; we already have lived and walked through it. Every corner of it, every stone and grass on it and every star in the sky above it are known to us. We have lived so much through it that it has become our home. The other path offers an amazing challenge that we cannot decline. This road is entirely unfamiliar to us as we walk through it for the first time. But its end point harbour awaits for us with our dreams. These are the dreams that we have been dreaming since we cannot even remember. And we cannot remember since when we have started to work hard with our sweat, flesh and bones to achieve these goals. This hardship was equally about mentality as it was for the physical body. But we have prepared ourselves psychologically – "We have sacrificed so many things in the courses of time during our voyages for the sake of our dreams. Nothing can stop us from catching it when we see it in front of our glaring eyes." Alas! We were wrong and definitely not so prepared at all. When we find ourselves in front of the two paths, we forget everything else. We forget why we have put our efforts so far, we forget the sacrifices. The first path has become dear to us. It has been there in each of our hard and soft times. It has been there to cheer after a victory, it has been there to clean our tears after a loss. The second path was absent during those times. And finally, when we get to see the second path for which we have been trying so hard with the first path, it becomes almost impossible to betray our old friend. Finally, we realise that during the times to achieve something else, we have fallen in love with our companions of the voyage. And thus, the destination does not look so appealing anymore; we fear to depart from our love. We finally realise why journey is always better than the destination.

Michael was not entirely happy. He just had been promoted to be the King's Man; it had been his dream, and James' dream. It had been the reason of their coming here from London, it had been the reason of their selecting the most dangerous regiment of all. Definitely it had taken the life of James, and Michael's this achievement was like taking care of James' dream too. But Michael was unhappy. He did not express it to others. He was acting like he was satisfied after being promoted. But, from now on, he had to live within the castle. From now on, he had to take care of more number of missions. He was never ever going to get the good times in the regiment, the trainings, the dinners, the chats and laughter in the tents. And he would not be getting much time, from now on, to spare, and even to meet Rose despite living within the stronghold.

"Molly and Tim are no more. Daniel and Ben have duties as leaders. I still can meet Rose after my work, may be once a weekend? And it has been my dream since long, it was James' dream too. And how can I forget what Molly said to me? It is the time to grow up, Michael. Those happy times of the past are gone. They will never come back. And it is worthless to try to bring them back, or to try to live with them," Michael tried to convince himself that he had taken the correct decision.

Michael saw Rose. She was wearing a beautiful white dress which was exponentially enhancing her charm. She was reminding him of something very dear. What was it? Was it the garden of white roses in the core of the forest?

Tonight Michael had grown to a man. He was more confident than ever. And so, tonight, he was not afraid of the crowd. He stood up, walked straight to Rose, neglecting the other people present, and asked, "Ms. Rose, will you lead me to a dance?"

In some other time, Rose could go surprised. She could hesitate to dance with Michael in front of the others, especially in front of her mother, the Queen. But tonight was different. Michael was admired by all tonight. And so she took his hands with a smile.

Michael and Rose went to the centre of the stage - the dancing floor. Some other couples also joined them. There were Gary and Jane, Daniel and his new girlfriend and many more. Music was being played vocally and with instruments. The dancers let the music flow through their bodies. The musical composition was making a fine adjunction between the precision movements and elaborate formal gestures, steps, and poses of the dancers with its own rhythm.

Michael and Rose were looking at each other's eyes. They were smiling, they were happy. And they were having the best time of their lives. They were wishing for the dance to never come to an end.

"I did not know you dance this well!" Rose expressed her surprise.

"Neither did I!" Michael replied.

-"So, how does it feel to be one of the strongest soldiers? To be a King's Man?"

-"Honestly, I am afraid. I am scared of what is ahead. I am missing the old times."

-"I also did not know that Sir Michael Chapman is afraid of something!"

-"I am afraid of a lot of things - mortal, immortal, physical, abstract. But one thing I am sure about is I am not afraid of anything while I am dancing with the most beautiful woman in the world."

At the end of the dancing, Michael, Daniel and Ben had a grand feast together. They took a lot of bread and potatoes, beef, pork, lamb, rabbit meat and sausage, cheese and custard, fruits and vegetables and alcohol for themselves. They were talking amongst themselves. They talked about the ceremony, the food, their future, Rose, Daniel's new girlfriend, and many more things. Michael and Ben laughed after hearing that Daniel already had been thinking about marriage. And they teased him. But they stopped after seeing the Queen. She had come to them.

"Sir Chapman, can I have a moment with you please?" she asked.

Michael left their table and followed the Queen.

They went out of the ceremony hall to a place calmer where they could have the privacy of talking.

"I want to thank you for your service and congratulate on your promotion," the Queen inaugurated.

"Thank you my Lady," Michael bowed.

-"I could not help notice that recently you have been spending a lot of time with my daughter."

Michael was waiting for this question, although he was not prepared for it. "Did you call me here for this question, my Lady?" he asked.

-"Yes, do you have any problem with that?"

-"Not at all, my Lady."

-"Tell me Sir Chapman. What is the deal?"

-"We are very good friends, my Lady."

The Queen sighed deeply. "I must remind you, Sir Chapman. You are just a soldier. And she is the Princess of the Kingdom. Her father is the King. Please do not violate the boundaries. Please do not forget the difference in statuses. I am requesting you. And besides, we are looking for her suitable mate. I personally have chosen one. He is the son of a Duke," she said.

The Queen left and Michael kept standing. He felt ashamed. He was wishing to go back in time and change the future. The reality got stuck into his head like lightning. He became aware of the fact that there indeed was the difference in statuses. There was no future for him with Rose. Who was the son of the Duke? Michael did not know if what the Queen had said was true. But he did not have a chance or an intention to verify its verity.

For the first time, Michael thought differently. He knew that after becoming the King's Man, he was going to have less time for Rose. And there had been a big part of him which had been wanting to decline the offer of King's Man because of this. For a moment, he got amazed at himself on why he had wanted to reject it; after all he always had known that there was no future with the Princess, but, becoming King's Man had been his only goal for a long time. He thought if he had never known Rose, how different his life could have gone? But what about the times that he had spent with Rose? Their first meet, their first talk, the trainings, the war? What about the time when Rose had held his hands tight as he had gone emotional while talking about his past? And what about the time when they were sitting by each other, holding hands, in the garden of Eden at the core of the forest? Michael did not know what to do, what to think.

It should have been dark; it should have been the darkest of all nights. The stars were lost. And the moon was shattered into pieces. On top of them, dark clouds had made colonies all over the sky. A storm was coming and the high wind was bringing its ultimatum. There was lightning in the sky but it did nothing to illuminate the ambience, as the lightning was blood red. Still, everything was not as dark as it should have been in this darkest night.

Michael found himself inside a forest. It was a dense one with many tall trees all over the place. But the trees were under flames, the forest was burning. Michael did not know how the wildfire had started, and why it was spreading so fast. He could hear the cracking of the thunder and the crooking of the burning leaves. The ashes of the gutted leaves and branches were falling down on the ground on which the dry leaves themselves were ablaze. And the trees were giving off lethal and suffocating black fumes up in the sky high as they ignited.

Michael recognised the place. He had identified the path. It directed towards a beautiful garden of white roses. The forest certainly was the Forest of Death, the Forbidden One.

Michael was running fast towards the core of the forest. He was running away from someone and something. He was being chased. Who were they? What was it that he was running away from? Were they the undead soldiers? And the hounds of the Hell?

"Where is Axilior?" Michael found himself alone, running barefoot. His feet were red hot as he was running on blazing ground. He could feel the pain, the unbearable one. But he could not stop. The hounds already had gotten the smell of their prey. And the undead were on their horses, chasing after their hunt.

They came very close to Michael. He could hear their voices, the neigh and he could feel the hot breath of the hounds. He did not turn his head back but kept running. Otherwise, for the first time, he could see them. They were the dead French and pirates who had been killed in the last war. They had waken up to take avenge, to complete their war. But they were not humans; they did not have flesh and blood and skin. They all were structures of rotting bones, decaying and disintegrating slowly. And the hounds had sizes of mountain wolves. Blood of their last prey was dropping from their fierce teeth as they kept chasing their next.

Michael fell down at the moment when the enemies almost had caught him. His legs were hurting. And he was exhausted. Moreover, he could hardly breathe and see through the fumes.

Michael could not identify this place. He never had seen or come here before. But he had been running for a long time now. He should be in the garden by now - the garden where there was no violence, the Garden of Eden, always guarded by Angels.

"Am I lost? But how could it be? I have been in this forest so many times!" Michael cried to himself.

He sat up and found that the enemies were gone. He was not being hunted anymore. The storm started. The burning trees were shaking like maniacs. And the blood red lightning in the sky increased rapidly. All of these enhanced the wildfire like how dry woods act as catalysts in spreading flames.

But Michael was not alone. He saw a very tall man, very far away from him. He was all inside flames. He had horns on his head. But he was a shadow in the thin air and Michael could not see his face. The man was looking at Michael sitting on the ground. Suddenly, the man started to run towards him. Michael felt an impulsive pain in his chest. He tried to stand to run, however, he could not. The storm had gotten stronger. It was getting even more strong with every step of the man. And with his every step, blood red lightning pierced the sky. Michael kept trying to stand up. He tried to ask for help. And he failed at both of them. He heard crying and screaming. Someone was calling by his name. She was asking him to run. Many people started to call by his name. All of them were telling something to him. Michael could not make out the indistinct calls. At last he heard something. It was clear even in the noise. Someone was saying only one word – "Lucifer".

Michael woke up. It was a quiet night. He was on his bed in his room in the castle. He felt pain at the back of his head. His face was sweaty and his hands were shaking.

"Was it a dream? But it felt so real," he thought to himself.

Suddenly, Michael had a look at his feet. He actually had felt an ache at them. And as he looked at them, he saw burning signs - like curse marks.

11
THE FINAL WARFARE

It did not take Michael much time to get his first job as a King's Man.

Michael reported about the last thing what Williams had said to him. There were colonies of French behind the Forest of Death and the English direly needed to destroy them in order to stop the invasions once and for all. It was certain that the colonies had gotten weaker since the last war because of their unexpected and conspicuously exterminating defeat. However, one could not be over confident because they had to pass through the death traps of the forest before reaching the colonies behind it.

King's Man Sir Michael Chapman reported to his commander Sir Black. And Commander Black called on a meeting with some other commanders and the Order.

"We have an information. There are some French colonies behind the forest. It supports how they can keep attacking us for years. And we need to destroy them now before they build their strength to attack us again," Black conveyed the agenda of the meeting.

"Who gave us this information?" someone from the Order asked.

"I did," Michael said.

"How did you come to know about this, Sir?" a commander of a regiment asked.

-"Actually, I got this information from late David Williams of the sixth regiment of the South. He told me this after our fight during the last war. He suggested me to come and destroy the colonies and stop the invasions forever."

"I am sorry, but I need to ask. Are we listening to David Williams?" another one from the Order asked.

-"Apparently, yes."

"But it is David Williams whom we are talking about. He was the one mastermind behind the last war and the biggest reason behind all the casualties," someone else said.

-"Yes, I know that. But still I trust him. In his last moment, he became one of us, a soldier of this nation. He even went to the colonies to attack them all by himself in order to prevent them from more invasions at that instant."

"So, you did not see him attacking the colonies. It is just your assumption, or rather a hope, based on what he has said to you, am I right? What if the reality is different? What if he is waiting there right now with an army? What if they are waiting with traps for us?" Ray said.

-"Yes, I understand your concern. But I know that this is not the reality. No matter how much plausible it seems."

"Michael, he was a master of tricks and traps. Did you forget how he had got you into the trial? I must say that I agree with Ray's concern," Daniel said.

-"I understand your concerns. But no, I am sorry but I cannot agree with you. I saw his eyes when he was saying these words. I saw regret and pain in them. The pain of being alone, completely alone, in this world. I felt the grief. He was desperate to make things right again. I do not know why but I understood his feelings. It was hurtful. But I also saw something else in the broken eyes. It was something that could heal any stabbed heart. It was love, a lost one, to his Kingdom. In a moment, he taught me the relationship amongst hate, sadness, love and joy. From being hated and misunderstood, he wanted to be loved and accepted. In his eyes, I read his last will. He wanted to sacrifice his life for his nation, like how any of our soldier does."

For the next few seconds, no one talked anything.

Michael did not have anything more to say. And the others did not have either. Some of the others wanted to disagree with Michael, but Michael's words were more powerful and convincing than their own thinking. The rest wanted to accept Michael's words, but they had such a bad impression of Williams that it was hard for them to imagine him as a good person.

"But can we take the risk?" someone asked.

"We have to," Walther started, "it is true that if we do not strike now, this war will never come to an end. But I will not completely agree with Chapman. I personally cannot trust Williams too, and it is not my fault. Therefore, I will come up with a strategy of a final warfare while keeping in mind the possibility of a killer trap. But we must not forget that we need to cross the forest. Can anyone help me by suggesting how we can cross it?"

"Yes, I can," Michael surprised everyone.

"We are listening," Walther wanted Michael to continue.

-"I do not know if you can remember, but I had a mission in the forest once - few months ago. The mission was a failure. And I refused to accept the result. That is why I kept going into the forest. So far I have been there some many times. I have been to its core. And I know the paths so well that I can find my way out even if someone drops me blindfolded at a random part of the forest. I can guide our soldiers safely to its core. And from there, we need to proceed with intuition and faith."

Daniel was angry with this surprising self-revelation.

"Michael, are you crazy? Don't you know that it is the Forest of Death? If you go in then you will die before the next sunrise?" he shouted at him.

"But I am alive, right?" Michael replied softly. He continued, "And so are the soldiers who fought and survived at the forest during the last war. The soldiers including me who had gone into the forest for the rescue mission were also alive for the next many sunrises, right?"

-"Is this your logic on why you put your life in the line like that?"

"Alright, enough!" Black had to interrupt, "I have decided. Chapman will guide us."

"And I have come up with the plan," Walther said.

He drew a rough diagram of the forest on the table with a piece of charcoal. The picture consisted of the forest, its entrance and an artist's imagination of the portion behind the forest. Walther drew three arrows starting from the entrance of the forest and ending to the portion behind it. One arrow went through the middle of the forest and the other two ran by the middle one's two sides.

"We will divide our soldiers into three groups. Chapman and some soldiers will be at this middle. The two other groups will be here and here," Walther said by pointing at the three arrows.

"At first, the group at the middle will attack. And they will judge if it is a trap. Based on this, they will create a smoke signal. The other two groups will know if it's a trap from the smoke signal and will decide whether to jump in or fall back," Walther completed explaining his fool proof plan.

The meeting ended with the formation of the three groups. All of Michael, Black, Daniel and Ben were enlisted in the middle group which unofficially was called as 'the group of decoy' and also as 'the group of death'.

At the end of the meeting, Ray caught Michael when he was leaving.

"Michael, I want to talk to you," he said.

"Of course, Sir," Michael said.

-"I want to ask you about your experience in the forest."

Michael shared with him his experience in the forest. He told him about the journeys, the trees, the supernatural feeling for the existence of the undead and hell hounds. But he deliberately did not tell about the garden. He wanted it to remain as a secret only to Rose and himself.

Ray did not show much interest in listening to Michael's experience which was strange.

"Now tell me. What do you think about the curse?" he asked. It was obvious that this was the question he had been willing to ask and the previous one was just a conversation starter.

"Frankly, I don't believe in it anymore. I should admit that there was a time when I believed in it too. But now, I do not see a point to believe it. I believe that either the curse does not exist at all or it just does favouritism," Michael said.

-"And you don't believe in it because of the result of that rescue mission, is it?"

-"There are so many more reasons, Sir."

Ray sighed and said, "Michael, I need to inform something to you. I guess you are not in touch with your comrades of that mission. It is unfortunate that, besides you, all the others are dead."

It took Michael as a shock. "What!" he exclaimed.

-"Yes, Michael. Two of them recently died of diseases. The rest died in the last war. Only you are alive. I am not sure and I hope I am wrong. But I think may be the forest is still acting. Slowly. But it is acting. So, I request you to be careful. Don't do anything hasty. And I request you to stop going into the forest."

Michael was stunned. He did not know of this news. Actually, the mission was so far in the past that he had stopped worrying about the aftermath long ago.

"Is the curse real? Am I cursed? Am I drowning slowly into the quicksand of death?" he thought.

-"Are you okay? Are you feeling any physical illness, mental trauma, abnormalities or anything like that lately? Or do you think that someone is trying to kill you?"

Michael took some time to think about it. He had not been feeling well lately. Moreover, he was having these nightmares. He had seen them twice more after the first one. Coincidentally, the stage of the nightmares was the Forest of Death itself. In the nightmares, the forest was burning as if it was the inferno of eternal damnation. Michael was in the forest and was chased by the undead soldiers and hounds from the Hell. He kept on trying to find his way out. He also tried to find the garden. But he kept getting lost. At last, he confronted the tall man figure with horns. He could not see the man's face. But he could hear the man's roar. And he could hear many people calling him by his name. And they shouted at him telling him to run. And someone was saying only one word – "Lucifer".

"No Sir. I am fine," he answered Ray.

It was the night before the big mission when Michael had his fourth nightmare. But there was a difference between this and the previous dreams. This one was even more intense.

The nightmare started as usual. Michael was in the burning Forest of Death. He was being chased by the dead and the hounds. He tried to find salvation but was lost. And he ended up in front of the tall man figure with horns.

The nightmare changed at this point. The storm got bigger than ever and more destroying. The burning and weakened tall trees which once had signified the symbol and symphony of strength started to break down. The barks and leaves of them ignited the blazing ground even more. Whirlpools of flames - burning hot gases of the atmosphere started to swallow the forest. The scorching and scathing fire was burning Michael's shirt and skin. And it was getting almost impossible for him to stand or kneel anymore with his injured and red hot feet and knees. He was hearing many people shouting, calling him, and asking him to run. Suddenly, Michael saw a child - a small boy. He was standing within the flames and looking at him. He was looking miserable in the burning clothes. And he was crying, covering his face with arms. Where was his mother? Had she left him like this in this inferno within the Forest of Death? Why was he crying? Was he tired of waiting and waiting for her to come back? Had he forgotten the meaning of joy and laughter and the reasons to live and love?

The boy was caught in fire. And he started to scream in agony. He was dying.

"Help! Somebody, please help!" Michael shouted asking for help. But nobody came, not even the ones who had been calling him by his name and asking him to run away.

The tall man started to run towards Michael. He was coming closer and closer. And his face was becoming clearer and visible. He had the face of a goat with horns of the same on the head. The legs were that of a goat too. But the rest of the body was of a human. Parts of the body were covered under dense fur.

Lucifer was coming. And he was saying something which was incomprehensible to Michael because of his roars. Unlike the previous dreams, tonight Michael could not wake up. He was on the ground on his knees like a lifeless sculpture.

He also had lost his voice to shout for help. And Lucifer was almost here.

Dong! Dong! Dong!

Michael woke up. The bell was ringing. This meant that it was the time to get ready for the battle.

Michael had trouble getting up from his bed. He felt pain in his whole body. His legs were hurting as if a demon had tried to bake them alive. His eyes were in a very bad condition too; they took a significant amount of time to adjust with the brightness. He touched his own forehead; he was burning with fever.

Michael did not take much time to get ready. He wore his uniform and the cloak with Sword on the Circle for his first mission as a King's Man. Then he joined the others in front of the forest.

Commander Black was there. Walther was there too. They let the others know of the entire plan once again. Black called Michael on. And he said that Michael had the experience of being in the forest many times. And so he was the best candidate to guide the team on this crucial mission. Black decided and announced that Michael would be the Captain for that mission. He would be Commander Chapman, commander of the King's Men.

From here the soldiers got divided into three groups as planned by Walther. Michael, Black, Daniel and Ben were in the group two as decided. And they started their journey into the Forest of Death, the Forbidden One.

Unlike the rescue mission of Young Junior, this mission had been kept confidential. The authority did not want any unnecessary attention that could alert the enemies. Moreover, Williams' last intention was not clear. Only Michael had faith in Williams which was very ironic itself.

The soldiers went in groups. There were about fifty soldiers in the second group where Michael and the others were there.

They headed towards the core and Michael was their leader and guide.

I must remind my readers that Michael Chapman was the only soldier who had previously come into the forest.

After a few minutes, the soldiers started to have the unusual sensations. They started to look behind as if someone was following them; they started to look at the branches of the trees as if someone was about to jump at them from there. They started to hear the sounds of running horses and the howling hounds. The Hell hounds were there too.

"Don't worry and don't look back. Just keep following me!" Michael ordered.

"Are you sure? It feels like someone is behind me!" a frightened soldier asked.

-"Yes, I am sure. Just trust me and keep your horse running."

"Sir Chapman! I just saw something on a tree! There is definitely something following us!" another soldier shared his concern.

Suddenly, they heard howling; it came from a place very close. And they could easily hear the footsteps of hounds and soldiers running towards them; the sounds were penetrating the heavy suffocating air.

Some boughs of the trees shook up violently. Leaves fell on the ground from them. The horses were acting strange which actually was not strange to Michael and Axilior at all.

"Keep following me. If you stop, they will catch you. You will be in a safe place as soon as we are at the core," Michael ordered. However, he was exaggerating and he knew it himself. He had been in the forest many times alone, but today the death trap was acting even deadlier. He had no idea what would happen at the core and beyond that.

"They will catch us? Who are they?" the frightened soldiers asked again. And Michael did not answer to this question.

Frankly, he did not know the answer himself. Who are 'they'? Undead? Hell Hounds? Unprecedented Soldiers? French and Pirates? He did not know. All he knew was that he had to keep Axilior running at its highest velocity.

Soon they reached at the core. Michael took a longer path to avoid the garden as he did not want it to be messed up by running horses. And after the core, the portion of the forest was new to him too. But they kept running forward, one horse after another.

All of a sudden, Michael stopped and so stopped the soldiers of this group who had been following him. Michael started to cough badly. He covered his mouth with his hand. He was feeling intense pain in his stomach. And with every cough, this ache was getting magnified by thousand times. He removed the hand from his mouth and looked at it - there was blood at his hand. He also felt that his fever had gone up. At last, Michael looked at the others.

The whole place had caught fire. The trees were burning and releasing smoke. The ground caught up in flames too. The other soldiers and their horses were screaming and trying to flee out. Unfortunate were they as spreading and sprouting flames and burning gases were seizing, catching, grasping and swallowing them one by one. It was burning them alive and Michael could not do a thing. He just stayed steadily still and watched his nightmare killing his friends and comrades. "Michael!" someone started to call him by name. Michael looked at somewhere. And his fear came true. The man with goat's face and horns was there. He just started to run at Michael. And more people started to call him by his name. "Michael, run!" They were saying.

"Michael! Are you with us or not?" Michael heard Daniel's voice.

"What? What is going on?" Michael asked.

"You started to cough and almost went senseless," Black replied.

Michael looked at his surroundings. No, it was not burning. Everyone was alright too. And there was no man with goat's face and horns running at him, neither was there someone calling by his name and asking him to run.

"Nothing. I just had a headache and head rush," Michael said. "Let's go. We are getting late," he ordered. However, he knew that it was no head rush. Was he hallucinating? Was he going insane?

It was no dream. He was wide awake. This was the fifth time he saw the scenes. The previous four were in dreams, but what about this time?

"What is happening to me?" he asked himself.

The soldiers kept going forward after this small delay. The density of the forest was decreasing. The supernatural feelings of being chased were declining too. After some time they got out of the forest and became the first and only people so far as of that date to perform the feat.

There were about fifty tents and two hundred armless French soldiers. The English soldiers dominated over them with swords and flamed torches. They started killing their opponents and gutting the tents. It was their only and final chance to stop the war forever.

Ben made a smoke signal to send the message to the other two groups to join the battle. And more English soldiers came into the front as soon as they got the signal.

The mission was over with a grand success very soon. All the enemies were slayed down and there was no casualty report for the attacking side.

"Hurrah!" the soldiers started the celebration of victory - a perfect triumph. They came down from the horses, shook hands and hugged. At the moment the soldiers were soulfully wanting glasses of wine, rum, hot drinks and delicious foods to be parts of their celebration. They also were hoping for music and women. Unfortunately, they did not have those with them. They needed to get back to a bar of their Kingdom to celebrate their victory. But all of them were very happy as the war finally had come to an end. They also were hoping that all the curses of the Forest of Death would finally lift up.

Michael was thinking about David Williams. His last words were stuck in his head. *"He did tell the truth,"* Michael thought. He himself was not sure if even for a second he had doubted Williams or not. But he knew that a big part of himself had wanted not to believe in Williams. Or, better to state that the big part was too afraid to believe what Williams had told.

Williams had died being misunderstood. The people of his Kingdom could not accept him. His guilts were not forgiven. His memories were alone, not remembered by anyone, just like how he himself was when he was alive. His last sacrifice had not gone in vain. He probably had been successful in preventing more invasions and attacks on the injured Kingdom. But his name would never be engraved in the stone of his grave. Nobody would even bother to search for his dead body. The body was alone without a soul exactly as it had been with a soul. David Williams, the lone and silent hero, a wicked and misjudged son of the Kingdom was lying somewhere, silently and forgotten.

Michael was glad that he had not disbelieved in his last words. He was grateful to Williams for being the one to stop the more-than-half-a-century old war once and for all. And he was feeling pity for him. But he never again remembered that Williams had been the reason who started the war of massive massacres.

★★★

12

"Goodbye, Sweetheart"

How was the Forest of Death? Was it really forbidden like the Adam's fruit of knowledge? Was it really cursed? What was the curse? "Anyone who trespasses into the territory will suffer a terrible death" - was this it?

It had been two weeks since the last mission. And it had been longer, actually almost a month, since Michael had last met Rose.

Michael had been so busy lately and he had decided to deliberately keep himself busier; he recalled what the Queen had said to him. Had she lied? Did Michael care? Why had not Rose tried to contact him from her side?

Michael now was the second in command in the army of the King's Men. In the absence of Black, he was Commander Chapman. Mostly his bravery and dedication had led him to be one of the youngest King's Men and the youngest Commander of them ever. The whole Kingdom and also lands beyond its border now knew his name. What Michael was liking the most was that women were showing interest in him. He was greeted by them every time he was out in towns or villages. They used to gather and form crowds to see him patrolling by riding his horse. He also got letters from them.

The other King's Men made fun of these moments during their dinners and Michael liked these talks too. He was also respected by all. Michael was loving being famous.

It had been some time since Michael had met Daniel and Ben. It had been that long since he had last visited the seventh regiment of the South. And it had been even more since he had last been in the memorial grounds.

But one should not judge him. He had been in an enormously tight schedule. From dawn to dusk, he had to work on his professional life. This included but was not confined to trainings, patrolling and official works. The only time he got for his personal life was during the dinner.

Michael had been right: there was not much time for him to spend for Rose. It had been such a while since they had been in the training. The good old days had been so beautiful and away from the harsh and cruel reality. They had not worried about the future back then; they had enjoyed the present.

Michael was so busy that he did not even have much time to think about the past as he once had used to, however, he still was hoping if he could meet her again.

As a King's Man, Michael no longer had to watch from the South Tower on every Monday night. Nevertheless, he had managed to pay visits to the apex twice in the last one month. He could not stay there for long as he had used to before, and he did not enjoy the world of night. He wrote to James in brief and returned to his room as he had early works on the next day.

Sometimes Michael had to work with the Order. Even someone with a strong cognitive mind as Walther also asked for and accepted his opinions during the meetings. In the absence of Black, Michael also performed his duty as a member of the jury in one criminal court case. Michael remembered that he had been in here on the platform allocated for the guilty more than a month ago. Rose, Molly, Daniel, Tim and a few others had proved that he was innocent. Michael was grateful to them.

One day, Michael had to go near the forest. But he did not enter. And he could not meet his friends from his old regiment either as he had to return to his superior Black and hand over a report. He passed the seventh regiment of the South gently by keeping a distance. He saw, from the distance, the soldiers training like the passed days from the past. He saw Daniel and Ben. And he could not overlook the tent where he had lived during his days in the regiment. The stables did not get away from his sight too. James' and his old horses were still there in one of them and that particular stable got caught in his vision. Before leaving the regiment, Michael had requested Ben to take care of them. He could gamble his life with that Ben was keeping his request perfectly. It really had been a while since he had seen the horses.

It was a good sign for Michael that recently he had not seen the nightmares again. He even had consulted a doctor and was under medication. The problems that he had been having, like the headache and coughs and pains in the back, were improving. It was even a better sign considering the fact that he was now working harder than ever. "No wonder that it is not anyone's job. No wonder that it requires so many qualifications," he made a compliment about the profession of a King's Man to himself.

Michael personally had met Ray. They had talked about the forest. Michael had assured him that he would not be visiting the death trap ever again.

It was one fine holiday. Michael got some time to spare and decided to go to a bar. Would he go to the old bar in the last village in front of the forest like how he had used to? But now he had the money to spend in an elite bar. Then why should he go to the old one and spend the time with farmers and blacksmiths and the soldiers of the regiments? He decided to go to a bar in a city with some other King's Men.

The bar was full of people on the occasion of the holiday. The King's Men were recognised as soon as they entered, because of the King's Crest that they were wearing. The people cheered for the devoted King's Men. They drank for their good health.

There was a large group of young and attractive women in the bar. They also were enjoying the holiday. They were wearing fashioned clothes and were having costly wines. One of them identified Michael. And started to gossip about him. They were looking at him, talking amongst themselves and laughing. The King's Men caught that in their eyes. And they influenced Michael to go and talk to the ladies.

"Go, man! Get your woman", "You are the man of the moment", "I don't know if I am proud of you or jealous" - they said many more.

At last one of the women called Michael herself, "Sir Chapman, please come over here."

Michael smiled, finished his drink and went to the table where the attractive women were sitting.

"The next round is on me," he offered drinks to them and the women shouted in joy.

Michael was enjoying being famous to them.

"Where is Rose? She did not contact me lately. I hope she knows how busy I am nowadays. Is she preparing for her wedding with the Duke's son? Why should I care? I already have cared a lot, and now I need to stop. Look at these beautiful ladies! I am having the best time of my life. And of course, I deserve it. I am the strongest. I am a King's Man. I deserve to be loved, not ignored."

Little Michael was looking at himself. How young was he? Ten years - the age when he had first heard of the King's Men. And this was the age when he had started to dream of becoming one of them. He had drawn pictures of how it might have been to be a King's Man. Was the King's Man Chapman really living his life as little Michael had dreamed of?

Little Michael was wearing a worn cloth covered in dirt and mud of the field that he had been working recently. The owners of this elite bar could throw him out if they had seen him and his clothes and the torn shoes. But they did not as they could not see him. He was just an abstract form from the past of King's Man Chapman.

King's Man Chapman did not fail to notice the little boy. It was he himself, but from a different time zone; it was he himself from his past, when he had lived and worked in the fields. It seemed like little Michael had just finished his day in the firm and was returning back to his room to have his hot soup, the tasteless liquid which he had been waiting for since the morning. It was clear that he also was interested in listening to the stories from his elders - the legends of the King's Men of the Kingdom in the south.

"If I knew this is what a King's Man's life looks like then I would never spend my nights listening to those stories. I would go straight to my dirty and old but warm bed," little Michael told Sir Chapman.

"Who are you?" Sir Chapman asked despite knowing the answer.

"I am Michael Chapman. Who are you?" little Chapman asked.

Sir Chapman tried to reply but he could not remember who he was. He started stammering.

Little Michael said, "I can see your cloak. Are you a King's Man? That is very impressive."

"Thank you," Sir Chapman said. He had trouble to say even these two words. He was feeling as if he did not know how to speak.

-"Why are you alone? Do you have no friend? Hey, do you know that I am a farmer boy. But I still have people with whom I can talk to. Why do not you have one?"

-"I have friends with whom I can talk."

-"Where are they? I cannot see any of them."

Sir Chapman tried to think of his friends. Where were they? What were their names? Why could not he remember any of them? Did not he have friends? He used to have, did not he?

"Are these beautiful ladies your friends? Or, are these King's Men who do not even know about your struggles, your feelings? They do not even know you. Are they your friends?" little Michael was asking.

Sir Chapman wanted to call them his friends, but, he could not. Even he himself knew that it was a lie. Little Michael came very close to Sir Chapman and did not sit on an empty chair. He did not want to make it dirty.

"Why can't anyone else see or hear you?" Sir Chapman asked. Little Michael could not care less about this question.

"I heard you were saying that this was the best day of your life. Tell me, Sir, how much better it is than the day James and you got recruited in the army? And then the day you first met the Princess? Your first talk, first training, the holding hands when you were crying, the moment in the garden of the forest, the dance?"

Sir Chapman was getting overwhelmed. He started to feel the old pain in his back. He was suffocating. "Get out! Get away from me!" he ended up shouting at the little kid.

Little Michael ran away from the bar. Sir Chapman felt ashamed for a moment. He wanted to talk to the little kid more. Where did he come from? Where did he go? Could he safely reach home?

Little Michael came in again, but not alone. He forcefully brought Mrs. Brenda with him by pulling her hand. How could he? Was not he an abstract?

Sir Chapman became embarrassed after seeing Mrs. Brenda. She, on the other hand, was shocked at Sir Chapman. She was stunned. And she could not watch anymore. She wanted to say something to Sir Chapman. But, instead, she covered her face with hands and left sniffing. Little Chapman followed her and left too.

A current of awareness hit Sir Chapman's head intensely and hard. And he found himself back to the reality. He again could hear the loud noise of the people enjoying their drinks and the holiday. He could again see the attractive women by his side laughing and talking and cheering. But Sir Chapman's concentration was fixated on Mrs. Brenda leaving the place, alone and crying.

"I need to go," he said to his beautiful companies and left without even listening to what the companies were saying.

"What happened, Sir?", "Where are you going?", "When are you coming back?" the attractive lasses kept asking. But, Sir Chapman did not care for them and left.

When he got out of the place, he could not see Mrs. Brenda. But he saw little Michael again. The kid was standing at a distance and was waiting for him while leaning on the wall of the bar. Upon seeing Sir Chapman, he stood straight and began to run away. Sir Chapman also took Axilior and chased him.

Little Michael was running unusually fast - like a squirrel on a tree, or a leopard on a hunt. Even a horse as quick as Axilior could not catch him. On top of that, little Michael periodically stopped only to ensure that Sir Chapman did not lose his track.

Sir Chapman was chasing the kid with torn clothes and shoes - the self from the past. And he kept meticulous eyes on the track and trail. He did not, or rather could not, notice where he was going to. The whole world had become irrelevant to him. The rest were oblivious of him too. And the only pertinent thing to him was little Michael.

It was as if the whole world was darkened by the shadows of the wings of a giant bat covering the sky. Was the air steady, or was it stormy? What was the smell? Or, was there any odour left at all? How was Sir Chapman feeling - cold, hot? Why was not he feeling anything?

Sir Chapman found himself in front of a stable of the South Bailey of the castle grounds. And he saw little Michael standing beside him and looking at the stable.

"Can you remember the place?" little Michael asked.

The brightness of the day declined in a blink of Sir Chapman's eyes. The air stopped blowing and so stopped the leaves undulating with its rhythm. And Sir Chapman saw himself, a third Michael Chapman, with Axilior in the stable. He saw Ms. Rose standing behind the third Michael Chapman. She called the third Michael Chapman. She was asking if he knew her. She was wearing a lovely dress, not an unusual gown of a Princess though. She was looking younger, and so beautiful. Why was the third Michael Chapman taking so much time to reply!

"Can you remember the place?" Little Michael asked again. "This is where and how you two first had your talk," he said.

The fading light got its brightness back again. And Sir Chapman could no longer see the third avatar of himself and young Rose. He turned his head around and saw little Michael running into the Greathall. Why was not anyone stopping him?

"You know where to find me," little Michael shouted while entering the building.

It was the night. Rose was in her room, lying on her bed. The room was small, but it definitely was the most beautiful of all rooms of the entire Kingdom. The furnished bed and furniture were made of costly wood exported from foreign lands of East. There were tiny idols of marble and stones to decorate. There were candle bars with twelve candlesticks in each of them. And there was a handsome-looking fireplace at the opposite side of the bed. The fire in there was warming the room. And the bed, made by Mrs. Brenda sometime ago with comfortable blankets, was where Rose was lying.

The tray of delicious dinner and bitter medicines on the table beside the bed was only partially empty. Rose could not have all the little foods and the lot of the medicines.

"You are standing for a long time. Why do not you sit? No, not there on the table. Come sit on the bed. Hey, no, not by my legs. I cannot see you like that. Sit beside me," Rose said to little Michael. Little Michael was in here, for how long? How was Rose seeing and talking to him? Was not he an abstract from Sir Chapman's past?

Little Michael sat beside lying Rose. And he looked at the tray with the half eaten dinner and the barely touched medicines.

"Why did not you eat?" he asked her.

Rose smiled but did not answer to his question. She wanted to avoid letting the kid know of the harsh truth at such an early age.

"Can I have the meatloaf? I am hungry," little Michael requested.

"Yes, sure! Just don't eat the ones that I have touched," Rose was sure that the disease was not infectious, but she could not afford to take the risk and let little Michael suffer like how she had been for the last thirty days. Little Michael picked up the meatloaf and a bread. He actually had already faced harsh truth of reality in life, and he understood everything. But he certainly was too hungry and little to quit eating and ask why Rose had not had the medicines.

"Tell me your story, little one. How is your village?" Rose asked.

"It is fine. I work in a mill. I work every day in the field," little Michael tried to prove how capable he was.

"Wow!" Rose was impressed. "And what do you do more?" she asked.

-"I listen to the stories of this Kingdom, the King, his Men. I listen to the stories about you. And I smoke too."

Rose sat up. It took her some time, a lot of effort and to endure severe pain. She patted little Michael on his head and said, "Aren't you a little young to smoke?" Little Michael did not answer but continued to eat.

"Tell me about your mother. Can you remember?" Rose asked.

Little Michael put the half eaten loaf on the tray, thought something for a moment and said, "She left me, Madam."

Rose quickly got up and hugged little Michael. She did not want to look at Michael crying once again while thinking about his past. She remembered the time, some long ago. Michael and she had been enjoying a little break after their training. And they had been sharing stories from their past. Michael had cried after thinking about his past, his mother, the hardship and the ignorance.

Little Michael did not cry. Rather, he asked, "Tell me about your mother."

-"My mother? Well, I cannot tell about her in a sentence, or even in many sentences. She is the Queen. But, she is simple. People say that I have gone after her. Sometimes, we fought. She wanted me to get married with a Prince, but I always denied. I sometimes have been unnecessarily mad at her. Later, she herself came to me with the dinner. We ate together in this room. She always thinks what is the best for me. I love her. I will miss her."

Now, little Michael was the one to quickly get up. And he cleaned the Princess's teary eyes with the unclean hands of his - the hands with dirt from the fields where he had worked that on-going day. Rose, in return, kissed at the little hands.

And she asked, "Will he come?"

Little Michael did not know the answer. He did not even know what and how to respond. He could only say, "I saw him today."

Rose remained silent. She knew what would happen if he would not come. Actually, nothing would happen. And nothing would ever happen. And everything would end, without a goodbye. She was only wanting to meet him one last time, tell him the things that she had never said, tell him not to cry and to fight well, and bid one last goodbye. And as the moon travelled in the sky from one side to the other, she realised how less time she had in her hands.

Suddenly, they heard a knock on the door.

"Let me," little Michael jumped up and went running to open it. And Rose kept looking as he opened it.

It was Sir Chapman Michael.

Michael ran towards Rose lying on the bed, sat on his knees, held her hands, closed his eyes and said, "I am sorry I am this late." He could not see little Michael anymore.

"No. You are not late. You are right in time," Rose held his hands back and said, smiling.

And she saw little Michael smiling too, and fading away to the world of abstracts. He faded in the thin air and went to from where he had come. His mission was over. Thus, Rose saw him for the last time - in the worn and dirty clothes, the torn shoes, still smiling and waving the hands.

Michael did not hesitate anymore. He was no longer afraid to love her. He kissed her on the lips, and she kissed back. She no longer was hesitant to express her feelings too. Michael put off his armour and kissed at her bare chest. And she kissed back on his head and asked him to the bed. The feeble candlesticks were dying and the fireplace was the only one to light the room as Michael and Rose made love.

The night progressed. Michael was sitting on the bed and Rose was lying.

"I wish we could have spent some more time together. I wish if I had stopped the time when we were in the garden of the forest," Michael sighed.

"Me too. And I wish if I could bear this child - our child," emotional Rose said.

Starshine was coming from outside through the window. Then he looked back at Rose. She was looking pale. And she saw teardrops in Michael's eyes.

"Hey, is the strongest soldier of the Island crying for someone like me?" Rose laughed, which was a fake attempt to hide the agony underneath - the agony of losing him forever.

"I should have told you. I should have forbidden you from entering the forest. It is the curse. And it is all my fault," Michael cried.

-"No. It is not. It was meant to be for me. My father called the best doctors of the Island. And they could not find a cure. But, they discovered that this disease had been generating since my days in Cambridge. So, do not blame yourself." Rose stopped for a moment. She held his hands for one last time. And then she said, "Live well, Michael. Eat well. You are looking weak nowadays. Are you working very hard? Take care of yourself. It was such an exciting journey so far with all the good and bad. But, you are the most beautiful thing that happened to me. Thank you for the training sessions. And thank you for coming here tonight. Thank you for everything."

Michael got up and kissed her on the forehead for one last time. And he was going out of the room for one last time. For one last time? Michael had been prepared for meeting Rose in her deathbed. However, he was not ready for this present time. As soon as he would get out from the door, he would not see her ever again. Her waving the hands to bid farewell would be for the last and lifelong farewell. She would become a past, a decaying memory, in his life. How would he live with that?

"Goodbye, sweetheart."

Michael left the room and never saw Rose again.

Michael met the King and the Queen at the stairways. They were silent as stone. The Queen's eyes had dried up some time ago. And they had been waiting here for the last few hours. They knew about Michael being with Rose. But, Michael did not get scared of the consequences. To his surprise, the King asked, "How is Rose, Michael?" And the Queen said in a very low and broken tone, "Thank you."

Michael had been sitting on a stair for the last one hour. And he watched the night progressing towards brightness from the dark. He watched the shadows of the idols of the Greathall to move as the moon travelled from one side of the sky to the other and so did its shine. But, the moonlight was sick. And there was no star. Clouds were patrolling in their victory ground and the heavenly bodies were dominated over.

The phase changed gradually. The clouds were erased. The moon and the stars started shining brightly again. And the Starshine came into the Greathall through the gigantic windows with ornate glasses. And the dust in the hall danced in the waves like the Stardusts in the Starshine.

Some people in black clothes passed Michael. They went towards Rose's room. And they were carrying a beautiful white coffin with golden patterns and impressions crafted on it.

★★★

13
His Last Pages

"Dear James,

How are you? How is Molly? Is she yelling at you? It is so funny that I miss her yelling, it has been a while since I have heard them. Tonight, I need to write many things. I don't even know from where to start.

As you can see, I am back with my job at the South Tower. And yes, today is Monday. You must be wondering how it is possible. You must be thinking that I should be elsewhere with a more important project assigned only to a King's Man. Well, yes, there are projects that only are assigned to a King's Man and watching from the peak of the South Tower certainly is not one of them. James, don't think that I am an odd exception. I am not a King's Man with such a mundane duty. But, the truth is, I am not a King's Man anymore.

Yes, I have resigned. I could not come back here where she had lived. There are these memories which haunt me even if I am miles away from this place. This castle, the South Bailey, that particular stable, the Greathall, the ball room, her room, and even this Tower - they smell like her, her fragrance, the smell of her hair. Therefore, I could not come back. I could not tolerate the torture of the haunting memories of the beautiful past.

So, why am I back here tonight? Did I get back my old job to watch? No. They had asked me, but I had denied. But tonight is an exception. I am coming here for the last time tonight.

He has caught me, James. Lucifer won it. I could not overrun him. The forest was burning. The storm was blowing. I was trying to run away from him and he was chasing me. The ground was in flames too. And I was barefoot and naked. Blaze was catching my feet and body; the fire of inferno was burning me alive. My legs were injured and I was in pain. I could no longer run or walk or stand. And Lucifer's conflagrating hand caught my shoulder. It gutted the flesh out. The skin was poisoned by the bites of a million snakes. The warmth dehydrated my underneath, ravaged my muscles, and liquefied my bones. And I screamed, but no one listened. Tears did not come out from my exploding eyes.

I have been feeling the old pain again, since she is gone. I feel the ache in my back. It is like a cruel executioner is breaking them by hammering. And the torment in my stomach feels like a witch had forced me to drink her toxic chemicals. I have not had a good sleep in some many previous nights. I wake up so early at the dawn that it is still dark and the sun is yet to rise. I am afraid of waking up this early when the whole world is sleeping and only I am the one suffering the abnormalities. I tried going to sleep very late at nights, but I ended up waking at exactly the same hour of the dawn. And I cannot go back to sleep anymore. Furthermore, because of the nightmares, I am frightened to sleep. Rather, I want to stay awake the entire long nights, watch the rest enjoying the peace when my soul gets tortured in the eternal damnation of the Hell. Sometimes,

I have different dreams too - about you, Molly, and my mom. But, all of them are nightmares. I see the night of your death, the days following that night, Molly's death, and my mom leaving me alone in the shelter. I recently saw Rose in a dream too. But, it was not about the day when we danced, or the days of the training. But, it was the moment when I was leaving the room, bidding her one last farewell. Although I was dreaming, I felt the sorrow. I sensed everything again - the despair and distress of leaving her forever. I left the room and could not turn to see her for a last time. I could not see her for one last time as I knew it was the end, but I wish if I had. I wish if I had seen her eyes and smile for that one more time. And I wish if I had not left the room, rather, stayed there with her until the very end. But, I could not.

James, tonight is the last time I have climbed up these long stairs to this summit of this Tower. In the past, I have climbed to here so fluently. Tonight was different - I felt agony with every step of mine. I was having trouble breathing, as if a demon had clutched my throat to smother me to death. My legs were shaking badly, as if the Devil himself was pulling them downwards to the perdition. I cannot climb up to here anymore. So, tonight is the last night I am going to enjoy the night from the South Tower. Tonight, I will enjoy the moon, the silvered spiders and sleeping birds, the greenish river and the Stardusts dancing in the waves of the Starshine one last time. And tonight is the last time I am writing to you, James. This is the end of my letters to you, my brother.

Hey, have you ever thought what to engrave in your gravestone? What to write in there? Something that will compel the people standing in front of it to think and remember you for centuries?

Daniel and Ben are the ones taking care of me nowadays. We cannot afford costly medication. But, whatever they are doing, I cannot repay them back. And I am ashamed that I almost had forgotten my friends while I was a King's Man. It seems like I ran after a wrong destination when my true destiny was right beside me. And it was very late when I fully came to the realisation that the voyage of hardship towards the dream of becoming a member of the Men was sweet, whereas the time post achieving the dream was not. I understood that I had wanted to be a King's Man, but had not wanted to receive it as my occupation. I had never wanted it to devour me from my friends and my love. What a fool I was!

I met our old horses yesterday. Axilior is there too in the same stable. They had been with me for such a long time. How is Warcress? The Black Beauty?

I bade goodbye to the King, the Queen, Commander Black and Walther a few days ago. They are aware of the poor condition of my health.

It was such an amazing journey so far. I am grateful to God for all that I have gained in this Kingdom. The days in the seventh regiment of the South, the training sessions, Molly's high pitch voice, Tim's soft calls, Daniel, Benjamin and You, the watches in this Tower, my times with Rose, and even the times as the member of the King's Men - I am glad all of them happened to me. Now I am prepared to finish this race. I am ready for the eternal rest. I am eagerly waiting to go and meet her again in the beautiful Garden of Eden at the core of the mesmerizing Forest of Joys as souls.

Is the curse of the Forest really the one to kill me? I do not even care anymore. All I care now is to be an integrated part of the Forest, to be a bee in the garden and dance around her as she blossoms as the loveliest rose.

Where is our old friend, the white owl? I have not seen her this whole night so far. Oh, there she is! She is coming from the Forest. Can you see her, James? She is dancing in front of the oceans of stars and the brightest of the moons in the sky above. Look at her unfolding the wings! She is foraging for food. Hear her howl!

This is it, James. This is where I need to stop. I need to go back and have the last drops of the medicines. Hereby, I want to thank all of you to make me feel special. All of you made my life worthy of living. And, thank you for hearing me out, even when I was talking nonsense.

Goodbye."

14

From Beyond the Diary of Michael Chapman

These were the last pages of the diary of Michael Chapman. I completed translating it from the medieval century common dialect to Modern English. It had been an arduous job as the diary was written by one ordinary citizen, not a scholar, and who had spent his whole childhood in villages. The entire tome, the diary of Michael Chapman, contains words, idioms, phrases and expressions not commonly used in scholarly articles of that century, but consists of a dialect of a rural vocal language. And it took me about two weeks to complete the work. It also deserves mention that I had to search and go through other books and articles from the library to buttress the statements of Michael Chapman and to find the information not highlighted in his tome.

It was one tough week and I had to spend the whole time working in the library. But at last, I achieved the goal which I had come for. I completed my dissertation successfully and mailed it to my supervisor while keeping Prof Tennyson in the 'cc'.

My goal of coming in this cathedral town was to find a topic for my Masters Thesis, and I got that despite having ambiguities at the beginning. However, later, I found that I have achieved something even more important for me.

I came to know about Michael Chapman, James and Molly Wheeler, Rose Scarlett, David Williams and many more. I came to know about love and hate, faith and distrust, friendship and antipathy, acceptance and rejection, loyalty and betrayal, synchronization and misunderstanding. I came to know about life and death.

What did Michael Chapman teach me? Firstly, he taught me resilience. If life is a race then he had to face so many obstacles so many times. But, he overcame the hurdles and started running again. If life is a sprint then he could only run for about a half of it. If life is a marathon then he could only run for about one-third of the allotted run before quitting, because of the broken knee may be? But the small part that he had run, he had been athletic. He had run, had been stopped by, had been run over, but he had stood up and started running again.

And what did the diary teach me? Well, it taught me how to live and love. It taught me about human lives.

After perusing through the tome, I reviewed my whole life - from the passed past to the future dreams. I put my life under the microscope where the tome was my scientific manual. How was my past? How pragmatic is my goal? Am I trying to become a King's Man and get detached from my loved ones because of the piles of professional responsibilities?

I met Prof Tennyson last month. He is retired now and is spending his time in a suburban county side of Texas, USA. I had an international seminar to attend in Texas A&M University last month and I managed some time out to meet him. We talked about our academics and works, contemporary researches, etc. My dissertation came out within a context as a pertinent part. And he advised me to write it down for the common audience.

Now, at last, there is something that is not written in the diary of Michael Chapman. However, without it, his story is not complete. This is something from beyond the diary of Michael Chapman. And I need to write it at the end, which is now.

After completing my translation, I had met Prof Tennyson. Looking at my face and realising my confusions, he himself said, "We never have found any trail of the Hell Hounds. However, recent archeological and biological evidences suggest that the forest had been the feeding ground of mountain wolves for long. The unprecedented soldiers? Well, I think Walther Livingston had been correct. There lived some savage tribes in the forest. Mass murders, rapes, human sacrifices, inhuman rituals were in their cultures. The Undead? Um, ah! I don't know. And the dreams of Michael Chapman, the curse - I think some things about the forest will always remain a mystery."

"What exactly was the curse?" I had to ask.

-"Well, from modern scientific point of view, there never was a curse. Citizens used to hear the howling of the wolves. And the unsolved murders within the forest were also committed by them."

I had to remember the signs of claws on the body of the temporary survivor of the forest - the horse, described in the tome.

"And the way Michael Chapman and Rose Scarlett died?" I had to ask again.

-"Ah! Actually, medical reports of treatments of Ms. Scarlett show that she had cancer and it got fatal and exposed only in its last stage. She had only four weeks to live after that. And,

Chapman already had some physical disorders for long. The death of Ms. Scarlett worsened his condition. It took his life."

I was a little upset with the outcome of the story and could not help expressing my dissatisfaction to Prof Tennyson.

"Is this ending all right, Sir?" I directly had asked as an amateur audience of a tragic soap opera.

He had not replied but asked me to follow him. We had got out of the castle and gone to the memorial grounds. The artistic beauty of the place had enthralled us - Mother Nature is such an artist! The gravestones and the tablets with the names of the fallen soldiers engraved on them had reminded how peacefully they had been sleeping their long rest, for centuries. The old grey gravestones had been telling us stories of those heroes, the myths and the legends. And the soldiers themselves had been sleeping while looking at their old yet undying Kingdom, for centuries.

Some stones had snatched my in-depth attention. I had found the names - James Wheeler, Molly Wheeler, and of Daniel, Benjamin, Raphael, the unsung heroes like Tim, and many more.

From there, we had headed to the Royal Graveyard at the North. Kings and their families from the reign of King Phillip V to King George IV had been lying here for centuries. The graves were there, one after the other. And we had to walk from the beginning of the yard to the end of it to get to our desired destination. Small pavements were there to lead us through the graveyard. And there were maintained green grasses at both sides of the stony pavements. At last, we had reached at the graves that we had come to visit. And we had found four graves, one beside the other. The first three were beautifully designed. They were cremated with painted white wood with golden arts crafted - the King George IV's, the Queen's and Rose Scarlett's. The golden arts were of lions indicating their royalty, of Christianity confirming their faith, of nature supporting their mortal existence. The Crosses were made of pure gold - the Royal Cross. And the last grave had not been this attractive. It was made of grey stones. And unlike the Royal Cross, this cross was relatively ordinary. It had the King's Crest - the Sword on the Circle that had indicated that it had been of a King's Man's.

Remember how Michael Chapman had asked in his final letter if James Wheeler had ever thought of what to write on his gravestone?

There on this gravestone, it had been engraved:

"If you are here, and you are crying
Do not cry, but smile
As I am smiling in joy because
You have been such a wonderful part of my life...
The faithful soldier, beloved friend and mighty King's Man
Sir Michael Chapman"

www.ingramcontent.com/pod-product-compliance
Ingram Content Group UK Ltd.
Pitfield, Milton Keynes, MK11 3LW, UK
UKHW041843190726
13854UKWH00002B/686